T0311274

THE

JAPAN–SOUTH KOREA
IDENTITY CLASH

CONTEMPORARY ASIA IN THE WORLD

CONTEMPORARY ASIA IN THE WORLD

David C. Kang and Victor D. Cha, Editors

This series aims to address a gap in the public-policy and scholarly discussion of Asia. It seeks to promote books and studies that are on the cutting edge of their disciplines or promote multidisciplinary or interdisciplinary research but are also accessible to a wider readership. The editors seek to showcase the best scholarly and public-policy arguments on Asia from any field, including politics, history, economics, and cultural studies.

For the list of titles in this series, see page 219

THE

JAPAN–SOUTH KOREA
IDENTITY CLASH

EAST ASIAN SECURITY AND THE UNITED STATES

BRAD GLOSSERMAN AND SCOTT A. SNYDER

COLUMBIA UNIVERSITY PRESS   *New York*

Columbia University Press
Publishers Since 1893
New York   Chichester, West Sussex

Copyright © 2015 Columbia University Press
Paperback edition, 2017

Library of Congress Cataloging-in-Publication Data
Glosserman, Brad.
The Japan-South Korea identity clash : East Asian Security and the United States /
Brad Glosserman and Scott A. Snyder.
pages cm. — (Contemporary Asia in the world)
Includes bibliographical references and index.
ISBN 978-0-231-17170-0 (cloth : alk. paper)—ISBN 978-0-231-17171-7 (pbk. : alk.
paper)—ISBN 978-0-231-53928-9 (e-book)
1. Japan—Foreign relations—Korea (South). 2. Korea (South)—Foreign relations—
Japan. 3. Group identity—Political aspects—Japan. 4. Group identity—Political
aspects—Korea (South). 5. National characteristics, Japanese. 6. National
characteristics, Korean. 7. United States—Foreign relations—Japan.
8. Japan—Foreign relations—United States. 9. United States—Foreign
relations—Korea (South). 10. Korea (South)—Foreign relations—United States.
I. Glosserman, Brad. II. Title

DS849.K6S68 2015
327.5205195—dc23
214029721

Book and cover design by Chang Jae Lee

To Fan and Reed
and to SoRhym, Elliana, and Elyssa

CONTENTS

PREFACE

AS THE ASIAN CENTURY FINALLY BLOOMS, THE PROMISE OF THE future appears increasingly subject to limits imposed by the past. For many observers, even those who understand their history, the lingering animosities that dominate relations between Japan and the Republic of Korea seem particularly inexplicable. It is hard for many if not most outsiders to understand why two countries that have enjoyed such extraordinary success in the postwar era would dwell on a more distant and ugly past. That is not to say that the past should be forgotten. Rather, given their many accomplishments and the opportunities they create, it seems strange and self-defeating that Koreans and Japanese focus instead on history. This focus is especially inexplicable and troubling for Americans, who see two countries with a remarkable convergence of values and interests, who share a worldview in many important respects, and who share geographic and geopolitical positioning that would incline them toward each other as an effective means by which to maximize their choices and options. It is troubling because both countries are U.S. allies, and those differences not only impede the protection and advancement of U.S. interests (and, we believe, those of their allies) but threaten to embroil the United States in their disputes.

The study that follows is an attempt to understand why the differences between Japan and South Korea overshadow their similarities and what those two countries can do, along with the United States, to overcome them. It is a work that has been a long time in the making, one that has gone through considerable revision and numerous iterations. The list of people to thank is a very long one, starting with Allan Song of the Smith Richardson Foundation, who originally suggested that we examine the role of national identity in these two countries and its implication for U.S. alliances. He has encouraged and supported us throughout the project's long gestation. We owe a great debt to those individuals who took the time to answer the surveys that constituted the starting point for our analysis, as well as the people in Japan and South Korea who sat down with us to flesh out the themes that emerged from those surveys. Thanks also go to the folks who attended roundtables in Washington, Tokyo, and Shanghai, where we presented findings and were corrected or admonished about our conclusions.

At Pacific Forum CSIS, virtually everyone affiliated with the organization or who has clocked time as an intern or fellow has contributed to this effort. President Ralph Cossa offered support and his own insights on both countries. Carl Baker has been a frustrating and invariably correct counter to the conventional wisdom. Brooke Mizuno and Georgette Alameida were essential to the production of the manuscript. We thank all of them and all the other fellows and interns who contributed to this product.

At CFR and the Asia Foundation, a host of interns have participated in and contributed to various stages of this project. Scott would like to thank See-Won Byun, Paul Choi, and Darcie Draudt in particular for their contributions and critical comments on various drafts. We also acknowledge the comments of the anonymous reviewers who took the time to read the draft and to provide their critical evaluation of the manuscript.

We are honored to be able to contribute to a Columbia University Press series led by close colleagues Victor Cha and David Kang, and we are grateful to Anne Routon for guiding this manuscript to publication at Columbia University Press.

Coauthorship carries with it both challenges and rewards. It can be a test of both collegiality and friendship, and it provides an opportunity to bring complementary skill sets and expertise to the subject at hand. It does not necessarily cut the amount of work in half, but it does make the research and writing tasks less lonely and more collaborative. Most important, our friendship has survived this test and has left both of us intellectually enriched by the experience.

THE

JAPAN–SOUTH KOREA
IDENTITY CLASH

I

THE JAPAN–SOUTH KOREA DIVIDE

AMERICA'S ALLIANCES WITH SOUTH KOREA AND JAPAN HAVE succeeded beyond the wildest expectations of their founders. Set up during the early 1950s, these two alliances have established a framework for Asian stability that has kept the peace, enabled prosperity resulting from economic take-offs in Japan and South Korea, and been flexible enough to manage and adapt to domestic political transformations in both countries. A study of alliances since the 1800s shows the average duration of such arrangements lasts just over a decade; these two alliances have survived for over six decades and are still going strong.[1]

They survived the Cold War, and their rationales have been successfully transformed from primarily threat-based instruments for deterring aggression by enemies to vehicles for promoting comprehensive cooperation on a wide range of regional and global issues. If anything, it might be said that the architects of the U.S.–Japan and U.S.–South

Korea alliances succeeded too well: more than a half century after their establishment, they remain discrete institutions, parallel parts of a "hub-and-spokes" system, despite efforts to knit these two alliances together as part of a regionalized framework for security cooperation.

This U.S.-led hub-and-spokes approach to security in Northeast Asia is increasingly under pressure from both within and without. On the one hand, despite a dramatic political and economic transformation and a convergence between America's two Northeast Asian alliance partners in values, interests, and stakes in global stability, the Republic of Korea (ROK) and Japan remain stubbornly apart from each other, divided by historical legacies that are themselves remnants of a messy, U.S.-led World War II settlement. In fact, issues surrounding unresolved historical legacies have become a tool for winning support in domestic politics, primarily on the basis of appeals to national pride. On the other hand, the U.S. hegemonic role that has guaranteed stability in East Asia is increasingly contested as a by-product of China's rise and accompanying demands for greater influence in regional affairs, as well as the inevitable erosion of U.S. hegemony in a world of increasingly distributed power.[2] The China challenge obliges Japan and South Korea to consider embracing a strategic rationale for cooperation to counter China's rising influence. The U.S. "rebalance" to Asia magnifies the pressure for U.S. allies to cooperate with one another, since this framework will bolster America's continuing role in the region while aiming to preserve and strengthen existing international norms as the primary basis for strengthened regional cooperation. The rebalancing strategy promotes intensified dialogue with China, but it also involves the revitalization of U.S. bilateral alliances in Asia with Japan, South Korea, Australia, the Philippines, and Thailand, as well as the establishment and strengthening of new partnerships with other players in the region, including India, Malaysia, Vietnam, and Indonesia.[3] The strategy has enabled the United States to reinvigorate relations with the Association of Southeast Asian Nations (ASEAN), to join the East Asia Summit, and to pursue multilateral trade negotiations through the Trans-Pacific Partnership (TPP).

But the rebalance has also had to face long-standing challenges in managing U.S. alliance relationships, especially with Japan and South

Korea. The internal dynamics of these parallel alliances have evolved in complex ways since the end of the Cold War. In particular, domestic political issues have become a challenge and a source of no small amount of frustration to alliance managers in all three countries in ways that did not happen during the Cold War. Some of these changes are the result of internal political transformations. For instance, as South Korea has industrialized and democratized, South Korean public opinion has become more influential in the formation of foreign policy, making the task of managing the relationship much more complex. Likewise in Japan, domestic constituencies or hot-button domestic political issues have occasionally superseded alliance concerns, paralyzing alliance management on the issue of the U.S. troop presence in Okinawa and complicating Japan's relations with neighbors. The rise of "intermestic" issues and their influence on alliance management started in the mid-1990s, at a time when the U.S. role in Asia was not subject to challenge, and it carried over into the early 2000s, when concerns about U.S. entrapment of allies in out-of-area obligations in Afghanistan and Iraq surfaced on the agenda of both the U.S.–Japan and U.S.–ROK alliances. More recently, heightened tensions between the two Koreas and between Japan and China over the Senkaku/Diaoyu islands have raised the prospect that the United States may face entrapment issues over the need to support allies in the event of "gray zone" conflicts that stop short of escalating into all-out war. These issues have not subsided, even as consciousness of China's growing economic and political influence and its implications for Japanese and South Korean security policies has risen among the publics in both countries.

The Puzzle of Persisting Tensions in Japan–South Korea Relations

The politicization of the alliance relationship with the United States—as a tool for attracting political support and winning elections—has challenged the assumptions on which the alliances have rested. But politics have proven an even more formidable problem in relations between Japan and South Korea. In fact, the persistence and continuing reemergence of conflicts in Japan–South Korea relations is a particularly interesting puzzle and challenge for U.S. security specialists. This challenge is all the more salient as the United States looks not only to strengthen its alliances with Japan and South Korea but also to support greater "horizontal" cooperation among alliance partners on regional political and security issues to strengthen regional stability and to maintain a balance in the region as China's power rises. The U.S. rebalance, with its renewed focus on Southeast Asia, appears to assume a certain stasis in Northeast Asia's security situation. That could be a dangerously mistaken assumption given rising tensions on the Korean Peninsula and surrounding the disputed Senkaku/Diaoyu islands and difficulties over history, textbooks, and territory that limit the potential of the Japan–ROK relationship.

In the 1990s and 2000s the rise of domestic political issues in South Korea and Japan as priorities that superseded alliance cooperation seemed to be a function of both democratization and the absence of an immediate regional threat. Even so, U.S. analysts took comfort in the fact that South Korea and Japan as fellow democracies were pursuing common values, and those values would ultimately strengthen the alliances as well as provide the glue for cooperation between Japan and South Korea as quasi-allies. The George W. Bush administration even attempted to frame alliance cooperation with both Japan and South Korea as a function of common values as it attempted to expand and apply alliance cooperation to both regional and global issues.

Yet Japan–South Korea relations have been turbulent, beset by political difficulties over history, territory, and textbooks. Despite repeated efforts starting with the Kim Dae-jung–Obuchi Keizo summit in 1998, attempts by Roh Moo-hyun and Koizumi Junichiro in early 2003, and a positive environment for Korea–Japan reconciliation afforded by the coming to power of the Democratic Party of Japan (DPJ) in Tokyo and Lee Myung-bak's positive attitude toward enhanced U.S.–ROK–Japan security cooperation from 2009, the South Korea–Japan relationship remains unable to overcome historical legacies.

Many observers are puzzled by these developments. Why are domestic political considerations a chronic flashpoint in Korea–Japan relations, and what has prevented these two countries—fellow Asian democracies and successful market economies with common values—from overcoming their tragic historical legacy? What would it take for the two countries to reconcile, especially given what appears to be a compelling convergence of strategic and security concerns in Seoul and Tokyo? Will commonly held threat perceptions occasioned by China's rise enable pragmatic cooperation between the two countries, or do their respective geographic positions and differing geopolitical calculations toward China limit such cooperation? And even if South Korea and Japan were to forge cooperation on a threat-based rationale, would that contribute to stability, or would it simply heighten tensions and exacerbate the possibility of confrontation with China? Is there a role for the United States in this process, or is it better for the United States to take a hands-off approach toward the relationship? These are some of the questions that arise from this effort to understand the impact of self-perceptions and perceptions of the other in both countries for the future of Japan–Korea relations, and to determine implications for U.S. management of its alliances in Northeast Asia.

The idea that domestic politics challenges the alliances or their conceptual underpinnings demands a reassessment of the U.S.-centered, alliance-based security network in Asia. Indeed, since the end of the Cold War, many scholars, analysts, and institutions have done just that.[4] None of those studies, however, focuses on national identity and its impact on U.S. alliances. This requires a deeper exploration of the root causes underlying changes in public opinion among U.S. alliance partners. New technologies, new methodological rigor, and the growing ease in conducting and comparing international polls have breathed new life into these efforts. The Pew Research Center and the Chicago Council on Global Affairs are perhaps the two best-known sources of data; many other polling resources, both private and governmental in the United States, Asia, and Europe, are also available.

Because South Korea and Japan are mature democracies, public opinion directly influences the parameters of foreign policy making in each country. It shapes, constrains, and potentially enlarges alliance-based cooperation with the United States. Many scholarly analyses of foreign policy in these two countries, while acknowledging the importance of democracy in Asia, nevertheless tend to emphasize systemic and structural factors and a model for understanding decision making that privileges elites over individuals. But it is apparent that the interaction between public opinion and political leadership increasingly influences national preferences in foreign policy and gives insight into relations with neighbors in the cases of Korea and Japan. Public views influence foreign policy, international relations, and the prospects for future conflict in Asia, with powerful implications for U.S. management of relations with these two allies.

When public opinion is taken into account, all too often it is used to provide a snapshot at a particular moment; unfortunately, extrapolation from that single moment cannot tell the whole story. There has been little effort to analyze Northeast Asian public opinion in an interactive way that paints a fuller picture of how elites and publics view relations with their neighbors. This book focuses on elite and public views in Japan and South Korea over time and tries to analyze available public opinion data in these countries as a means to better understand how Asian neighbors view themselves, each other, and the United States. In other words, the data provide insight into how the Japanese and Koreans see themselves and their place in the world.

These views, we argue here, represent a sense of identity that helps shape and bound national choices. It sets parameters for political interaction among neighbors that have a complicated shared history. No understanding of the relationship between Japan and South Korea—or its potential—is possible without a firm grasp of that legacy. Interaction between the two societies has occurred over two millennia, with indications of cross-border influence from the fifth and sixth centuries AD (which way the influence flowed isn't clear). There is speculation that the Japanese imperial family has Korean origins; Japan's emperor has "all but declared his own Korean ancestry."[5] While the formulation of the Korean Peninsula as "a dagger pointed at the heart of Japan" is of modern origin, that notion has shaped regional thinking for generations as regional powers for centuries fought for control of the area through a series of bloody invasions. This experience has molded Korean thinking to this day and fostered the belief among Koreans that their country is "a shrimp among whales."

While China has been the most persistent invader, Japan was the most recent. Its conquest and bloody occupation from 1910 left an indelible mark on Korean memories. The jubilation over Japan's defeat at the end of World War II and the restoration of Korean sovereignty was tempered by the division of the peninsula by the Cold War. Japan was blamed for that as well. Tensions were downplayed when diplomatic relations were normalized in 1965, and the Cold War and South Korea's authoritarian government forced remaining tensions between the two countries into the background. Meanwhile, Japanese economic accomplishments proved an important—albeit disputed—source of inspiration for South Korea's own development. Since then, the two nations have warily eyed each other, with the economic relationship dominated by competition. Korea has long viewed Japan as a business and economic benchmark; as the economic pacesetter, Japan historically paid little attention to the country in its rear-view mirror, but that attitude is changing after two decades of stagnation.

Today members of each public are increasingly interacting directly with each other, through business relationships, tourism, education exchanges, sister-city relationships, and even marriage. *Hallyu* (the "Korean Wave" of popular cultural outflows) has played a critical role in creation of favorable images of Korea and has even prompted pilgrimages by Japanese fans to Korean locales where favorite television shows and films were made. Middle-aged female fans have rioted when Korean TV stars visited Tokyo. But there is a paradoxical downside to this increasing interaction between the two countries. Exposure has heightened expectations of the other as the two societies recognize similarities between themselves. They now expect their partner to understand and appreciate their concerns. When that does not happen—when one country does something that hurts or offends the other—the feeling is more akin to betrayal and the pain seemingly more acute.

Sadly, there have been ample opportunities to feel betrayed in recent years. Whether the trigger is a territorial dispute, contested views of history, or memories of the treatment afforded Korean civilians during the long period of occupation, the offense taken and the subsequent reactions have become more intense. An aggressive and unfettered Internet culture, a polarized political landscape, and a growing sense of alienation among voters have all fanned the flames of discontent.

The United States is in the middle of these disputes, despite efforts to avoid being caught in the crossfire over territorial disputes that have been fanned by the U.S. failure to more definitively settle ownership claims following the end of World War II. Not only does each ally measure itself against the other, but both use relations with the United States as a benchmark as well. Accustomed to seeing their alliance as the cornerstone of U.S. engagement in Asia, many Japanese were confounded when U.S. president Barack Obama and then ROK president Lee Myung-bak in 2009 declared their relationship "a lynchpin" of U.S. relations with the region; Japanese sought out native English speakers to discover if lynchpin was a plural or singular noun. For their part, Koreans use U.S. legal agreements with Japan as the gold standard for their own documents, whether the issue is Status of Forces Agreements (SOFA) or civilian nuclear cooperation deals. (The United States is not above playing this game. Some strategists believe one of the goals of the Korea–U.S. Free Trade Agreement (KORUS) was to prod Tokyo to do its own deal with Washington, which is now playing out via Japan's decision to join multilateral Trans-Pacific Partnership trade negotiations.) Each government seeks U.S. backing for its position in the various bilateral contretemps, whether it is the Dokdo/Takeshima territorial dispute or the treatment of sex slaves during World War II. Since 2013 the competition between South Korea and Japan has even played out at the state level in Virginia and other states in the form of lobbying over whether U.S. textbooks should refer to the water separating the two countries as the East Sea or the Sea of Japan. While the United States has avoided taking sides on any particular issue, the effort to evade entrapment in historical disputes between Japan and South Korea has become more difficult in recent years.

Japanese and South Korean perceptions of China also play an important role in this analysis. Assessments of China are multidimensional. First, there are objective measures of power and influence: the fact that China is now the world's second largest economy and is slated to overcome the United States as number one in a decade or two (if not in years) if present trends continue; growing scientific and technological accomplishments; its possession of a rapidly modernizing military with growing conventional and nuclear capabilities; its status as a permanent member of the United Nations Security Council and the readiness to play a more prominent role in regional diplomacy as part of its effort to reclaim its place as the regional hegemon; and its nationalist public that is ever ready to engage when it feels national pride has been impugned. These calculations will ultimately include estimates of Chinese intentions—the reality of which the Chinese themselves may not even know. Is China a revisionist power? Will it try to settle on its own terms the grievances accumulated after a century of humiliation? Or will it support the existing regional and global order, norms, and institutions alike?

Second, Japanese and South Koreans must also assess the current and future state of their bilateral relationship with China. How do they characterize that particular balance of power? Will it change and how? Is China viewed more as a partner or a competitor—and in which arenas? How will economic relations influence the overall bilateral dynamic? These calculations take on particular importance since both Japan and South Korea have disputes with China over trade, foreign policy, and territory. How will those conflicts be resolved and on what terms?

A third level of assessment involves calculations of the regional balance of power, or how each country sees China within a broader constellation of interests and actors. Perhaps the most important of these is perceptions of the U.S.–China balance of power. Is the gap between the two nations closing? At what pace and with what effect? Is China's rise coming at the expense of the United States? Can a new balance of power be reached, and how will it operate? In Tokyo there is fear that Washington will reach an accommodation with Beijing that sacrifices Japanese interests for those of a broader U.S.–China relationship. In Seoul policy makers wonder if the road to Pyongyang runs through Beijing and to what degree China can help forge a better relationship with North Korea. It should be noted that both Japan and South Korea are not mere onlookers as the new regional balance emerges. Both are substantial actors in the own right, and their behavior will have a power-ful effect on outcomes, with the potential to influence stability through-out East Asia.

That same logic applies to Japanese and South Korean assessments of the United States and its future role in and relations with the region. The regional balance of power depends on Chinese and U.S. behavior; too often calculations focus on China without a corresponding examination of American strengths and weaknesses. In recent years weaknesses have been most evident as the United States reels from a financial crisis, a self-inflicted political wound that suggests political paralysis and a failure to appreciate larger issues of American status and standing in the world, and a new sense of limits as a result of a decade of war and all the domes-tic turmoil such conflict invariably triggers. Yet for all those weaknesses, the United States has demonstrated a surprising resilience and a capacity to adapt. It continues to exercise considerable diplomatic influence, has played leading roles in humanitarian operations including responses to the December 2004 tsunami and the March 2011 triple catastrophe in Japan, and has reinvigorated its Asian presence and policy through the rebalance adopted at the end of 2011. Washington is just one budget deal away from a modernized and sustainable policy that positions the United States to play an enduring role in Asia for decades.

But the perception is otherwise. The rise of new security threats, talk of the need for new cooperative approaches to counter those threats, and the seeming desire for new security mechanisms in Asia are seen as cover for a diminished U.S. role in the region. Finding new equilibria within alliances that recognize political demands for equality and new financial capabilities is viewed not as an attempt to accommodate the new realities of Asia but instead as evidence of retreat. Perceptions can shift if Asian nations see themselves as subjects in this drama rather than mere objects. Publics in South Korea and Japan must recognize that the way they define their own stakes, role, and interests vis-à-vis the United States and China will strongly influence the balance of power between those two countries and the future of the alliances as well.

Asia faces extended uncertainty as the United States and China test each other's capabilities across the full spectrum of national power and intentions. The two countries will simultaneously cooperate and compete in a wide range of endeavors and will be sending mixed signals as they do so. Attempts to create new regional architectures to deal with security will be evaluated not only on their records of success or failure but on the assessments of imputed signals they send. Is the U.S. championing of the TPP really an attempt to set "gold standards" for trade negotiations? Or is it a means to contain China and develop an economic architecture that locks in U.S. dominance and its preferred rules? Or is it intended to block other Asian trade initiatives?

Regardless of the outcome—which is uncertain for many reasons, not least of which is the fact that neither the United States nor China is guaranteed to continue on its current trajectory—the region is set for a prolonged period of uncertainty and increased volatility. In these circumstances, the U.S. alliance system will be tested more than ever before. This U.S.–China competition will place new and contradictory demands on allies, both as a result of conflicting interests in the economic versus security spheres and as a result of heightened expectations between alliance partners regarding their contributions to the alliance, their behavior within the alliance, and their relations with each other.

The Theoretical Challenge of Explaining Japan–South Korea Relations

Most strategic thinking starts with realist assessments of power and relative gains: how do alternative courses of action advance or impinge on national interests in an anarchic world? It should not be surprising that straightforward calculations of material power dominate foreign policy and national security thinking. The state has been the key feature of the international order since that phrase existed. For all the diversity among nations, realists assume all states are and act alike. Their preeminent interest is survival. To do that, they must maximize power and acquire resources. Looking at the particular characteristics or defining features of a state makes no sense if all states share the same objectives: particular identities are irrelevant since the bottom line for the black box is protecting itself and ensuring its continued existence. Absent some authority that could impose structure and procedures and ensure predictable outcomes, states have the freedom to act as they wish. Since the international arena is an anarchic system, constraints on state behavior either are self-imposed or come from stronger states that compete with them. In other words, relations between states are determined by their comparative levels of power, usually derived from military and economic capabilities. Other states cannot be counted on to help because there is no way to ensure that agreements to cooperate will be honored. International institutions have a limited role as they have no power and are unable to compel behavior. Not surprisingly, clashes are common: the shared aim to acquire power sparks conflict when two nations eye the same prize. This is an amoral world: since power is all that matters, there is no room for principles that might limit a state's room to maneuver in specific circumstances. Pragmatism and flexibility, the ability to exploit opportunities, are the lodestars for foreign policy and diplomacy.

Objections to realism spurred the development of another school of thought: liberalism. Liberals are not convinced that states are unitary actors that have one simple motive. A state's preferences are not fixed but differ from state to state and even from situation to situation. As such, liberals shift their focus from state capabilities to state preferences. This shift in perspective also extends the range of interactions to be studied. Political and diplomatic interactions, which involve the highest levels of state authority, are important but so are economic interactions, which include a much broader range of actors. This shift in focus and operating principles has critical implications. First, it means that each particular state has to be studied—operating principles cannot be assumed. Second, states may discover that they share characteristics or preferences. There may be common features among states—type of government, culture, economic order, ideology—that provide them with a shared outlook. This commonality could provide a basis for cooperation. Third, this broad assessment of state concerns and interests suggests that power is more diffuse than realists assert. There is more to power than wealth and military capabilities. Finally, this school believes the appropriate baseline for state behavior is not relative gains—who wins or loses by virtue of a particular action—but absolute gains. In other words, does cooperation provide advantages to all states, even if some benefit more than others?

A third school, constructivism, argues that important elements of international relations are socially and historically contingent—constructed—rather than invariable outgrowths of the structure of an anarchic state system or human nature. This theory rejects the idea that there are permanent and immutable forces that shape state behavior. Rather, beliefs and practices are shaped by history and the very process of interaction itself. Even if states maximize power and influence, they choose to do that, and that choice is the result of learning; it is not innate. Similar evolutions can result in similar value structures and shared approaches to problems; geographic proximity, and the similarities it creates, can lead to cooperation rather than conflict. Shared values can emerge, and they can provide a basis for cooperation, informally or through institutions. This, argues constructivism's proponents, better predicts and explains state behavior.

This cursory sketch will no doubt irritate many theorists; it is a broadbrush attempt to sketch the key features of the schools and what distinguishes them from one another. But as should be clear, abstractions have their limits. As one colleague has noted, when officials have to make decisions, the decision makers don't ask what school they belong to and then fashion a response accordingly. The utility of a theory depends on its ability to explain or predict behavior. Being locked into one single paradigm/framework/perspective makes no sense it if prevents the analyst from solving problems. This impatience has led to the rise of analytical eclecticism, whose supporters argue that "the complex links between power, interest, and norms defy analytical capture by any one paradigm. They are made more intelligible by drawing selectively on different paradigms—that is, by analytical eclecticism, not parsimony."[6]

In the case of Japan and South Korea, realism has been useful for explaining the origins of the alliances with the United States—they were an antidote to the threat of communism—but it has not been useful in explaining their durability following the end of the Cold War and the dissolution of the Soviet threat. Nor is realism useful in explaining the barriers to cooperation between South Korea and Japan, either in response to the Soviet threat or against the backdrop of China's rise. A liberal approach might anticipate a better South Korea–Japan relationship than currently exists given the extensive network of trade and investment relations between the two countries and the role of Japan's investment as a catalyst for South Korea's early economic development. Shared values between the ROK and Japan should make the two countries ripe for constructivist approaches to bilateral or trilateral cooperation, but aside from trilateral statements on North Korea, the development of habits of cooperation among the United States, Japan, and South Korea has proven to be more difficult than expected. The problems in the Japan–South Korea relationship point to an additional factor not well captured or espoused in theoretical approaches to international relations: the role of gaps in and opposing conceptions of national identity, or an image of one's own national community forged by historical experience and imagined common values and interpreted through the ritual life of the nation. These nationally inculcated values, historical experiences, and narratives come together to create a sense of national communal life around which a sense of identity is forged.

State behavior depends on history and culture, as well as capabilities.[7] Raw power is important, but so too are beliefs, values, and norms.[8] How states define themselves, who they think they are (their identity), and what they think is important (their interests) are critical issues. And the answers to those questions differ from state to state, and even in single states over time. A society's conception of itself shapes what it thinks is important. Identity shapes interests, and interests determine foreign policy. Martha Finnemore explains that "interests are not just 'out there' waiting to be discovered; they are constructed through social interaction."[9] But identity can also shape conceptions of what power is and how it ought to be used; this seems to be the case in Japan, where the image of a peace-loving nation provides bounds on the exercise of state power and diplomacy. Whether a state even considers itself a practitioner of realism can be a function of its identity. This activist role by government and elites to construct identity and subsequent interests creates opportunities for manipulation and is one to which policy makers need to be alert. As Kenneth Pyle explains, "Although universal ideals and abstract principles were relatively weak in Japan, shared ideas of national identity and the social construction of the world they had entered were powerful determinants of their international behavior."[10]

Consider, for example, the work of Gilbert Rozman, who has done some of the most extensive analysis of national identity in Northeast Asia. Rozman deploys a six-dimensional analysis that includes ideology; time (or more precisely, history—prewar, postwar, and post–Cold War); cultural, political, and economic factors (what he calls "sectoral"); a vertical dimension that looks at groups from families to gender; a horizontal dimension that deals with international relations ranging from those with the United States to the wider global community; and depth of national identity, which emphasizes the "intense emotionalism over identity."[11] Focusing on Japan, he sees a country at "an identity crossroads" that is reeling from blows to its pride and well-being.[12] He differentiates four schools of Japanese thought—statism (*kakkashugi*), ethnic nationalism (*minzokushugi*), internationalism (*kokusaishugi*), and pacifism (*heiwashugi*)[13]—that battle for preeminence. He espies shifts as he applies each of his six dimensions to Japan. For example, politics is increasingly superseding cultural and economic identity; there is growing disillusionment with or questioning of historical accomplishments, along with doubts about the value of the culture and the groups that characterized Japanese society. Rozman argues that clashes among the competing identities can create an image of pragmatic adaptation that suggests a lack of identity, when the reality is a standoff among fiercely opposed ideas.

Likewise, South Korea has several identities derived from its own origins of state formation: anticommunism, anti-imperialism, the incomplete identity of a divided state, mixed with the newly emerging identities of a model developmental state and mature capitalist democracy. Aside from state-centric identity constructs, Korean conceptions of national identity have historically revolved around concepts of shared ethnicity, although upward immigration and international marriage trends have recently engendered public support in Korea for the concept of a civic national identity as an alternative to an ethnicity-based conception of national identity.[14]

Historically, identity has been marginalized and largely overlooked in the field of international relations.[15] Only recently has identity "as an explicit concept" moved into the mainstream of international relations research, and a growing number of scholars now pay attention to identity in their research and are publishing their results.[16] One assessment concludes that this trend "is likely to grow in the coming years."[17] Unfortunately, however, the concept is elusive. It is "the subtext for almost any argument in international relations," and those scholars often construct theories of identity "on the fly, sometimes for the purpose of a single article, without searching for existing theories."[18] A sociologist concludes that "the notion of identity is of no great help in the social sciences. It is rather a portmanteau term that does not possess the status of a concept."[19] Even after noting that "identity" is both "a category of analysis and a category of practice" and outlining five key uses of the term, two critics conclude that "whatever its suggestiveness, whatever its indispensability in certain practical contexts, 'identity' is too ambiguous, too torn between 'hard' and 'soft' meanings, essentialist connotations and constructivist qualifiers, to serve well the demands of social analysis."[20]

Ultimately, however, it is hard to disagree with the survey that concludes that, despite the confusion and the amorphous quality of identity as a concept, there is "a degree of coherence that should be noted . . . all identity scholars share the notion that identity is a source of an actor's behavior, and therefore fundamental."[21] Identity defines a group, a process that incidentally and necessarily also creates "others" who do not share that identity. Identity is important in a global order that privileges self-determination; identity forms the very basis for the states that follow its assertion. But that effort at differentiation has been the source of considerable violence in the twentieth century. "Identity politics" has negative connotations because it has been used to drive wedges in societies, to exploit divisions, and to rally support against another group. When identity becomes nationalism and otherwise healthy patriotism becomes chauvinism, troubles usually follow. When political platforms are based on the exploitation of differences, they often engender hostility.[22]

Of course, identity differences do not have to lead to conflict. Peter Hays Gries argues that intergroup conflict is a highly contingent outcome; instead, the social psychology of intergroup relations explains whether cooperation or conflict will prevail.[23] If identity is constructed, then the inclination to choose cooperation over conflict can be encouraged and embedded in the identity itself. Erik Gartzke and Kristian Skrede Gleditsch believe that conflict is actually more likely among states with similar, and not different, cultural and identity ties.[24] That argument may have particular resonance for Japan and South Korea, given their close history and extensive ties.

Yet, as the diplomacy of the early twentieth century reminds us, identity does matter, even if the term lacks rigor or clarity. A group's ability to identify itself as a nation has been the starting point for claims of self-determination. Even if it was honored in the breach, national identity was a core element of foreign policy in the first two decades of the last century. In the 1960s the United States began a culture war, whose participants fought over the very nature of U.S. society, what it stood for, and how it would conduct its foreign policy. This struggle continues to this day. It is a debate over how the American people see themselves and how their society is to be idealized. For instance, both sides in the debate over the war against terrorism and the way that the United States has treated prisoners believe that torture is wrong and fundamentally alien to "who Americans are" or "what the country stands for." Of course, other issues are part of this debate, but all agree that torture is somehow foreign to the U.S. conception of national identity.

Public Opinion and Its Influence on Formation of Foreign Policy

It is intuitive that a nation's conception of its identity, of "who" it thinks it is, and the values that it considers important if not integral to its being shape its behavior. Identity determines what a society thinks is important—in essence, identity forges interests. As one recent study concludes, "State identity is a lens through which citizens determine a framework for a state's appropriate response to the demands and challenges of the international environment."[25]

But how does one identify and define the contours of a national identity? There are four possible ways to get at national identity: careful analysis of public opinion polls, examination of national literature expressive of a country's underlying values, examination of historical narratives, and analysis of national textbooks as a window into how societies remember the past. We have chosen to focus on polling data analysis as our primary means for exploring national identity. Opinion surveys are one way to get insight into collective thinking on important questions. Of course, they are subject to a well-known list of concerns: the sample size has to be large and diverse enough to be representative; questions can be subject to multiple interpretations; the data reflect findings only at a given point in time. Good polling should be supplemented by follow-up questions and interviews to add depth and nuance.

In addition to providing a measure of public response to various security trends in Asia, public opinion provides important insights into conceptions of national identity and values. How a nation sees itself has a profound impact on the identification and definition of its national interests, whom it sees as friends and enemies, and how it wishes to comport itself domestically and in its foreign policy. In democracies, public opinion influences the policy direction of leadership through elections or through withdrawal of support for particular national policies, but it can also be a lagging indicator, at least by demonstrating (or exposing) public satisfaction with government policies and perceptions of how the government is managing relations with neighbors. A close analysis of trends in public opinion in Japan and South Korea may be particularly useful in understanding how perceptions of the interaction between self and other interact in ways that frame the parameters for their international relations.

Even after the components that contribute to a nation's sense of identity are identified, one must grapple with additional challenges. First, how tightly coupled is identity to national policy making in general, and foreign policy in particular? Are there other factors that mediate between outcomes and identity? For example, how important are bureaucratic politics? Second, national identity can change. In the main, national identity is assumed to be enduring. If it reflects core conceptions of a society, it should not be ephemeral. Nonetheless, identity is not static; it is contested and constructed. A changing conception of national identity can reflect changing circumstances that put different features in relief, or it can signal a change in core beliefs. How can the two be distinguished? How is it possible to know which is taking place?

This study uses public opinion surveys and elite interviews and commentary to understand foreign policy in Japan and South Korea. It focuses on how public perceptions of national identity influence foreign policy choices and the interaction of these countries with China, the United States, and each other.

To better understand Japanese and South Korean perceptions of themselves and their country's role in the world, we have conducted an in-depth review of more than a decade of public opinion surveys on major foreign affairs issues conducted in each country, talked to a cross-section of Japanese and South Korean opinion leaders, and conducted our own survey of elite opinion that was distributed to Japanese and South Korean security analysts and professionals.[26] Overall our conversations with Japanese and South Korean interlocutors and the experience of preparing and conducting our own elite survey greatly assisted us in our interpretation and assessment of the major trend lines that characterize broader samples of public opinion that have accumulated in both countries. These experiences helped us to identify the contours of and influences on the national debate about identity and foreign policy that has been underway in both countries.

For instance, one striking aspect of our experience conducting directed interviews in South Korea and Japan was the relative unity of Korean respondents, who without hesitation and without fail rattled off in various forms a list of economic and political accomplishments that they associated with Korea's national identity. In contrast, we found that Japanese required clarification of the meaning of identity to the point that we were forced to rephrase the question: it became, "How do you think other countries see Japan and its place in the world?" This was a surprising outcome, given Kenneth Pyle's trenchant observation that "throughout their modern history, the Japanese have been compulsive in their preoccupation with their national character, with the question of what makes them Japanese." He cites critic Shuichi Kato, who famously asked, "Who are the Japanese? They are a people who are always asking who they are."[27] As one interviewee noted, "Our identity is like the air we breathe, the earth we walk on. It is not something we are conscious of." To the extent that Japanese responses were forthcoming, they associated their country's identity with the country's postwar economic success and its democracy, a tradition of pacifism that emerged from the disaster of World War II, an insular and conservative culture that posits a fundamental difference between Japan and the rest of the world, and a pragmatic approach to policy that puts results above principle.

Chapters 2 and 3 analyze trends in Japanese and South Korean public opinion, respectively; reveal how those countries think about themselves, their Asian neighbors, and the United States; and analyze what the data reveal about national identity and its influence on the direction of Japanese and South Korean foreign policy. Chapter 4 is devoted to an analysis of how Japan and South Korea interact with each other, with special reference to the difficult history that both share and influences on politics and public opinion that impact their bilateral relationship. Chapter 5 analyzes the implications of these trends for U.S. alliances in Northeast Asia and the future of security in the region. We conclude in chapter 6 with suggestions for the United States and speculate about how the future will unfold.

Most foreign policy analysis begins with the identification of national interests and then explains how institutions of the state act to protect those interests. The prevailing tendency is to use a realist framework that focuses on threats and the national assets available to counter them. The concordance of interests and the convergence of threat perceptions usually define the contours of cooperation by governments. Shared interests and common threat perceptions encourage states to act together. But "national identity," as revealed by values, beliefs, and resulting social systems, provides an equally compelling basis for cooperation. Governments would do well to focus on these areas of convergence to form more resilient bonds between states. The ties that bind are much stronger when they reflect a fundamental agreement between societies. When there are similarities with others at the most basic level—that of identity—there is a more compelling relationship. Equally important, a distance between ourselves and "others" will impede coordination and cooperation. This is not to make the case for a purely values-based diplomacy, nor does it argue that interests are irrelevant. It does suggest that there are ways to use identity to consolidate U.S. alliances in Northeast Asia. More significantly, this research shows that the United States, Japan, and South Korea are bound together by powerful ties that go much deeper than "mere" national interests.

These three countries have a moment of opportunity. After relations between Japan and South Korea arguably reached their lowest point in decades, elections in Tokyo and Seoul returned new governments. In both cases a conservative administration returned to power; both have histories that recognize the need for common action and reconciliation. The individuals making and administering policy in each capital understand the value of each country's alliance with the United States and the need for a robust and forward-looking relationship with each other.

Because of this situation, we propose a Grand Bargain for the three countries that addresses the long-standing issues that bedevil relations between Seoul and Tokyo and have recently ensnared Washington as well. This requires that the United States be more engaged in the resolution of the issues that unsettle the Japan–Korea relationship. While many insist that U.S. involvement will force it to take sides between allies, we disagree. Washington can facilitate without mediating. More significantly, it is important to acknowledge that the United States has long played a critical role in shaping Northeast Asian politics, and the idea of remaining above the fray is misguided. Our solution—or any solution for that matter—must rest on a clear-eyed understanding of each country, who the citizens think they are, what they and their society stand for, and under what circumstances it will be possible for the three countries to cooperate toward a common purpose. This recognition of national strengths and weaknesses produces a narrative that can be used to guide policy. Shared values and concerns should be identified to mold and shape relations, locating rallying points for concerted action and alerting policy makers to sensitive areas to avoid.

2

JAPAN'S IDENTITY CRISIS

CONFUSION IS TO BE EXPECTED. WHETHER THE OPERATIVE time span is 150 years, 75 years, or 35 years, Japan has spiraled through a series of ups and downs that have shaken the nation to its core, along with Japanese notions of national identity. Over the past few decades, the country has gone from world-beater to beaten down, from trendsetter to treading water. At the beginning of 2014, Japan appeared to be enjoying a recovery, one whose durability may well depend on ideas of national identity. A national consensus on power and purpose will help direct the country's energies in constructive and productive ways. This chapter attempts to explain what the proper conception of Japanese national identity is, how it manifests in policy, and why it matters.

The post–Cold War era has not been kind to Japan. A nation that rebuilt itself from the near total devastation of war to become the world's second largest economy and reclaim a prominent role on the international stage has suffered a series of blows that shook the pillars of Japan's post–World War II national identity. The first, and most debilitating, was the prolonged period of economic stagnation between 1991 and 2001 that became known as "the lost decade." During that time Japan's average annual economic growth plunged to less than 1 percent, a stark contrast to the 4 percent average annual growth of the previous decade and the jaw-dropping 8 percent growth registered from 1960 to 1975, resulting in "the deepest slump of any developed economy since the Great Depression."[1]

The economy recovered somewhat in the first half of the new millennium but was again hammered by the Lehman Shock of 2008. In a blow to national pride and confidence, China overtook Japan in 2010 as the world's second largest economy. By the close of 2013, Japan's real GDP had expanded 0.8 percent on average year-on-year over the past two decades, and nominal growth averaged negative 0.2 percent.[2] The Japanese belief that they had endured not one but two "lost decades" prompted voters in 2009 to turn their backs on the Liberal Democratic Party (LDP) for the first time in half a century to give the opposition a shot at ruling the country. The effort failed miserably. The Democratic Party of Japan (DPJ), which took the reins of government with such high hopes, proved hapless and incompetent, lurching from one crisis to another. After three disappointing years, the LDP regained its majority in December 2012 and consolidated its grip on power in the July 2013 Upper House elections.

The stunning reversal of Japan's economic fortunes and the seeming inability of the political leadership to do anything about it sapped Japanese self-confidence, which had rested on a belief that the country had developed a superior version of capitalism that overcame the tensions of the Anglo-American model and would result in "Japan as Number 1." (This success provided the foundation for one of the key pillars of postwar Japanese identity—that of a "mercantilist" or "trading" state.) Not surprisingly, a survey in 2002 revealed that a stunning 86 percent of Japanese were dissatisfied "with the way things are going in the country today." That number had dropped to "only" 71 percent five years later, but it has climbed steadily since: by spring 2012 it stood at 78 percent.[3]

The unease created by these developments has manifested itself in social phenomena, such as falling birthrates, growing unemployment, homelessness, a rising suicide rate, and increasing crime.[4]

Economic stagnation produced other, equally painful, results. The contraction of the economy deprived the Japanese government of funds needed to finance its diplomacy. As they battled recession, businesses retreated and tax revenues slumped. This robbed Tokyo of the economic largesse—in the form of both overseas development assistance and its extensive overseas private-sector business networks—that it had used to compensate for its refusal to use the military as an instrument of state power. The slump also devalued the Japanese economic model in the eyes of other nations, especially those in Southeast Asia. This undermined Japan's "soft power" and diminished its political and diplomatic influence as a country once viewed as a beacon for its accomplishments became "just another nation." A country accustomed to seeing itself as the rightful leader of Asia discovered its role had been usurped as it struggled with its own troubles. While primarily focused on a growing list of domestic woes, Japanese were acutely aware of China's rise and worried about its impact on the regional balance of power.[5] In particular, the Japanese public and policy makers alike worried about the prospect of the United States once again "passing" Japan to work with more vibrant and engaged governments, with Beijing topping that list.

Other core components of Japan's postwar identity eroded at the same time. At the end of the Cold War, Japanese were buoyed by the belief that international law was ascendant and that international institutions would be the arbiters of international disputes. This was a comfort for a nation whose constitution, in the form of Article 9, abjured the use of military force as an instrument of state policy; it also validated that decision and positioned Japan as a leading-edge country in this "new world order." The commitment to diplomatic solutions for international problems was not just a pillar of Japan's foreign policy, it was a cornerstone of the Japanese conception of who they were, a peaceful people who knew better than other nations the price of war and conflict. The world's reaction to Iraq's invasion of Kuwait confirmed Japanese optimism, although the Kuwait government's response after the war—omitting Japan from the list of nations it thanked for support—also exposed limitations inherent in Japan's willingness to provide only economic and not military contributions to multilateral efforts to maintain international order. Developments in East Asia would ultimately burst the Japanese bubble. Two North Korean nuclear crises, a Taiwan Strait crisis, the *Taepodong* missile that flew over Japan in 1998, and other incidents convinced many Japanese that Northeast Asia was a dangerous neighborhood. The South Asia nuclear tests of 1998, the failure of the Nuclear Nonproliferation Treaty (NPT) to deal with North Korea, and the United Nations' inability to resolve international crises damaged Japanese faith in international institutions. The promise of a post–Cold War world and a new world order evaporated.

At home Japanese were shaken by the failure of their national security apparatus during the Great Hanshin Earthquake of 1995 and the sarin gas attack on Tokyo subways several months later. Both underscored vulnerabilities in Japan's response to emergencies and shook confidence in the leadership's ability to deal with crises. A series of mishaps in the nuclear industry and a string of product safety fiascoes demonstrated that the shortcomings extended to the corporate sector as well. All those failings were again made manifest on March 11, 2011, when a triple catastrophe—earthquake, tsunami, and subsequent nuclear accident at the Fukushima Daiichi nuclear facility—occurred. As they assessed the Great Tohoku Earthquake, Japanese were forced to acknowledge a systemic failure that included parts of the government, the bureaucracy, and the corporate world. The impact of this blow to Japanese confidence was magnified by the knowledge that some fifteen years of preparation had little impact on the Japanese government's ability to respond to a crisis, and subsequent revelations that the nuclear *mura* (or village that included politicians, the nuclear industry, and regulatory authorities) had systematically shortchanged public and safety concerns in the name of industry profitability.[6] At the same time, however, the extraordinary response of Japanese citizens directly affected by the events of March 11—their dignity, stoicism, reserve, and resolve—also corresponded to the image many Japanese have of themselves and their society: a resolute citizenry prepared to struggle through hardship with quiet determination.

This image reflects a core element of Japanese identity: a population that will "suffer the insufferable" with dignity.

The collapse of the Soviet Union undermined the consensus that stabilized Japanese politics throughout the Cold War. Japan had nine prime ministers—and twelve governments, or cabinets—from the end of the Cold War (June 1989) until Koizumi Junichiro took office in April 2001. Koizumi ushered in some stability, holding on to the Kantei (the Prime Minister's Office) for nearly five and half years. But Japan has had seven prime ministers and seven cabinets (and four additional cabinet shuffles) since he stepped down in 2006.

The split in the LDP in 1993 was one crushing blow to the system. While a new government was created by defectors from the ruling party (as opposed to rejection by voters at the ballot box, as occurred in 2009), the new group proved unable to hold itself together, ushering in a period of political instability and uncertainty that shook the nation's faith in its political system. The LDP reclaimed power within two years, but it was no longer invincible, assured neither of winning elections nor of fashioning solutions to the country's problems. Electoral reforms passed during that brief eighteen-month interregnum contributed to the instability. At the same time, the Socialists abandoned bedrock positions—such as opposition to the Self-Defense Forces (SDF)—to permit party leader Murayama Tomiichi to become prime minister as head of a coalition with the LDP. This act of opportunism discredited the Left, a development that helped shift the center of Japan's political spectrum to the right. Over time progressives recaptured their constituencies, but policy gyrations by the DPJ—once thought to be a progressive alternative to LDP rule—again subsequently undermined the appeal of the Left when it was in power, as did the party's adoption of many LDP positions on issues ranging from taxation to security policy. This, combined with the rise to power of a younger generation of politicians with different thinking about Japan's international role, forced the nation to reopen debates about national identity and its place in the world.[7]

The conventional narrative argues that the end of the Cold War lifted many constraints on Japanese nationalism, which in turn yielded a more assertive foreign policy. Proponents of this view point to the expansion of the role of Japan's SDF, including its participation in overseas peacekeeping operations, the extension of Japanese responsibilities for regional security under its alliance with the United States, and more aggressive diplomacy, evidenced by Tokyo's demand for a permanent seat on the United Nations Security Council, its refusal to buckle under to Chinese and South Korean criticism of the behavior of its politicians, in particular the visits of Prime Minister Koizumi to Yasukuni Shrine, where the souls of those who died in the service of the empire of Japan reside—including, most controversially, fourteen convicted Class-A war criminals. Talk of constitutional revision to change Article 9, legislation to honor the national flag and anthem, Ministry of Education–approved textbooks that "whitewash history" and efforts to promote traditional values, the assertion of Japanese claims to disputed territories, and the erosion of taboos about the discussion of defense options such as nuclear weapons and offensive-strike capabilities are all rolled out as proof that Japan is changing and becoming more nationalistic. Moreover, an opportunistic leadership in Tokyo is poised to exploit this new environment.

A more extreme variant of this view argues that the "the Japan that can say 'No'" is a harbinger of Japanese ambitions and worries that the reassertion of Japanese nationalism will lead the country back down the path of militarism and the mistakes that led to the Great Pacific War. To be clear: while Japanese nationalism had been loosened by the end of the Cold War, and Japan is assuming a higher-profile security role in the region, expression of this nationalism within official policy remains circumscribed. The extreme variant identified here is an extreme. There remain powerful political, social, and ideational checks on the practice of power politics (in domestic or foreign policy) within Japan. As Professor Soeya Yoshihide of Keio University has argued, "Were a desire to revive Japan's prewar aspirations actually articulated clearly as a strategy, the Japanese public would be the first to reject it."[8]

A more judicious approach—and more widely shared view—acknowledges the emergence of a new security policy perspective in

Tokyo in the post–Cold War era but emphasizes the evolutionary nature of that change. Its proponents argue that Japan has embraced "reluctant realism,"[9] a slow and hesitant embrace of a more traditional approach to security policy, with Tokyo prodded by Washington to be a more active partner and shoulder a larger burden. While much of the credit for this has gone to Koizumi, whose vision for his country befitted its economic might and interests, the beginning of Japan's evolution predated his term in office. Koizumi did, however, seize opportunities in the aftermath of the September 11, 2001, terrorist attacks, using his relationship with President George W. Bush to raise Japan's international profile and push the boundaries of its international security role. For this school, Japan is to be applauded for breaking free of constraints that stunted its international stature and deprived the world of the substantial contributions that Tokyo could have made. Progress will continue to be made, but it will be measured, restrained, and careful not to destabilize the region. In his important work on Japanese public opinion and security policy, Paul Midford argues that "its recent evolution does not live up to the radical transformation many analysts see. . . . Japanese public opinion toward security is stable and coherent and evolves in intelligible and generally rational ways."[10] To be fair, however, Midford also insists that "Japanese public opinion was never pacifist or as opposed to all forms of military power as has often been claimed."[11]

For a third group, there was considerably less to Japan's evolution than meets the eye. Yes, Prime Minister Koizumi was especially adroit at exploiting the opportunities presented by the George–Jun relationship, but that interregnum was destined to be temporary, the high-water mark of the bilateral partnership. Japan was evolving, but change would be minimal and grudging, the product of exterior forces rather than an internal drive to find a new place in the world. This group reckons that Japan's future should be shaped by a considerably diminished set of expectations, one more suited to a "middle power" rather than one of the world's leading economies.[12] This outlook obliges Tokyo to find common cause with other like-minded states, searching for cooperative, multilateral solutions to international problems. It melds the idealism of Japan's postwar pacifism with a practical, if not somewhat pessimistic, emphasis on the limits imposed by Japanese circumstances and characteristics. As Soeya explains, "Changes in Japanese security policy since the Cold War have been possible only because they have been sustained by international inspirations and aspirations. Traditional nationalists have attempted to take advantage of these changes to advance their own agenda, but without much success."[13] To the degree that Japan is activist in the pursuit of its diplomatic ideals, that activism is made manifest via larger institutions. In this world Tokyo is content not to lead but to find partners and let them take the credit, if not the initiative, for policy innovation.

Finally, a fourth group would like Japan to continue on its earlier postwar trajectory, keeping its pacifist constitution, avoiding a high international profile, and focusing on its economic development. Its preference for a low profile means that this group sometimes finds common ground with the third school, but some of its members prefer that Tokyo avoid all international engagement—typically viewed as entanglement—out of fear that it would unleash a militarist and hegemonic leadership. It is deeply antimilitarist (as can be members of the third group) and, concerned that Japan's democratic roots are not deep, it rejects all temptations that might push the country off its rails. This group lost adherents in the late 1990s with the discrediting of the Left following the Socialists' venture into government and the admission by Pyongyang that North Korea had in fact kidnapped Japanese citizens. It retains a presence in Japan and has experienced something of a resurgence in recent years as the first group becomes more vocal and visible. While this group has a reflexive distrust of the United States in many cases, fearing that Washington will involve Japan in its misadventures, it has on occasion called for greater U.S. intervention in Japanese politics to tamp down the more adventurous elements on the right.

There have been several attempts to organize and categorize these responses. Hirata Keiko has provided a comprehensive assessment of perspectives on Japan's state identity, at least in regard to the security discourse.[14] She notes that Kenneth Pyle identifies four groups: the progressives, who embrace the postwar pacifist constitution and backed unarmed neutrality and nonalignment; mercantilists, who back the notion that Japan should focus on economic interests and can best protect them and promote peace through mercantile activities; liberal realists, who support incremental rearmament; and new nationalists, who believe in autonomous security policy that includes robust rearmament, even nuclear weapons, if necessary. According to Hirata, Mike Mochizuki echoes those categories but uses different names, calling them unarmed neutralists, political realists, military realists, and Japanese Gaullists, respectively. For Richard Samuels, the four groups are best labeled pacifists, middle-power internationalists, normal nation-alists (the hyphenation is Samuels's), and neoautonomists. In his formulation, the key factors that distinguish the groups are the value placed on the U.S.–Japan alliance and the willingness to use force in international affairs. Hirata herself uses the terms pacifists, mercantilists, normalists, and nationalists and believes that the two dimensions of the security debate are positions related to armament (pro or anti) and autonomy versus internationalism.

The tensions and contradictions in these positions have not been resolved; indeed, they have been compounded by political uncertainty in Tokyo. In a 2007 interview, a Foreign Ministry official concluded that Japan is "in crisis" and that Japanese are engaged in "soul searching" as they try to reach a consensus on answers to twenty-first-century issues and concerns.[15] Since then the level of dissatisfaction with the country's direction has continued to rise, with nearly 80 percent of respondents admitting that they weren't happy in a spring 2012 poll. Some of that unease has been further magnified by the March 11 triple catastrophe. The serial failures that followed the natural and (in particular) the man-made disasters forced the Japanese to look hard at their society and how it worked. Kyoto University professor Nakanishi Hiroshi explained that "March 11 put us into a very serious reflection of what postwar Japan is and where it should go. Japanese society as a whole hasn't come up with any good answers to these questions."[16] The debate over foreign policy—and Japan's contemplation of becoming a "normal" country—is part of this larger effort. For us, the vital question is whether and how debates over national identity issues provide clues to the ultimate resolution of these questions.

Understanding Japanese National Identity

Japanese Values

It is difficult to credit the assertion that nationalism is resurgent in Japan from public opinion data. Cabinet Office surveys from 1980 to 2013 show roughly half the respondents (peaking at 58 percent in 2013) agreeing that they have "strong affection" or patriotic feeling for their country.[17] (See figure 2.1.) Comparative studies show that Japanese exhibit the lowest sense of patriotism among Asian nations. According to Asia Barometer, 27 percent of Japanese are "proud of their own nationality," considerably less than the 46 percent of Chinese, 75 percent of Malays, and 93 percent of Thais. In the World Values Survey, Japan has the lowest percentage of people (24 percent) "proud of their country" and willing to fight for their country (16 percent) among all countries polled.[18] One interviewee suggested Japanese demonstrate *puchi* (small) nationalism, a "feel-good nationalism" characterized by flag waving at soccer games or sporting events. This tendency likely reached its apex

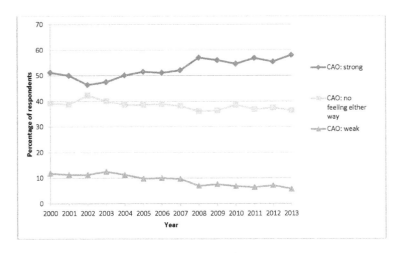

FIGURE 2.1 Japanese Views on Nationalism
Sources: CAO—Cabinet Office, Government of Japan

in the summer of 2011, when the Japanese women's soccer team, Nade-shiko Japan, won the FIFA women's World Cup. The team served as a rallying point for national sentiment and pride just four months after the triple catastrophe that slammed the country. Another interviewee characterized Japanese nationalism as a form of "cultural confidence." A university professor noted this tendency in his students: "They think we (Japanese) are cool enough."

Conversations with Japanese interlocutors reveal disagreement over whether nationalism is on the rise. While a Tokyo University professor was reluctant to say the Japanese were less arrogant fifteen years ago, the majority of our interlocutors felt the country was exhibiting more patri-otic sentiment. There was a spike in the aftermath of March 11, when Japanese were urged to come together in response to that tragedy. The government's emphasis on *kizuna*—a word meaning "bonds" or "con-nections" that was so ubiquitous that it was recognized at the end of 2011 as "kanji of the year"—highlighted the unity of all Japanese and by extension the idea of a single shared identity.[19] Several interviewees attributed rising patriotic sentiment to a more sweeping phenomenon: the country's changing international status. As Japan's relative power diminished, its citizens compensate by boosting national sentiment. A left-leaning journalist blamed "rising frustration and dissatisfaction with our position in the world. There is an unhealthy victim sentiment—despite all our goodwill, our intentions and contributions, we are not appreciated." That sentiment—the sense of a lack of appreciation—is borne out by Pew data: in 2013, 60 percent of Japanese felt that their country should be more respected in the world than it is.[20] Equally inter-esting is the prospect of a reaction to the seizing of the nationalist high ground by the Right. Sudo Reiko, a textile artist in Japan, noted that "after March 11 we started to think about our country seriously. We look at ourselves and we feel we are Japanese and we have to think about our country, but there is no nationalism, only the right wing. The Right monopolizes the flag and the country. We started to be concerned about nationalism in a positive way."[21]

There is a fear among Japan's neighbors—and even on the left within the country—that the rise to power of a younger generation with no direct experience of war and increasingly nationalist sentiment could produce a "normal" Japan that makes the same mistakes of the 1920s and 1930s. The *Mainichi shimbun* fretted about the resurgence of "narrow minded nationalism," which, it warned, "could block international cooperation. Although patriotism is important, exclusionary nationalism only causes friction and conflicts. If Japan pursues such nationalism, it would lose out entirely the benefits to be had through international cooperation and both Japan and the rest of the world would suffer."[22] Not only is it reassuring that a major Japanese newspaper would warn against that outcome, but none of the interviews we conducted substantiated that concern. All of them felt that rising nationalist sentiment in Japan was good for relations with the United States as it would spur Japan to be a better partner. The debate over the modernization of Japanese security policy underscores this point. While there are some in Japan who seek a more independent Japanese security posture, the majority position even among reformers seeks changes in policy and doctrine so that Japan can work more closely with the United States, shouldering a larger security burden (both for itself and for the region) within the alliance framework. This issue is taken up in more detail below and in later chapters.

Pew polls show steady frustration among Japanese regarding their country's direction: in 2013 just 33 percent were satisfied with the direction the country was heading (a 13 percent jump over the previous year), although 40 percent expect the economic outlook will improve.[23] Seventy-six percent of Japanese think that children will be worse off economically than their parents.[24] Pacific Forum CSIS respondents were decidedly more optimistic, with 63 percent believing that Japan will be a better country in a decade.

Mood matters, but more important is what kind of country Japan will be. Traditionally, Japan has had an activist state that promoted the notion of an egalitarian society. Famously, as many as 95 percent of respondents label themselves "middle class" when asked about social status.[25] Pacific Forum CSIS survey respondents confirmed that faith in egalitarianism by dividing 48–50 when asked if Japan ought to be a society where the gap between rich and poor is small regardless of one's achievement.

When Abe Shinzo became prime minister for the first time in fall 2006, one opinion survey showed that 80 percent of respondents considered a growing income gap a serious problem for Japan.[26] The same inclination is evident in a national poll in which a clear majority (58.4 percent) expressed preference for "a Northern European–style welfare model"; the "U.S.-style competitive society model" garnered only 6.7 percent support.[27] University of Hokkaido professor Yamaguchi Jiro, an adviser to the DPJ, believes that "The Japanese people want a welfare state. In government public polls people say they will pay more taxes if social security benefits are assured. Two-thirds agree with that direction."[28]

Other polls agree. A survey from 2008 shows overwhelming support—84.1 percent of respondents—for the idea that "the government should actively engage in closing the economic gap between citizens."[29] When those same respondents were asked "what kind of country Japan should be in the future," the top response (57.3 percent, and the only one garnering more than 50 percent support) was "a country focused on enhancing welfare."[30] Again, Pew data concurs: in 2011, 55 percent of Japanese respondents favored a state that played a more active role to guarantee that no one is in need, while just 37 percent wanted more freedom to pursue life goals without interference, results that had grown more lopsided over the decade.[31] Japanese demonstrate a general skepticism toward free-market economics. In a 2012 survey just 38 percent of Japanese agreed that "most people were better off in a free market economy," the second lowest of the twenty-one countries surveyed (only Mexico demonstrated lower support).[32] Not surprisingly, unable to see tangible rewards from growing diversity, many Japanese find the image of a united, homogeneous nation increasingly appealing.[33]

This is one of the most important tensions in Japanese politics. In 1997 Prime Minister Hashimoto Ryutaro launched economic reforms that some—critics and supporters, both at home and abroad—said would transform Japan into a "more Western" economy and society. Four years later Prime Minister Koizumi made reform the cornerstone of his administration, promising "structural reforms without sacred cows," and eventually even ran "assassins" against his own party's candidates to defeat LDP stalwarts who opposed his plans to overhaul the postal insurance and finance system. He booted the "postal rebels" out of the party if they survived that challenge. When Koizumi left office, however, his successor, Abe Shinzo, welcomed the rebels back to the party. Not surprisingly, the postal reform bills, along with similar legislation, were pushed aside. When the LDP and Abe reclaimed the reins of government in 2012, they promised to focus on economic rejuvenation, recognizing that an extended stay in office, and the realization of their entire political agenda, rested on revitalizing Japan's stagnant economy. This prompted the prime minister to push his "Abenomics" program with its "three arrows": monetary expansion, fiscal stimulus, and structural reform.[34] The third arrow represents the unfinished business of the Hashimoto and Koizumi governments and remains the most bitterly contested—on both ideological and political grounds—item on the prime minister's agenda, with Abe conceding in the summer of 2013 that there was not yet public and political support to push it through.[35] A year later, complaints about a lack of progress on the reform agenda were still being heard, but supporters of the Japanese government argued that the groundwork was being laid and that a forthcoming cabinet shuffle would help deliver on those changes.[36]

The difficulties launching the third arrow of Abenomics are the product of political concerns as well as a split among Japanese about the type of society they want to inhabit. According to the Pew Global Attitudes Project, 82 percent of Japanese agreed that "our people are not perfect, but our culture is superior to others" in spring 2011.[37] Similarly, 74 percent lamented "the loss of our traditional way of life" (in spring 2007) and agreed that "our way of life needs to be protected against foreign influence" (in spring 2009). This protection extends to foreign investment in Japan, with 69 percent agreeing in spring 2008 that the purchase of Japanese companies by foreigners has a bad impact on the country.[38] The evidence suggests far more skepticism may be warranted regarding the success of reform. Many Japanese, if not a considerable majority, not only prefer the status quo but actually oppose change that could undermine Japanese tradition and culture.

Looking back at the Koizumi years, it appears that he was popular not because of the policies he championed but because of the image of a leader he projected. Koizumi halted the revolving door in the Prime Minister's Office, and providing stability is a political asset in its own right. His ability to stand shoulder to shoulder with President Bush was a signal to the Japanese (and the world) that their government was again prominent and respected and sought out by world leaders (even if the Japanese themselves were ambivalent about Bush and his policies). It also helped that the economy was regaining its footing while Koizumi was in office. And, finally, while he talked of reform, there was a considerable gap between Koizumi's rhetoric and his accomplishments. In a telling indication of where his party's "center" of gravity lay, the "postal rebels" were reinstated once Koizumi stepped down.

The Japanese may only be flirting with Western ideas about structural reform. When faced with the social consequences of economic change, they reverted to more traditional and comfortable positions. This is not to say that Japan resists all reform; no society can. But the Japanese identify with a state in which all members are equal, there are few disparities, and the state plays an active role in ameliorating those that do exist. This combines with a respect (and periodic reverence) for tradition, another integral component of Japanese identity, to act as a brake on change. The government's readiness to exploit those traditions for economic purposes in the "Cool Japan" program emphasizes and reinforces the importance of traditional culture to the population at large.[39] Perhaps the most revealing indication is the fact that Japan has struggled to implement the same package of reforms for over a decade. The price of inaction—two lost decades—is clear, yet politicians and the public refuse to accept substantive change. The country's trajectory remains largely fixed, and that says a great deal about national preferences and national identity. Indeed, one interviewee explained that the turmoil of the lost decade has pushed many Japanese, especially the younger generation, traditionally the most adventurous cohort, to seek security and to become increasingly conservative. As a former LDP politician explained, "reform has another face: traditional Japanese values." Economist Sawa Takamitsu even argues that Abenomics rolls back reforms that were in place, insisting that targets that the Abe plan provides and the call for government intervention to achieve them constitute "an attempt to build state capitalism." He concludes that "Abe has completely overturned the moves by former Prime Ministers Nakasone Yasuhiro and Koizumi toward small government, in which economic results were to be left to the workings of free, competitive markets . . . it's as if Abe has resurrected the old LDP as well as an administration controlled by bureaucrats, both of which Koizumi set out to destroy."[40]

Foreign and Security Policy

Japanese believe that they should be engaged in the world. Yet after peaking in 2004 at nearly 83,000, the number of Japanese students overseas has fallen considerably: in 2010, the last year numbers are available, just 58,000 Japanese were studying abroad, with just under 20,000 of them in the United States.[41] One interviewee—the professor whose students were "cool enough"—suggested their cultural confidence was causing them to lose interest in the outside world. One journalist blamed "globalization fatigue" for encouraging them to focus inward. Yet another journalist suggested that Japanese were so comfortable at home, in both job prospects and daily comforts, that they had lost the appetite to venture outside the "bubble" of Japan. Agawa Naoyuki, a lawyer and former diplomat in Japan's embassy in Washington who is now a vice president of Keio University, suggested there is "a big lie about 'international Japan.' The common feeling is 'Everyone should be international but not me.'" This reflects, he said, "the real dividing line in Japan—those who want to be international and those who don't."[42] Agawa makes an important distinction. While there is little support for isolationism among Japanese, that does not mean that individuals are prepared to be the leading edge of engagement.

Fears of entanglement aren't prominent among respondents, but the terms on which Japan should engage are particular. When Pacific Forum CSIS asked respondents to rank priorities for Japan's role, "helping solve environmental problems" was far and away the first choice. "Developing new technologies" was a distant second, followed by "developing and stabilizing the Asian economy" and "developing and stabilizing the global economy." These findings are consistent with other research.

In the annual Cabinet Office Survey on Foreign Relations in 2012, when asked to identify "what role Japan should play in international affairs," the top response was "humanitarian relief and peacekeeping," followed by "environment and climate change" (this category topped the list in 2009). In 2012 no other role won majority support.[43]

These findings reflect an enduring consensus in Japan: with the exception of environmental issues, few Japanese believe their country should play a regional role, and even fewer believe it should play a global role. At the turn of the century, the only international role that more than 50 percent of Japanese could agree on for their country was "contributions to the improvement of the global environment" (which 77 percent endorsed). In that survey, less than 40 percent backed the "arbitration of interests and opinions in the region," 28 percent supported "arbitration of interests and opinions of the international society," and still less— 26 percent—felt Japan should contribute to solving international conflicts. All three numbers represented declines from a survey done two years earlier.[44] Plainly there is support only for a limited Japanese role, one that plays to traditional (postwar) conceptions of Japanese strength and identity. There is a powerful preference for peaceful forms of conflict resolution and prevention.

Again, other polls agree. When asked about national policy priorities in the Pacific Forum CSIS poll, respondents ranked "assert international leadership" sixth of nine choices. In a 2008 poll, just 8.2 percent of respondents wanted Japan to "contribute to international society"; all other choices focused on domestic concerns.[45] Interviewees blamed Japan's weak self-image for the reluctance to step forward or a disposition toward modesty. Another argued that the problem was cultural: "Japanese are not aware of national power, not taught to think in those terms. National security has been given to us." Japanese are, in the memorable phrase of one analyst, "*Asahi*-reading realists."

There isn't support for the idea that Japan should be more assertive in international affairs. Eight-nine percent say Japan should assert its interests, but an even higher number—92 percent—believe Japan should be sensitive to other countries' feelings. Consistent with that, 71 percent of Pacific Forum respondents believe that the Japanese prime minister should not visit Yasukuni Shrine if other countries object. That figure has changed only a little over time. On the commemoration in 2013 of the end of World War II, 63 percent of respondents in an *Asahi shimbun* poll said that it was "appropriate" for the prime minister to skip ceremonies at the shrine, more than three times the number of respondents who said it was "inappropriate" (20 percent).[46] Only 62 percent in the Pacific Forum poll agreed that "there can be no compromise in territorial disputes with other nations." At the close of 2013, Prime Minister Abe made a surprise visit to Yasukuni, angering both Seoul and Beijing. In a snap poll by *Kyodo News* immediately after the visit, nearly 70 percent of respondents thought Abe should take diplomatic relations into consideration when visiting the shrine. This figure is considerably larger than the 47.1 percent who said "it was not good" that the prime minister went to the shrine; just 43.2 percent appreciated the visit.[47]

Article 9 and "Normalcy"

For many the bellwether of change in Japan is the debate over revising the constitution. Long a target of nationalist resentment for being imposed by the United States in the aftermath of defeat in World War II and depriving Japan of one of the essential attributes of statehood, a majority of public opinion in Japan appears to positively assess Article 9.[48] In the early 1990s, as the country grappled with the implications of a post–Cold War world, then LDP secretary general Ozawa Ichiro proposed that Japan become a "normal nation," which required a reconsideration of the restraints imposed by the constitution.

This is a dense and complex topic. When Ozawa argued for "normalcy," he was focused on politics: the alternation of power that would result from a two-party system. The "security" component of this evolution was secondary. Moreover, the degree to which the constitution has actually constrained Japanese security policy is unclear. A host of politicians, cabinet interpretations, and court decisions have suggested throughout the postwar era that Japan could do considerably more than it does; the constitution's constraints have proven quite flexible.[49] More intriguing still, however, and more pertinent to this discussion, is

Swedish scholar Linus Hagstrom's argument that Japan's "abnormality" is a core component of its national identity. Drawing on the work of Michel Foucault, Hagstrom asserts that the claim of abnormality is itself a form of "identity discourse" that relates to the notions of "(1) Japan as an Other in the international system; (2) the Japanese Self as an Other—at the same time illegitimately 'abnormal' and legitimately 'exceptional'; and (3) Japanese Othering both of its own alleged 'abnormality' and of China/Asia, as a way to secure a more 'normal' Japanese Self."[50] A key point of Hagstrom's analysis is the convergence of seemingly incompatible left and right perspectives—"although narratives of 'exceptionalism' and 'abnormality' are diametrically opposed, they are both conditioned on a notion of Japanese 'difference,' and so is the political right's replacement idea that Japan should become 'beautiful,' 'correct,' and 'strong' "[51]—a demonstration of how this notion of identity transcends positions on the political spectrum.

While there seems to be growing sentiment that backs constitutional revision, it is premature to assert that change is coming. First, there does not yet appear to be a consistent majority that favors revision. Second, results often depend on the poll, its sponsor, and the particular questions it asks. Finally, it is important to recognize that many Japanese favor changing the charter for reasons that have nothing do with Article 9—a desire to protect human rights, to change the role of the imperial family, to prevent environmental destruction, and so on. In a Department of State survey of Japanese opinion in October 2006, revising Article 9 was only fifth in a list of reasons people would back constitutional change, mustering a 59 percent support rate (a 7 percentage point increase from July 2002). Topping the list was strengthening of environmental protection (94 percent in favor), direct election of the prime minister (71 percent), strengthening of individual privacy rights (67 percent), and giving more power to regional authorities (61 percent). In a *Nikkei shimbun* poll from 2008 in which 48 percent of respondents favored amending the constitution (and 43 percent wanted to keep it as it is), the major justification for backing change (54 percent, the only option to top 25 percent) was "it is necessary to incorporate new ideas." And for that group, key problems with the current constitution were the failures to account for privacy rights and the environment (31 percent), failure to include local autonomy (28 percent), the idea of a bicameral legislature (24 percent), and the failure to limit government intervention in the economy (23 percent). Complaints about Article 9 were only the fifth reason.[52] When the *Nikkei shimbun* reported in May 2013 that 56 percent of Japanese agreed that the constitution should be amended, the results again showed this need to be cautious about the data. In this case, 54 percent of respondents wanted to change Japan's parliamentary system (reform the two chambers), but just 38 percent endorsed revision of Article 9.[53]

Focusing on Article 9, 75 percent of Pacific Forum respondents felt it should be revised, but just 39 percent said that it should be rewritten entirely. Forty-four percent endorsed keeping the first paragraph—which renounces the use of force as a means of settling international disputes—and merely changing the second paragraph, a move that would, in essence, legalize the SDF. Other surveys show greater opposition to constitutional amendment, but those that show (relatively) high support for revision echo these results. For example, a *Yomiuri shimbun* poll in April 2008 found that just 42.5 percent of respondents said it would be better to amend the constitution, while 43.1 percent were opposed. Nearly 82 percent of respondents opposed changing the first paragraph, while 54 percent opposed changing the second; 36.8 percent supported that revision.[54]

That division endures. A September 2013 poll by the right-leaning *Sankei shimbun* showed 52 percent of its respondents favoring constitutional amendment generally, with just 36 percent opposed.[55] (The poll addressed security issues so it can be assumed that amendment was interpreted by readers to concern Article 9.) A survey at the same time by the more centrist *Mainichi shimbun* reported 56 percent favored amendment to Article 9, while 37 percent believed that no change is needed.[56] Predictably, a poll by the progressive *Asahi shimbun* a few months earlier showed a 52 percent majority opposed to changing Article 9, with 39 percent favoring such a step.[57]

Public positions on changing Article 9 fit well within the political and social framework outlined here. Interviewees explained that the call for constitutional revision was a way to make Japan a more reliable security partner for the United States and the region. Several complained that changing the interpretation of the constitution, as was done by Japanese administrations to permit Japanese contributions to international peacekeeping and security efforts, undermined Tokyo's international credibility and the legitimacy of the constitution itself. But they also recognized that a changing security environment demanded more of Japan and that a failure to act would have been equally damaging to Japan's international standing. In other words, for them, constitutional revision was not intended to provide a blank check for Japanese security policy makers or the SDF but would provide a more robust and stable framework for contributing to international efforts to provide security. After all, in 2007, 60 percent of Japanese conceded that "it is sometimes necessary to use military force to maintain order in the world."[58]

Constitutional revision remains a challenge, even in 2013 when conditions were about as favorable to reform as can be imagined. After the March 11 triple catastrophe, the performance of the Self-Defense Forces pushed public approval of the military to the stratosphere, with opinion polls showing 91.7 percent of respondents had a favorable impression of the SDF.[59] Meanwhile, support for the alliance with the United States is plumbing new heights at the same time that anxieties about neighbors are mounting (both topics will be discussed in more detail below). Prime Minister Abe has made clear his desire to amend the constitution, calling it his "historical mission,"[60] as well as making it a core component of the LDP's 2012–13 election platform. And finally, an overwhelming majority of Diet members favor constitutional revision: 75 percent of Upper House members and 89 percent of Lower House members have said that they back reform, meaning that more than two-thirds of Diet members—the threshold for initiating a constitutional amendment—are theoretically ready to back such a move.[61]

And yet the constitutional amendment juggernaut has been confounded. Despite those high support levels in the Diet and his own inclinations, Prime Minister Abe has tabled plans to revise Article 96 of the constitution (which deals with how the charter is to be amended) and is focused instead on economic revitalization and mustering more support among the public. He may be playing the long game, recognizing that he has to get the economy in gear to stay in power, but it is a bet neverthe-less. The historical record is not good, and if the economy sputters and stops, he may never again have the support ratings to push through a proposal this controversial.

The opposition is also evident in the debate over the exercise of the right of collective self-defense, where resistance has proven more entrenched than Abe and his supporters may have anticipated. Since (re)broaching the subject, the advocates of reinterpretation have been forced to go slow, narrowing the scope of the proposed changes and engaging in a public debate in the Diet and in the media. The public remains deeply divided even after the pump was primed and a strong case was made for reform.[62] The government made an aggressive push to make the case for reinterpretation, but a *Nikkei shimbun* poll in May 2014 showed that 47 percent opposed the exercise of collective self-defense, with just 37 percent in support, results that echoed a *Mainichi shimbun* survey of the week before in which 54 percent opposed the idea and 39 percent backed it. Abe himself conceded that "it's difficult for the general public to understand, and there is strong opposition."[63]

In other words, the political and social constraints against constitu-tional reform are powerful, which is not surprising if the Japanese have internalized the peace constitution and its ideals in their national identity.

China in Japanese Eyes

China looms large in Japanese thinking. Kenneth Pyle notes, for example, that as early as the seventh century, "the rise of an expansive China spurred Japan to adopt Chinese institutions and create the first unified Japanese state."[64] Historically, at least until the Meiji Restora-tion, "Japanese identity was constructed primarily by differentiating Japan from Asia, and particularly China."[65] Today, in many respects, China is everything Japan is not: large, dynamic, confident, possessed of a nuclear arsenal, with a permanent seat on the United Nations Secu-rity Council, and prepared—if not anxious—to play a leading role in the region and the world. China's assumption of second place among global economies in 2010, overtaking Japan, only drove the point home.

The two have been rivals for centuries, with Japan emerging as Asia's leading nation at the beginning of the twentieth century, losing its position in war, and then reclaiming that role, for a few decades, from the 1970s. After China emerged from its self-imposed isolation in the late twentieth century, it has squared off with Japan over regional supremacy. While China has been a source of Japanese anxiety for some time (scenarios involved either a conflict with Taiwan or some event on the mainland triggering a flood of refugees), in recent years China's strength has occupied Japanese security planners. Territorial disputes, historical grievances, and the tensions prompted by day-to-day interactions have been a toxic cocktail.

The first decade of the twenty-first century was an especially turbulent time for Japan–China relations. While there were hopes that this vital relationship would consolidate and provide the axis for Asian integration, the first half of the decade was troubled as Prime Minister Koizumi insisted on visiting Yasukuni Shrine, a gesture that honored one of his campaign promises but managed to infuriate and offend China and South Korea.[66] At the time of the Pacific Forum survey, there was widespread agreement that the Japan–China relationship was improving, a product of the policy shift that occurred when Koizumi left office and his successors abjured visits to the shrine. Nevertheless, a deep reservoir of mistrust was evident: 76 percent of respondents in the Pacific Forum poll did not trust China to act responsibly in the world. Moreover, 58 percent identified China as the biggest threat to Japan. The 2008 Japan Defense White Paper captured popular sentiment, noting that "Japan is apprehensive about how the military power of China will influence the regional state of affairs and the security of Japan."[67]

The improvement proved to be temporary, and relations between Japan and China soon deteriorated again. A series of incidents kept the relationship frosty,[68] but tensions boiled over in 2010, when a Chinese fishing boat captain was arrested by the Japanese Coast Guard for fishing in waters near the disputed Senkaku/Diaoyu islands. Normally in such a case the offender would have been released without charge, but this time the captain rammed two coast guard vessels while trying to escape. The authorities felt compelled to arrest the suspect, triggering an international confrontation that continues to this day. China demanded the captain's release (eventually obtained), and then an apology (not given). During the height of the standoff, Chinese exports to Japan of rare earths, minerals critical to production of high-tech items, were cut off. While Chinese authorities dispute any connection between the cut-off and the faceoff, Japanese drew their own conclusions, interpreting the move as a form of economic warfare. Soon after, Tokyo governor Ishihara Shintaro decided to stir the pot by launching a campaign to buy the islands (held by private Japanese citizens) to reaffirm Japanese sovereignty over them (and tweak both the Chinese and the DPJ government, which he considered weak-kneed). The Japanese government subsequently nationalized the islands, a move intended to head off Ishihara and defuse the controversy, but which nevertheless inflamed the Chinese government and public alike. At the end of 2013, the two governments continued to wage a high-stakes diplomatic battle over the islets, with China sending aircraft and naval vessels routinely into territorial waters surrounding the islands to challenge Japanese "control" over them while Tokyo repeated that there is no territorial dispute.[69]

Not surprisingly, Japanese feelings toward China are not good, as is evident in figure 2.2. In 2008, when relations were supposedly on the rebound, Japanese feelings toward China were cool: when asked to gauge the relative affinity toward China, the overall rating was 44.66 (out of 100)—and 50 was "not warm or cold." Respondents were evenly split on whether China's role in Asia will be positive or negative; consistent with that view, respondents gave China an average score of 5.06 (out of 10) when asked how much influence they would like China to have in the world. The Chicago Council on Global Affairs poll in 2008 revealed a slightly more positive assessment of China, with 62 percent of its Japanese respondents viewing China as having a "very positive" or "somewhat positive" influence in Asia.[70] By 2012 just 5 percent of Japanese in one authoritative poll had a favorable opinion of China, a 24-point plunge since 2007. Eleven percent of respondents saw China as a friend of Japan, 47 percent considered it an enemy, and 47 percent were undecided.[71] The Japanese government's annual Survey on Foreign Affairs reached similar conclusions, with 18 percent of respondents

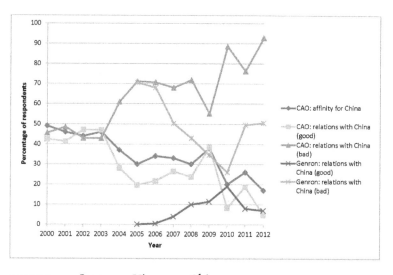

FIGURE 2.2 Japanese Views on China

Sources: CAO—Cabinet Office, Government of Japan; Genron NPO

saying that they had friendly feelings toward China, a drop of 8 percentage points from the year before, and 80 percent professing to have unfriendly feelings, an increase of 9 percentage points from 2011. Only 4.8 percent of respondents considered the Japan–China relationship "good" (compared to 18.8 percent the year before), while 92.8 percent agreed it was "not good" (a jump from 76.3 percent in 2011).[72] In the ninth Japan–China survey by Genron NPO, a Japanese civil society group, 61.8 percent of respondents said that they actually viewed China as a military threat to Japan; only North Korea (73.4 percent) evinced greater concern, and no other country topped 17.5 percent.[73] This bilateral relationship is increasingly adversarial, and the key to a sustainable reversal—a reservoir of goodwill toward the other country among the public—is nowhere in sight.

Despite growing antipathy toward China, however, Japanese feelings about its neighbor remain complex, for not only is it a rival—and increasingly considered a threat—but it is also a partner. In July 2008 Japan's exports to China overtook those to the United States, making

China its number one export partner.[74] When asked which country would be Japan's most important economic partner in the next five to ten years, slightly more than half (53 percent) of Pacific Forum CSIS respondents pointed to China; the United States was second.[75] (This is part of a larger trend: 78 percent believe there will be greater economic integration among Asian countries; 56 percent anticipate creation of an East Asia free trade area (FTA) that includes Japan, China, and South Korea. That process has taken on additional momentum in recent years, especially with the launch of a study of an FTA and the realization of common rules on investment among China, Japan, and South Korea, as well as the creation of a secretariat for their various trilateral endeavors.) In the *Asahi shimbun* Japan–China joint poll taken in September 2012, 50 percent of respondents backed deepening economic exchanges with China.[76] Two-thirds of respondents in the Genron NPO poll in 2013 said the two countries should cooperate and work on East Asian issues together.[77]

When asked "which country was more important to Japan—the U.S. or China?" 43 percent of Pacific Forum poll respondents said "both are equally important." More recently, 52.2 percent of respondents in the Genron NPO poll agreed that "both relationships are equally important"; in contrast, a little over 37 percent said relations with the United States were more important for Japan, while just 2.9 percent put China first.[78] This contrasts with Pew data in 2013, which show that 84 percent of Japanese think it is more important to have strong ties with the United States, while just 6 percent picked China as their preferred partner.[79] What is potentially more troubling is the fact that 44 percent of Pacific Forum respondents said Japan and China are equally important *to the United States*—while only 32 percent picked Japan as more important. The seeds of insecurity are deep in the U.S.–Japan relationship, and U.S. policy makers must be attuned to Japanese fears of "Japan passing."[80]

China's rise poses several important issues for Japanese identity. Most obviously, China is a direct challenge to the Japanese belief that it is the most successful country in Asia and the de facto rightful leader of the region. China's continuing growth is a pointed contrast to the stagnation in Japan and compounds the malaise that gnaws at Japanese self-confidence. Equally important, a mounting sense of threat from China forces Japanese to examine their commitment to the conception of their nation as inherently peaceful; the risks of that position are magnified when a potential challenger or threat is nearby.

Relations with the United States

While China is seen as Japan's most important economic partner, 91 percent of Pacific Forum respondents identified the United States as Japan's most important security partner over the same 5–10 year period.[81] That could reflect the belief that Japanese *values* are most similar to those of the United States (34 percent agreed; South Korea was named second with 32 percent) or the belief that Japanese *interests* are most similar to those of the United States (56 percent; nobody else comes close on this question). When asked which country is most important to Japan, 55 percent said the United States, while 42 percent identified China. The Pew data cited above, in which 84 percent of Japanese identified the United States as their preferred partner and just 6 percent selected China, suggests the frictions of the past decade have undermined Japanese readiness to partner with China.

In addition to—or perhaps because of—the convergence of ideas and values mentioned earlier, in the Pacific Forum CSIS poll Japanese have the warmest feelings for the United States when compared with all other countries: 81.11 (out of 100) versus 71.77 for the United Kingdom, 69.96 for Australia, and 68.12 for Southeast Asia. (These results also suggest a strong identification with the West, at least among elite respondents.) Again, the Pew data confirm this positive assessment: 69 percent of Japanese respondents gave the United States a favorable rating in 2013, a decrease from the peak of 85 percent in 2011 but strongly positive nonetheless.[82] (See figure 2.3.) Seventy-six percent of Japanese consider the United States a friend. That tracks results from the Japanese Cabinet Office: in its 2012 survey, 84.5 percent had positive feelings toward the United States, a 2.5 percent increase over the previous year. Consistent with that finding, nearly 80 percent (79.6 percent) of those respondents characterized the relationship with the United States as "good," a jump of 4.9 percent from the previous poll.[83]

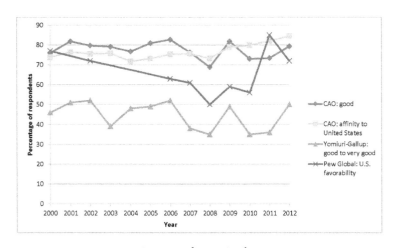

FIGURE 2.3 Japanese Views on the United States

Sources: CAO—Cabinet Office, Government of Japan; Yomiuri-Gallup Poll; Pew Research Global Attitudes Project

Not surprisingly, support for the U.S.–Japan alliance is strong across all surveys. In the Pacific Forum CSIS poll, 96 percent said that the alliance is vital to Japan's security, and 62 percent of respondents said the alliance is the most important contributor to Japan's security. That figure is almost twice as high as those who put Japan's own efforts as most important; only three respondents were prepared to put their faith in the United Nations and other international organizations. Eighty-eight percent believe U.S. bases in Japan are important to the country's national security, and 82 percent believe the United States should keep them there. Seventy-eight percent credit those bases with increasing stability in East Asia; 94 percent believe the U.S.–Japan alliance is a force for regional stability and security.[84] In 2012, 81.2 percent of respondents to a Cabinet Office survey agreed that the alliance is "beneficial" for Japan, a number that reflected the positive evaluation of U.S. forces during *Operation Tomodachi*, the bilateral response to the March 11 disaster.[85]

Still, there is some ambivalence toward the alliance among Japanese, however. The alliance provides Japan with security, allows Tokyo to "cheap ride" and devote more resources to economic development, and provides cover for Japan's growing regional security role: the alliance reassures regional governments that Japan's assumption of new responsibilities does not represent the first steps toward remilitarization. But the unbalanced relationship serves as a constant reminder of Japan's defeat in World War II, Tokyo's subordinate status, and the limitations on Japanese sovereignty embodied in Article 9 of the U.S.-imposed constitution. Little wonder then that the alliance has been both the cornerstone of Japan's postwar security and a lightning rod for criticism from the Left—who decry an alliance with the capitalist and militarist United States that undermines the country's pacifism—and the Right, which complains that Japan's independence is compromised and its status diminished. And both appeal to core components of Japanese identity as they do so.

While Japanese recognize the importance of the alliance, that does not mean they accept it as is or that Washington has a blank check when it comes to alliance policy. Japanese have had "sticker shock" when considering the cost of realigning U.S. forces in Japan. A survey showed 72 percent of respondents agreed it is important to strengthen U.S.–Japan security cooperation, but 69 percent think Japan should pay less than its ¥700 billion share.[86] Moreover, more than half (56 percent) think local interests should take priority over national interests—think "not in my backyard"; only 36 percent put national interests first.[87] This makes readjustment and realignment problematic. The ongoing failure to move the Futenma Marine Air Station to northern Okinawa is the most visible manifestation of this tendency. Widespread public support for the alliance and rising concern about the regional security environment notwithstanding, Japanese politicians have shown precious little inclination to spend political capital on hard decisions. Even an avowed conservative like Prime Minister Abe initially courted Washington's anger by going slow on Okinawa issues.[88]

While almost all interviewees thought Japan should be more self-reliant and better able to assert its interests within the alliance, they all agreed that this stronger Japan is best served by the alliance. "Japan wants to be able to say no, but we don't want to fight with the United States," explained a young security analyst. "We want more equality within the alliance." As one former LDP official elaborated, the security alliance is leverage for Japan. The debate over the interpretation of Japan's right of collective self-defense in 2013–14 is illustrative. Traditionally the Japanese constitution has been interpreted as affording Japan the right of collective self-defense but banning its exercise. In other words, Japan, like all states, *has* this right but is unable to *use* it. When Abe Shinzo first occupied the Prime Minister's Office in 2006, he pressed for a reinterpretation that would allow Tokyo to exercise this right. He left office before the idea gained traction. In his second administration, Abe picked up that battle where he left off, pressing again for a change. Abe and like-minded conservatives prefer to rewrite the constitution, dropping or changing Article 9 (along with other provisions), but, having recognized that goal is too ambitious at present, they are pushing for change on collective self-defense. Significantly, proponents argue that a new interpretation is needed so that Japan can be a better partner and ally of the United States and make more contributions to regional security.[89]

There remain reasons for concern, however. More than a quarter of Pacific Forum respondents (25.56 percent) disagreed with the statement that "the U.S. respects Japan." That is a worryingly high number for foreign policy specialists who otherwise demonstrate a predisposition toward the alliance. If they feel "dissed," that sentiment may be even more widespread among the general public. As one journalist explained, "There is a fatigue with U.S. annoyance." That sentiment is also evident in a 2013 survey that shows just 38 percent of Japanese respondents think the United States considers Japanese interests "a great deal" or "a fair amount"; a far more substantial 59 percent think the United States largely dismisses Japanese concerns, either taking them into account "a little bit" or "not at all."[90]

There have been long-standing problems for the U.S.–Japan alliance—the Futenma Air Base, environmental pollution, burden sharing—but alliance frictions often reflect issues of the day. At the time of the Pacific Forum survey, there were mounting complaints in Tokyo about U.S. reliability as the negotiations over North Korea's nuclear program proceeded. Japanese officials and observers charged that chief U.S.

negotiator Christopher Hill was moving forward with a deal despite a lack of progress in bilateral Japan–North Korea dialogue. In strategic discussions at the unofficial level, Japanese participants asked whether the United States was ignoring Japanese interests. At the same time, Japanese noted Washington's readiness to work with Beijing on issues such as the Six-Party Talks, the fight against terrorism, and "capping" Taiwan's independence ambitions and worried that this might portend a diminution in the U.S. commitment to defend Japan. In 2013, Tokyo's focus was the Senkaku/Diaoyu dispute and U.S. readiness to back its claim to sovereignty over the islands, which became a proxy for larger concerns about the alliance and relative weights Washington afforded the U.S.–Japan and U.S.–China relationships.

At a time when Japan faces hardening sentiment and periodic hostility from its Northeast Asian neighbors, the relationship with the United States takes on new meaning and value. While many Japanese (and some foreign observers) initially applauded efforts by the first DPJ government to invest more energy in relations with Asia, when it became clear that the U.S.–Japan relationship might suffer in the process, support for this new orientation quickly evaporated. While growing numbers of Japanese acknowledge that their future lies in deeper integration within Asia, there is near unanimity that this must occur in tandem with a strong alliance with the United States.[91] This is not a zero-sum relationship among the United States, Japan, and Asia.

Explaining Japan

The portrait of Japan that emerges from these data should be familiar. Japanese are proud of their country and their culture, but that pride does not equate with nationalism or chauvinism. Rather, it is a sense of belonging to a distinct group. Japanese are conservative in the traditional sense of the word, meaning status quo oriented. That conservatism is evident in the continuing overwhelming support for an egalitarian society and the call for state action to make that ideal real. While that social structure is usually equated with "liberalism" when describing politics, in the Japanese case it comports with the prevailing image of postwar society as predominately middle class and homogeneous. The introduction of "Anglo-American capitalism" with its inequalities is a departure from the norm for Japan and seems to have little popular support other than in a very abstract sense.

Japanese national priorities focus on improving conditions at home rather than the projection of power or dealing with external issues. (This is consistent with the notion that Japanese pride should not be equated with nationalism.) When Japanese contemplate ways to help the world beyond their shores, their preferred answers seem to be the extension of domestic efforts beyond their borders—exporting environmental solutions or technology, or letting the region enjoy the fruits of Japan's economic success. There is little interest in mediating or solving problems. In other words, there is little desire for assuming responsibility. Rather, Japanese want to export their good behavior.

Periodic frictions in the bilateral relationship notwithstanding, support for the alliance with the United States remains strong. That makes sense as the United States is seen as the country whose values and interests best align with those of Japan. The United States is viewed as Japan's most important security partner, and the U.S.–Japan alliance is considered to be the best guarantor of Japanese security. The value of that alliance has been buttressed by the rising sense of threat emanating from China and North Korea. The importance of the alliance is evident when seen through the prism of the national debate over the constitution. To the degree that there is support for revision of Article 9, it is intended to make Japan a better ally, not loosen the ties that bind it to its partner.

Equally significant is the language used to validate this new outlook: the changes Japan is making are intended to allow it to become a "proactive contributor to peace," a phrase that appears eight times in the new National Security Strategy.[92] Even more revealing is the explanation offered by Kitaoka Shinichi, an adviser to numerous government panels on Japanese national security and vice chair of the advisory panel on the exercise of the right of collective self-defense. Kitaoka uses the phrase "proactive pacifism" to explain the new policy, noting that "proactive pacifism is not a new outlook." Pointing to Japanese ODA and its advocacy of the concept of human security, he concludes that "all these are manifestations of proactive pacifism and we are now trying to push it further."[93] Michael Green is right to point out that some skepticism is in order here. In some cases policy makers "manipulate the rhetoric of security identity to mask significant changes in security practice."[94] But there is another way to interpret that "deception": the resort to the language of pacifism is an attempt to demonstrate continuity and an acknowledgment of the depth of pacifist sentiment within Japanese national identity.

The features outlined here are not just descriptive. The identity they reveal helps explain the trajectories of Japanese politics and the broad contours of Japanese foreign policy in recent years. It underscores the "reluctance" of Japanese to be realists when dealing with foreign and security policy, the readiness despite—or because of—political instability for over two decades to cling to existing security and foreign policy frameworks, and the hesitance to take on new commitments. Thus, "forward deployment" of the Japanese security presence is increasingly difficult. This may seem anomalous as Maritime Self-Defense Forces have joined antipiracy patrols off the coast of East Africa and an SDF "camp" in Djibouti has been created. However, the mission is tied directly to Japanese national interests, the protection of its shipping,[95] and the camp serves as infrastructure for the effort. In the absence of this strong, direct connection to Japanese national security interests, there are likely to be fewer such ventures in the future. This reflects a number of factors: completion of the mission in Iraq, a diminished sense of urgency in addressing these foreign problems (from the Japanese perspective, especially as the United States shifts its attention to focus more on Asia), increasing budget constraints, and a growing sense of threat closer to home. Each could be overcome, but the Japanese "identity" that emerges from these data raises the bar for doing so.

The political turmoil that Japan has experienced since Koizumi left office in 2006 has increased resistance to change by obliging the public and policy makers to focus on more immediate concerns. The turmoil is an assertion of the traditional Japanese identity. The rise to power of the DPJ reflects, in some ways, a response to the transformative impulses of the LDP. Koizumi's economic reforms challenged the egalitarianism that most Japanese support. In foreign policy his successor, Abe Shinzo, confused public support for Koizumi's distinctive international profile with support for an assertive foreign policy. There is little stomach in Japan for leadership—as opposed to status—in most fields of international endeavor. The tolerance for departures from that low profile shrinks even more when the Japanese government cannot deliver on fundamental services like pensions or economic growth. While his successors, Fukuda Yasuo and Aso Taro, retreated from the more extreme elements of Abe's policies, neither handled those bread-and-butter issues. The policy swings under DPJ governments, its mishandling of the March 11 triple catastrophe, and the continuing failure to get the economy on track doomed the brief experiment in opposition rule.

Understanding Japan requires an appreciation of its sense of vulnerability. For some it is the product of the "island nation mentality" and it is nurtured by the constant reminder that Japan has no resources other than its people. The March 11 catastrophe hammered home this point, as was explained by writer Murakami Haruki in a 2011 speech. For Murakami, the Japanese outlook is captured by the word *mujo*, a Buddhist concept that means that everything is ephemeral, and nothing is immutable or eternal. He believes that this concept has been "burned into the spirit of Japanese people beyond the strictly religious context, taking root in the common ethnic consciousness from ancient times." For him, acceptance of the fleeting nature of life and beauty is an integral part of the Japanese aesthetic; for us, it is another indication of the outsized role of vulnerability in the Japanese psyche.[96]

This sense of vulnerability takes more visible forms, too. In recent years Japan has experienced moments of real isolation within Northeast Asia; the fact that Japanese action (or inaction in some cases) has created that situation is secondary. Recall that the data show that Japanese values are most closely associated with those of the United States. And there are rising external threats. Not surprisingly, then, ties to the United States have become even more important. In this environment the call of the first DPJ prime minister, Hatoyama Yukio, for more balance between

Asia and the West in Japanese foreign policy may have made sense, but not if that meant downplaying the alliance with the United States. And no matter what his intentions, when it looked like his policies might jeopardize relations with its ally, Hatoyama lost public support and was forced from office.

His disastrous term in office reflected tactical mistakes, but an equally compelling explanation for the response to his policies can be found in its rejection of the basic tenets of modern Japanese identity. While Japanese understand that their fates are increasingly intertwined with those of their Asian neighbors, there is still a close identification with the United States, for reasons of protection, prosperity, and profile (alliance with the United States permits Japan to stake out a distinctive role in the region). Economic relations may demand closer ties to Asian neighbors, and China in particular, but national pride remains important, and getting too close to China risks Japan's eclipse by its neighbor. Consistent with this analysis, we anticipated and saw Hatoyama's successors, Kan Naoto and Noda Yoshihiko, work to get relations with the United States back on track, a task that was facilitated (ironically) by Japan's problems with its neighbors and the horrific events of March 11, after which *Operation Tomodachi*, the U.S.–Japan relief effort, demonstrated the depth of the U.S. commitment to Japan's security. In other words, ties to the United States are reinforced by Japanese values and a sense of vulnerability, because they validate Japan's identity as a peace-loving state (by reducing defense burdens) and promote Tokyo's status as a leading nation in Asia.

Japan's New Nationalism?

It isn't possible to predict political outcomes on the basis of identity alone, but this notion constrains decision makers and helps explain and anticipate the success (or failure) of various policy outcomes. Japan's fall 2012 parliamentary campaign and the results of the December 16, 2012, poll offer a valuable test case.

When Prime Minister Noda took office in September 2011, his first task was halting the free fall in the DPJ's popularity, a plunge that was accelerated by the government's hapless response to the events of March 11. He promised to practice a "politics of decision" (*kimeraru seiji*) that put the interests of the people and the country ahead of short-term political calculations. He made the unpopular decision to raise the consumption tax, a step toward putting the nation's finances in order, and signaled his intention to join the Trans-Pacific Partnership.[97] Unfortunately for Noda, his party proved less capable of accommodating such positions. A large number of DPJ members left the party in protest, forcing the prime minister to reach out to the opposition LDP, which backed his efforts on the condition that he call an election before the Diet's term expired.

All observers expected the DPJ to take a shellacking in the ballot. Not only had it performed poorly in the aftermath of March 11, but the economy continued its slide as well. A few weeks before the election, the government announced that Japan had marked its seventh quarterly downturn since the Lehman Shock in 2008, and the fifth "technical recession"—two consecutive quarters of contraction—in fifteen years.[98] The party was very unpopular—cabinet approval ratings dropped to under 20 percent—and it shed almost enough members to lose its majority.

The LDP won the election, claiming a stunning 294 seats, which, when combined with those of its ally the New Komei Party (Komeito) gave it a supermajority of 325 seats, allowing it to overturn vetoes imposed by the Upper House. The LDP repeated that victory in the July 2013 Upper House vote, with its ruling coalition winning 76 seats (an increase of 31 over the last legislature). Its 135 seats give it a majority in the Upper House and control of both chambers. Many observers worry that this outcome presages a new nationalism in Japan. They fear that a second Abe administration will take up where the first Abe government left off, pushing an aggressive rightwing agenda that modifies the constitution, unleashes the SDF, and antagonizes its neighbors. They point to Abe's campaign call for constitutional change that would allow the country to exercise the right of collective self-defense, renaming the SDF as an army, visits to Yasukuni Shrine to honor Japan's war dead, and ambivalence about the Kono Statement in 1993 that acknowledged Japan's responsibility for using women as sex slaves during

World War II and the apology for Japan's conduct in World War II issued by Prime Minister Murayama Tomiichi in 1995.

Our conclusions—and the data—suggest that those fears are unfounded. Abe may hanker for a more conservative Japan, but the public is not likely to follow him. First, it is important to recognize that the election results did not represent so much a vote *for* the LDP as a vote *against* the DPJ. After all, many voters didn't even turn up: turnout was ten million less than the previous two general elections. Then there is the Japanese electoral machinery. With imbalances that favor rural districts, and its two-vote ticket—one for individual districts, one for preferred party—it rewards large parties with organized machines. That is the very essence of the LDP. And remember, too, that DPJ defectors scattered rather than organizing around a single party. That helped the LDP as well. As a result, while the LDP in 2009 received 26.7 percent of the proportional representation (PR) vote and received 119 seats, in 2012 it received only slightly more (28 percent) PR votes yet won 294 seats in total. In contrast, the DPJ received 308 seats in 2009, with 42 percent of the PR component of the vote. Finally, exit polls show that more than 80 percent of voters focused on domestic issues; only 12 percent cared about foreign policy and security.[99] To insist, then, that the results anticipate a swing to the right overstates the case.

The evidence thus far backs this claim. When asked about the government's priorities, LDP sources insist that "it's the economy, the economy, the economy," and they have stuck to that plan.[100] Their preferred tool of recovery is old-fashioned pump priming, with a hefty dose of public works projects. Consistent with our analysis, there is little stomach for the reform that once seemed popular. On foreign policy the Abe administration has been firm without being belligerent. Before taking office Abe announced that he was sending special envoys to Seoul and Beijing to try to get those relationships on firmer ground. (That effort failed and is taken up in more detail in later chapters.) Recall too that in Abe's first term as prime minister—and he was no less nationalist then—his first overseas trip took him to Korea and China to smooth those relationships. This time, however, the prime minister hoped to first visit the United States, and his first foreign policy priority has been getting the alliance back on track. (Because President Obama was unable to schedule a meeting, Abe visited Southeast Asia at the end of January 2013 instead; his Washington visit occurred a month later.) Again, that is very much what these findings predict.

Notions of national identity are not dispositive: they do not necessarily determine policy outcomes.[101] We do believe, however, that an understanding of who the Japanese think they are allows us to better understand the national debates they engage in and the choices they ultimately make.

3

SOUTH KOREA'S GROWING CONFIDENCE

THE END OF THE COLD WAR COINCIDED WITH POWERFUL changes in South Korea's domestic political system. The country's democratic transition and its international economic emergence occurred at the same time that the Berlin Wall came down and the Soviet Union collapsed. But the end of the superpower competition did not end the long-standing political confrontation on the Korean Peninsula. After Seoul hosted the 1988 Olympics, South Korea's diplomatic horizons expanded as a result of normalization agreements with the Soviet Union in 1990, Eastern European countries, and eventually the People's Republic of China in 1992. South Korean president Kim Young Sam pursued a policy of *segyehwa*, or globalization, and South Korea entered the Organization for Economic Cooperation and Development (OECD) in 1996, successfully breaking into the ranks of industrialized nations despite the setbacks of the Asian financial crisis in 1998–1999. Along with the economic achievements that followed industrialization, the consolidation of Korean democracy resulted in the strengthening of civil society and a greater ability to hold the South Korean government accountable to public preferences, including in foreign policy.

Alongside South Korea's political transition from authoritarianism to democracy, the end of the Cold War and economic modernization provided the basis for the country to pursue a wider range of foreign policy interests than before. During the Cold War, South Korean foreign policy was primarily consumed with managing the U.S.–ROK alliance and competing with North Korea for international legitimacy. But with the end of the superpower competition and normalization of relations with the former Soviet Union and China, South Korean foreign policy was no longer tethered primarily to U.S. interests, and its economic modernization made South Korea an attractive trading partner for many developing countries and economies in transition from socialism to capitalism. As a result, the aperture of Seoul's foreign policy widened with the adoption of a framework that incorporated a regionwide approach to peninsular security concerns that prioritized relations with the four major powers surrounding the peninsula: the United States, Russia, China, and Japan.

In the wake of the 1998 Asian financial crisis, South Korea experienced its first democratic political transition from the ruling to the opposition party with the election of Kim Dae-jung. A democracy activist who had fought authoritarianism, Kim successfully managed South Korea's economic and financial recovery while simultaneously ending policies of containment toward the North in favor of his Sunshine Policy, which promoted inter-Korean engagement and cooperation. The cornerstone of this policy was a growing sense, in the wake of South Korean economic and political success, that North Korea was no longer an equal competitor and that the dangers associated with the North emanated more from its weakness than from its strength. These developments gave South Korea under Kim Dae-jung the confidence to shift from a zero-sum approach to the North, in which the only options were victory and defeat, into a more magnanimous policy involving reconciliation and cooperation as a possible step toward a reunified Korean peninsula. This policy initially yielded an apparent success in the landmark inter-Korean summit on June 15, 2000, which catalyzed a range of inter-Korean social and cultural exchanges, transformed South Korean attitudes about inter-Korean relations, and had profound implications for relations in Northeast Asia. South Korea's cohosting (with Japan) of the 2002 World Cup and the unprecedented performance of its soccer team—it reached the semifinals—fed confidence about the country's capacities and its potential to play an active regional and global role. Shortly after the World Cup, Kim Dae-jung announced that South Korea should aspire to join the ranks of the top four economies in the world. Meanwhile, its economy continued to globalize, and its largest companies, such as Samsung and LG, began to compete toe-to-toe with Japanese companies on the international stage.

Identity and Korean Nationalism

South Korean identity had long been shaped by anticommunism, anticolonialism (focused on overcoming Japan's 1905–1945 rule), or antihegemonism. Another powerful theme that has shaped Korean conceptions of identity since the beginning of the twentieth century has been the concept of ethnic nationalism. This theme is reinforced both through extensive genealogical records dating back centuries that capture the history of Korea's leading family and bloodlines and in narratives about overcoming divisions and thwarting external invasions from its neighbors, including Japan and China. Shin Gi-wook argues that Korean identity is "based on a common bloodline and shared ancestry." He cites polls he conducted in the fall of 2000 that show that 93 percent of respondents agreed that "our nation has a single bloodline" and that returned large majorities identifying North Korea and Koreans living overseas as part of the nation owing to their shared ancestry.[1]

More recent polling by Kim Jiyoon at the Asan Institute of Policy Studies shows growing support among the younger generation for a Korean identity based on civic nationalism, in which nationality, linguistic ability, understanding of tradition, and obedience to national law have surpassed measures of ethnic nationalism as components of that identity, although her results show that at least two-thirds of respondents also still strongly support ethnicity-based measures in thinking about Korean identity.[2]

In their attempt to develop a modern national consciousness, Korean intellectuals in the early 1900s conflated concepts of race and nation, perhaps as a result of Korea's loss of its national identity following Japanese colonialism in the early years of the twentieth century. Scarred by that experience, Korean nationalists such as Shin Chae-ho based the concept of nation on racial homogeneity as they justified the struggle to recover national independence.[3]

This equating of race and nation is clearly reflected in nation-building efforts of Kim Il Sung and Rhee Syngman. Although these two Korean post–World War II nationalist leaders were divided by ideology and implacably opposed to each other, they both embraced the reunification of Korea as their unwavering objective. Ethnocentric conceptions of Korean identity are reflected in the virulent xenophobic nationalism that infuses North Korean ideology as well as in the strong sense of communitarianism that is a critical component of South Korean national consciousness.[4] A modern manifestation of the privileging of ethnicity over nation as the central component of national identity occurred during the ice skating competition at the 2006 Asian Games in China, at which time South Korean protestors laid claim to the mountain between China and North Korea, forcing South Korean diplomats to issue apologies since South Korea has no legal basis on which to assert a formal claim over territory that lies between China and North Korea.

The primary divisions over identity and nationalism have historically occurred between conservatives and progressives. These divisions have antecedents that go back to the Korean colonial period, although they were masked under Korea's conservative authoritarian leaders, who tended to oppress progressive tendencies as pro–North Korea. But with democratization and especially with inter-Korean rapprochement in 2000, divisions between progressives and conservatives emerged much more clearly than before as central dividing lines within national identity debates. A central theme of this debate revolves around disputes over identity, namely, whether to prioritize reconciliation and ethnic unity over ideological and system differences or whether ideological and system divisions must be dealt with as a prerequisite to achievement of Korean reunification.

Identity Shift Under Kim Dae-jung

South Korea's power transition from conservative to progressive and its economic modernization, despite the setbacks posed by the Asian financial crisis, enabled Kim Dae-jung to challenge South Korean identity on two fronts. First, Kim sought to redefine the relationship with Japan by reconciling with its former colonizer on the premise that definitive Japanese statements of remorse would enable the pursuit of a "future-oriented relationship" through the establishment of a Korea–Japan Joint Partnership. But this partnership, agreed to in 1998 with Kim's counterpart, Japanese prime minister Obuchi Keizo, foundered over the reemergence of history issues that hit directly at politically sensitive and conflicting conceptions of identity in both countries (these difficulties are treated in greater detail in chapter 4).

Second, Kim Dae-jung's Sunshine Policy and the realization of the inter-Korean summit raised hopes among progressives—who for the first time since the founding of the ROK in 1948 wielded sufficient influence to take political power through the election of Kim Dae-jung—that a long-cherished "unified" Korea might finally be attainable. The 2000 inter-Korean summit—and particularly Kim Dae-jung's declaration that the summit had eliminated the possibility of renewed military conflict on the peninsula—deepened internal divisions within South Korea over how to deal with the North, with conservative skeptics of prospects for inter-Korean relations labeled "antireunification," while progressives optimistically insisted that tighter ties would strengthen the capacity and role of a reunified Korea to promote regional peace and prosperity. Divisions between progressives and conservatives over how to deal with North Korea reveal diametrically opposed assumptions about Korean identity. The progressive view prioritized the idea of reunification based on a concept of grand national unity over historical efforts by outsiders to keep the Korean Peninsula divided, while conservatives held to a view that North Korea's bankrupt ideology must be defeated so that a market-based, democratic reunification (with Seoul at the helm) can finally be achieved. The progressive view represented a classic ethnic nationalist impulse for unity of the race over division at all costs, while the conservative view argued that reunification would be meaningful only if it were to occur on the basis of an ideology that also embraces freedom and democracy. The deepening identity debate between progressives and conservatives over North Korea policy has ramifications both for inter-Korean reconciliation prospects and South Korea's broader foreign policy orientation, particularly as it relates to the U.S.–ROK alliance.

On the one hand, Kim Dae-jung's Sunshine Policy provided a progressive rationale for pursuing cooperative engagement with North Korea that would induce change inside that country. On this basis President Kim argued that South Korea should be willing to provide North Korea with benefits of economic engagement in the initial stages of interaction so that the North would become dependent on cooperation with South Korea, thereby generating leverage that would be used to restrain North Korean belligerency and forge a mutual path toward peaceful coexistence. Kim Dae-jung supported a tourism project in Mount Kumgang based on the separation of economics from politics and also sought to reconnect inter-Korean railways and roads that had been cut off since the Korean War. The inter-Korean summit declaration in 2000 emphasized that the two Koreas would pursue better relations without being subject to outside interference and paved the way for a stream of inter-Korean sports, cultural, and economic exchanges but made little, if any, tangible progress on political and security cooperation. The Kim Dae-jung administration also introduced the cooperative construction of a special economic zone at Kaesong that was further developed under the Roh Moo-hyun administration. The development of that zone was also premised on the belief that inter-Korean economic cooperation would lead to social and economic changes inside North Korea, both by exposing North Koreans to the nuts and bolts of capitalism and by inducing dependency on foreign cash as an incentive for broader economic reform and opening.

South Korean progressives who supported inter-Korean rapprochement have also tended to see the U.S.–ROK alliance as an obstacle to cooperation and, by extension, to the recovery of a unified Korean identity. They see the alliance as a tool to be used but not a security blanket to be depended on, and some progressives believe that the U.S. alliance structure is an obstacle to cooperative security arrangements in Northeast Asia. The successful development of a multilateral cooperative security arrangement would dilute the prospect of conflict and promote enhanced economic cooperation. Kim Dae-jung himself saw utility in continuing U.S.–ROK alliance cooperation, but his administration did little to dampen South Korean public criticism of the U.S. force presence in the months following the inter-Korean summit. The criticism culminated in public protests in late 2002 surrounding the deaths of two Korean middle school girls in a traffic accident involving a U.S. military vehicle that was returning from participation in exercises. Kim Dae-jung was also an active proponent of East Asian and Northeast Asian multilateral cooperation, both through his government's support of the nongovernmental recommendations of the East Asia Vision Group and through his vision of South Korea as a hub for regional economic, transportation, and energy networks.

Korean conservatives opposed Kim's progressive approach for several reasons, claiming that it was naïve and that it provided valuable financial support that sustained the North Korean regime and its nuclear development. Opponents also argued that cooperation with North Korea stood in the way of North Korea's imminent collapse, removing the possibility that reunification might be achieved on South Korean terms. While the Asian financial crisis tilted the scales in favor of a gradualist versus a sudden approach to reunification due to the perception that a financially recovering South Korea would be unable to bear those costs, Kim Dae-jung's failure to bring any opposition members on his historic visit to Pyongyang subjected the effort to criticism on a partisan basis, deepening divisions within South Korea. Conservatives further criticized the Sunshine Policy once it became clear that Kim's Pyongyang visit was secured by a transfer of hundreds of millions of dollars via Hyundai channels; this criticism became even more strident as it became known that North Korea continued to invest in a covert nuclear program at the same time that Kim Jong-il welcomed Kim Dae-jung for their historic summit.

Conservatives continued to believe that a strong U.S.–ROK alliance was the backbone of South Korean security and worried that better inter-Korean relations might come at the expense of the alliance. They saw the alliance as a necessary support for South Korea's diplomatic efforts in the region and focused more on raising South Korea's profile on the global stage rather than diplomatic initiatives to strengthen regional coopera-tion in East Asia. While they were willing to take advantage of economic opportunities associated with the opening of the China–ROK relation-ship, they did not trust China's intentions or Beijing's willingness to cooperate with South Korea on security issues, including North Korea.

Swing Toward Populism Under Roh Moo-hyun

Divisions between progressives and conservatives deepened in the run-up to South Korea's 2002 presidential elections, which pitted progres-sive candidate Roh Moo-hyun against establishment conservative Lee Hoi-chang. During the 2002 presidential campaign, U.S. Forces Korea (USFK) ruled that the two soldiers driving the army vehicle that killed two Korean schoolgirls were not guilty, catalyzing widespread candle-light demonstrations among South Koreans who felt that the verdict exhibited highhandedness and impunity on the part of USFK. This inci-dent fanned the perception that the United States did not appreciate the extent of South Korea's modernization, democratization, and emergence as a global partner.

These demonstrations had a direct impact on the South Korean presi-dential election in 2002. As an outsider to South Korea's government and business elite, Roh Moo-hyun had greater credibility as a candidate who might stand up to the United States while continuing reconciliation with North Korea, while conservative Grand National Party candidate Lee Hoi-chang had sought and gained a high-level audience in Washington with Vice President Richard Cheney in the course of his campaign, giv-ing the impression that he was the U.S.-favored candidate. Changes in South Korean public opinion appeared to be turning South Korea away from the United States, and the populist Roh administration, under the phrase "participatory government," appeared willing to adapt to anti-American preferences in South Korean public opinion, however volatile or reactive to current events, as Roh implemented foreign policy.

The influence of populism on the Roh administration resulted in further politicization of South Korea's alliance with the United States. Although the task of managing alliance relations between the conservative George W. Bush administration and the progressive Roh administration proved to be challenging, both sides were able to maintain the veneer of coordination toward North Korea while initiating major adjustments to the operational structure of the U.S.–ROK alliance, including plans to change the combined command structure of the alliance to two separate structures in which South Korea would play a leading and the United States would play a supporting role. While these plans also reflected serious frictions between the two administrations, they were handled in a fashion that preserved institutional coordination between the two militaries and catalyzed a needed review of a wide range of capabilities, functions, and responsibilities within the alliance.

During the Roh–Bush interregnum, there was an ongoing debate among South Korean conservatives and progressives over how South Korea should position itself between the United States and China, and what South Korea should expect from Washington and Beijing vis-à-vis the relationship with North Korea. During this period, some U.S. analysts argued that South Korea would inevitably side with China as its natural ally, forsaking the alliance with the United States.[5] These trends were connected to the question of whether South Korea's sense of self was changing in ways that would force significant adjustments in South Korea's foreign policy and its role in Northeast Asia. Reflecting South Korean popular sentiment, Roh Moo-hyun seemed quick to exploit tensions with Japan—drawing on historical animosities—whenever his popularity sagged. Tokyo was an easy target for pent-up frustration, and few Koreans were prepared to defend relations with Japan, despite the many seemingly compelling reasons for the two neighbors to cooperate.

In response to rising tensions between China and Japan in early 2005, President Roh promoted the notion of South Korea as a "balancer." Roh's National Security Council articulated several principles that revealed its thinking about South Korea's role vis-à-vis larger regional powers, including that (1) Korea is "a major actor, not a subordinate variable" in Asia, (2) Korea can be trusted in the region since it has no history of hegemonism, (3) as a "balancer for peace," Korea can play the roles of mediator, harmonizer, facilitator, and initiator, and (4) through "hard power plus soft power," Korea can maintain existing alliances while also promoting establishment of regional cooperative security institutions.[6] Although the balancer concept was subsequently discredited, its boldness and the effort to try to shape the regional environment rather than allowing others to set the tone are notable. Other values that the Roh administration emphasized as part of the policy have been recast as core objectives within the context of the U.S.–ROK alliance, including the idea that the alliance will be built on mutual values and trust and will promote peace in the region.[7] It was also the product of an identity for Korea that sought autonomy and release from dependency on the United States through the alliance.

Conservative Efforts to Roll Back a "Lost Decade" Under Lee Myung-bak

South Korea's second democratic transition from ruling party to opposition in 2008 followed a decade of progressive rule. President-elect Lee Myung-bak signaled that a conservative return to power would entail major changes when he described a "lost decade" under progressives. This characterization reflected frustrations with perceived shortcomings of the Roh administration but also reflected increasing South Korean frustrations with the low returns on investment South Korea had received from a decade of engagement policies toward the North. The Lee administration was able to raise South Korea's profile in world affairs through pursuit of a "global Korea" and by hosting several major international gatherings in Seoul. The pendulum of Korean identity and preferences had shifted through the elections back to a conservative vision of the future, but Korea's identity was also undergoing an evolution from being defined in negative terms to an identity based on South Korea's accomplishments and contributions to the international community. In part this shift was a reflection of a South Korea that had become more globally exposed and trade dependent, and therefore not focused on a weakening North Korea as a benchmark for judging South Korean performance. At the same time, South Koreans had become weary of North Korean efforts to shake down their country during inter-Korean cooperation programs, initiatives that were supposedly designed to lead to reciprocity in inter-Korean relations.

The Lee administration campaigned on a "Denuclearization, Opening, 3000 Policy" toward North Korea that envisioned unlocking significant economic benefits to North Korea if the North would recommit to denuclearization, describing its inter-Korean strategy as one designed to "advance mutual benefits and common prosperity."[8] An early step toward reciprocity involved pulling the plug on annual provision of 500,000 tons of fertilizer that had occurred during the Roh administration. Subsequently, the killing of a South Korean tourist in 2009 closed down the Kumgang tourism project, and the South Korean government's conclusion that North Korea was behind the sinking of its navy vessel *Cheonan* in 2010 led to strict sanctions on all inter-Korean trade outside of the Kaesong Industrial Zone. It is notable, however, that by 2012 over 123 South Korean firms were generating almost $2 billion in inter-Korean trade and $90 million per year in hard currency for North Korea.[9]

The Lee administration took important steps to broaden and deepen cooperation within the U.S.–ROK alliance. Presidents Lee and Obama announced a Joint Vision Statement in June 2009 that not only discussed U.S.–ROK security cooperation in peninsular terms, with a special emphasis on Washington's commitment to extended deterrence against North Korea's nuclear threat, but also envisioned regional and global cooperation on nontraditional security issues such as antipiracy, nonproliferation, development, and international security. The two presidents also pledged to ratify the ROK–U.S. free trade agreement in their respective legislative bodies. The U.S. Congress ratified it in October 2011, and South Korea's National Assembly followed suit the following spring, allowing for the FTA to go into effect in spring 2012. Lee's emphasis on strengthening the U.S.–ROK alliance and his emphasis on "global Korea" provided a positive identity for a country that was confident as a partner of the United States, had overcome the pain of hardship through development, and was looking toward a future in which it would assert itself as a responsible leader in the international community. This assertion of a new, positive identity for South Koreans was particularly remarkable because it hinted at a way out from identity formulations that either defined South Korean identity in negative terms or seemed to entrap Korea permanently as a victim of its own past.

Park Geun-hye: Entrapped by Her History and Identity?

The election of conservative Park Geun-hye as Lee's successor has resulted in relative continuity in South Korea's foreign policy framework, priorities, and approaches. Park made her first visit to the United States and strongly reaffirmed the importance of the alliance as the foundation of her foreign policy. Curiously, her own family history and identity have appeared to impose new constraints on South Korea's policies, especially as related to North Korea and Japan.

As a candidate, Park advocated a policy of Trustpolitik toward North Korea, an approach she describes as having two strands: North Korea keeping its commitments to South Korea and the international community, and clear consequences for breaches in those agreements.[10] She also identified poor inter-Korean relations, Japan's failure to take a "correct view of history," and the prospect of a Sino–U.S. arms race as three primary concerns that contributed to the "Asian paradox" of strong economic growth against the backdrop of lingering and even intensifying regional political tensions. In the case of both North Korea and Japan, the legacy of Park's father appears to overshadow or limit her maneuverability. Park Chunghee took the unprecedented step of opening dialogue with North Korea, but his outreach to Pyongyang appears to have been much more a function of distrust than of trust. His controversial decision to normalize relations with Japan in 1965 appears to have constraining effects on Park Geun-hye's own approach to addressing concerns about historical revisionism in Japan. For her, Korea can experience true liberation from the past only if history has been dealt with correctly. While this approach to Korea's identity may ultimately provide a way out from the past, it also runs the risk of focusing on a correct assessment of the past at the expense of the need to move past history and prepare for the future.

Current Public Debates on Foreign Policy

Despite shared inclinations among South Korean conservatives and progressives regarding the need to take the initiative to strengthen South Korea's ability to shape its external environment, bitter debates over the best means to do so remain an integral part of domestic politics. Conservatives and progressives may agree on the need to promote South Korea's influence both regionally and globally, but the ROK presidential election campaign of 2012 showed deep differences among candidates over the relative priority of engagement with North Korea and the extent to which South Korea should align itself with the United States (and Japan) or China to attain national objectives. Although the campaign was primarily about domestic policy and South Korea's foreign policy choices remain constrained by North Korean militancy, rising regional tensions, and the durability of institutional ties underlying the U.S.–ROK alliance, the differences between progressive and conservative candidates reflected the persistence of deep divisions over policy toward the North and Korea's broader strategic position and orientation. These differences are directly associated with long-standing debates over Korean identity.

Public opinion has been a steadily growing influence in discussions of the direction and rationale for specific South Korean foreign policies as a result of democratization. South Korean public opinion holds the government accountable to its expectations, projects a South Korean sense of identity based on its own self-perception, and shapes its responses based on the perceptions of others. Citizen groups have exercised increasing influence as stakeholders in foreign policy as a result of democratization.

Conversations with leading South Korean foreign policy analysts reveal widespread pride in the country's recent political and economic development and a resulting confidence derived from its accomplishments. However, South Koreans also harbor a sense of vulnerability deriving both from South Korea's history and from its inability to control its destiny as related to its most important foreign policies and objectives. Despite the nation being a leading economy, many older Koreans continue to think of themselves as a small country surrounded by larger powers and subject to geopolitical constraints, while younger Koreans hold a much more ambitious view of Korea's position in the international order and what it should be expected to accomplish.

Korean National Identity and Its Influence on Foreign Policy

In considering the influence of South Korean public perceptions on its foreign policy, two questions seem particularly relevant. First, to what extent does perception of similarities in values and interests with those of its neighbors affect foreign policy? Second, to what extent do South Korean expectations of the future affect foreign policy?

Interviews with South Korean opinion leaders reflect a positive tone and optimism about the future. This sense of satisfaction derives from the perceived success of the country's economic and political development over the past two decades and transcends Korean ideological divisions between conservatives and progressives. These accomplishments have positioned the country to play a greater role in international affairs. Interviews with opinion leaders confirm that economic and political development "has given many Koreans a sense of unique pride," "confiden[ce]," and "success." One scholar even worried about public "over-confidence about our national capability." This comes into play when the public expects the government to have influence on international issues disproportionate to that which South Korea is able to wield, given its size and geographic circumstances. The younger generation appears to have higher expectations for South Korean performance on the international stage since they "are citizens of a rich country with a powerful army. . . . This has precipitated a fundamental shift in national identity and expectations for how Korea ought to behave."[11] That outlook reflects an increasingly international Korean public. A South Korean specialist on the political attitudes of younger-generation Koreans reports that people in their twenties "feel we are now one of the main members in the global economy so we can walk or act or play in world terms."

A Pacific Forum CSIS survey in 2007 showed that South Koreans believe their country excels in comparison with other countries on the level of education, economic power, and science and technology. Most Koreans support an international role for Korea, a role that promotes Asian economic development, develops new technologies, and serves as a bridge between East and West. Korean internationalism is reinforced by the fact that the path to success in South Korean society often includes graduate and postgraduate education in the United States. According to statistics from the Institute of International Education, 72,295 South Korean students enrolled in U.S. universities during the 2011–12 academic year, up from 45,685 Korean students in the United States during 2000–2001. In addition, large numbers of Korean students are studying in the United States at a secondary level as a result of perceptions that the U.S. education system is superior to the education available in South Korea. Korean students have represented the third largest foreign student group in the United States since 2002, trailing only India and China.[12] More than 65,000 South Korean students were in China in 2010.[13]

On the other hand, South Koreans show relatively high levels of frustration with their democratic system, despite development of vibrant democratic institutions in a relatively short time since transitioning from authoritarianism in 1988. In fact, public dissatisfaction with politics has been a major driver for democratic consolidation and domestic political reforms especially because public protest drove the country's political transition from authoritarianism to democracy in 1987–88. Since that time, South Korea has developed a vibrant civil society that has played a major role in holding politicians accountable and in serving as a catalyst for political reform. For instance, a civil society coalition successfully launched a blacklisting campaign against candidates for the National Assembly in 2000. A combination of public expectations and the adoption of strict oversight of election processes by the South Korean National Election Commission influenced the process by which political parties selected candidates for the National Assembly in 2004.

In spite of these civil society–driven reforms, South Korean opinion polling shows continued dissatisfaction with how politics works in South Korea. A Chicago Council on Global Affairs/East Asia Institute

(CCGA/EAI) survey in 2008 showed high levels of dissatisfaction about South Korean politics, with 89 percent of respondents saying that they are "not very proud" or "not at all proud" of their political system. An Edelman Trust Barometer in 2012 also showed high levels of dissatisfaction, with 67 percent of respondents saying that they "do not trust" or "do not trust at all" their political system.[14] While an Asan Institute–German Marshall Fund of the United States (GMFUS) poll in the same year showed that two-thirds of Koreans feel confident that their elections reflected the will of the voters, the poll also indicated considerable dissatisfaction over government policies that are perceived as having failed to address economic inequality, with 70 percent of South Koreans expressing dissatisfaction with South Korea's economic policies and over 91 percent saying that the economic system is not fair.[15]

While South Koreans are proud of their economic and political accomplishments, the younger generation has come of age in an industrialized democracy, unlike their parents, who grew up in a poorer, less-developed, and even war-torn South Korea. Reflecting these harsher experiences, some older Koreans believe that members of the younger generation do not appreciate the freedoms they enjoy. Younger South Koreans don't appear to have the chip on their shoulders that came from perceived historical injustices that their elders had cultivated. While the experience of Gwangju that shaped the political activism and antiauthoritarian mobilization of Korea's "386" generation (now in their forties and fifties), the defining event for Korea's *N-sidae* (the generation in their twenties and thirties) was the Asian financial crisis, during which they saw their parents and other family members lose their jobs and tighten their belts. But the financial crisis does not appear to have triggered a fear of globalization in Korea's younger generation, despite perennial concerns about employment opportunities; instead they embrace a dynamic Korea that is going out into the world, not a defensive, protectionist outlook.

South Korea's generational divide is most clearly present in its political preferences, with the older generation trending conservative while the younger generation supports more progressive political leadership. Notably, the generational political cleavage, if anything, worsened between the 2002 election of progressive Roh Moo-hyun and the 2012 election of conservative Park Geun-hye. A comparison of 2002 and 2012 election results shows that a greater percentage of Koreans in their twenties, thirties, and forties voted for Park's opponent Moon Jae-in in 2012 than voted for Roh Moo-hyun in 2002, with voters in their fifties having turned markedly more conservative in their voting patterns than they were ten years earlier. Support from this cohort, along with South Korea's aging society and higher turnout and support rates for Park among older Koreans, enabled her election as president (table 3.1).

The Asan Institute–GMFUS poll reveals interesting differences among generational cohorts in South Korea. On the one hand, despite strong support for U.S. leadership in world affairs, only 57 percent of those in their thirties see U.S. leadership as positive compared with 83 percent of respondents in their sixties and older. On the other hand, older South Koreans are much more likely to view China favorably (54 percent) than those in the younger generation (27 percent). Younger South Koreans feel more at home in the world, but they also appear to be more critical than their seniors in their attitudes toward major powers and toward North Korea. It remains to be seen how these attitudes will play out in specific terms, but the evidence shows that the rising generation is prepared to play an international role but will also be sensitive to perceived unfairness, hegemonism, or discrimination toward South Korean interests on the part of major powers.

South Korean Values and Interests

Given cultural similarities between South Korea and its neighbors and the ROK alliance with the United States, one data set of particular interest in the Korean case is the extent to which South Koreans perceive their values and interests as compatible with those of neighboring countries. A survey conducted by the Chicago Council on Global Affairs in 2006 asked to what extent Korea "shares similar values and a way of life" with China, Japan, and the United States. Respondents said that they shared similar values and a way of life with China (56 percent) or Japan (58 percent) "to a great extent or to some extent," while only 14 percent said that they shared similar values and a way of life "to a

TABLE 3.1 ROK Voter Turnout by Age Cohort, 2012 and 2002 Elections (in percent)

AGE GROUP	2012 ELECTION (40,507,842 VOTERS)				2002 ELECTION (34,991,529 VOTERS)			
	VOTER SHARE	VOTING RATE	PARK SUPPORT	MOON SUPPORT	VOTER SHARE	VOTING RATE	LEE SUPPORT	ROH SUPPORT
20s–	18.1	65.2	33.7	65.8	23.2	56.5	34.9	59
30s	20.1	72.5	33.1	66.5	25.1	67.4	34.2	59.3
40s	21.8	78.7	44.1	55.6	22.4	76.3	47.9	48.1
50s	19.2	89.9	62.5	37.4	12.9	83.7	57.9	40.1
60s+	20.8	78.8	72.3	27.5	16.4	78.7	63.5	34.9
Total	100	75.8	50.1	48.9	100	70.8	46.6	49.2

Source: Asan Institute–German Marshall Fund

great extent or to some extent" with the United States.[16] These data suggest that South Korean perceptions of common values do not necessarily play a significant role in reinforcing public perceptions of the importance of the U.S.–ROK alliance. Instead, perceptions of common interests, possibly derived from a common sense of threat if not a common source of threat, appear to serve as an important bond in the alliance. Among Americans, a CCGA poll in 2012 showed that almost half of those polled view South Korea as sharing similar values and a way of life with the United States, compared with only 35 percent in 2008.[17]

The Pacific Forum CSIS survey from 2007 shows an interesting convergence between South Korean perceptions of values and interests. More than 43 percent of respondents said Korea's interests were most compatible with those of the United States, and 23 percent indicated that their country's interests are most compatible with those of Japan; only 10 percent chose China. Thirty-eight percent perceived common interests with the United States, while 34 percent chose Japan. A plurality of respondents also showed strong identification with Japanese values and interests, a finding that might be considered surprising in light of the historical difficulties between the two countries, especially as perceived by the Korean public. These findings suggest that there is a reservoir of goodwill at the elite level that appears to contrast with historical animosities toward Japan reflected in Korean public opinion. This differs from South Korean views of shared values and interests with the United States, a tendency demonstrated by a joint report from the Asan Institute and the GMFUS in 2012.[18] Seventy-six percent of South Koreans surveyed in that poll felt that they held sufficient shared *values* with the United States to be able to cooperate on international problems. Seventy percent of South Koreans thought they held sufficient shared *interests* with the United States to cooperate on international problems.

A second potential indicator of how public opinion may influence South Korean foreign policy is related to South Korean expectations for the future. Pacific Forum CSIS survey data from 2007 underscore the continuing strength of South Korean expectations of China as an economic partner, with over two-thirds of South Korean respondents agreeing that China will be South Korea's most important economic partner within a decade. However, the survey also revealed a strong desire among elites for continued security relations with the United States. As noted, this inclination is also reflected in the Asan Institute survey data since 2010, which show a continued desire for the United States to remain as South Korea's ally.

Attitudes Toward North Korea

South Korean attitudes toward North Korea have fluctuated dramatically in concert with government optimism or pessimism about prospects for the relationship. In other words, it appears that government policy has led South Korean public opinion of the North, depending on whether the government pursued a policy characterized by either cooperation or confrontation with Pyongyang. However, public opinion also reveals divisions and constraints that have inhibited unconditioned pursuit of policy extremes with the North. Prior to the 2000 summit, over 34 percent of South Koreans surveyed viewed Kim Jong-il as a dictator; that figure dropped to less than 10 percent immediately after the summit, and over 97 percent indicated that they would welcome a visit by Kim to Seoul.[19] Korean expectations for reunification also rose as a result of the summit, with over 71 percent of Korean students expressing optimism about the possibility of unification when polled in July 2001 compared with only 59 percent a year earlier.[20] Public opinion polls from the end of 2000 show that almost 80 percent of the public supported a policy of cooperation and reconciliation with North Korea; the public gradually turned skeptical of Kim Dae-jung's generous approach to the North, however.[21] A year after the summit, a *Chosun ilbo* poll on June 11, 2001, showed that 50.1 percent of those surveyed believed that North Korea had not changed much. Moreover, 43.9 percent thought that the Kim Dae-jung government was not managing policy toward the North well, compared with 33.9 percent who believed that the government was doing well.[22]

Inter-Korean rapprochement had significant implications for South Korean identity. If the inter-Korean summit in 2000 marked a dramatic turning point in South Korean public attitudes toward North Korea, it also launched a deep conflict within South Korea between conservatives and progressives, who responded in different ways to the meeting. While conservatives criticized Kim Dae-jung for naïveté and a failure to gain reciprocity from the North, progressives made emotional arguments for a Korean nationalism defined by reunification and argued that the end of inter-Korean conflict would bring a "peace dividend" as well as lay the foundation for economic cooperation that would benefit both Koreas.

The *nam-nam kaltung*, or "South–South conflict," pivoted on whether South Korea should side with North Korea or the United States, given the long-term security implications of the levels of trust that would be necessary to carry out rapprochement. The domestic political implications of inter-Korean reconciliation influenced educational policy regarding North Korea and budgeting for inter-Korean economic cooperation projects. It also affected perceptions of the longer-term U.S. role in South Korea, given the fact that the rationale for the U.S. presence was directly tied to deterrence against a North Korean threat.

Under the Roh Moo-hyun administration, public concerns regarding security shifted away from North Korea and toward the United States, especially in the initial phase of the second North Korean nuclear crisis. A KBS poll in 2006 showed that 43 percent of respondents blamed the United States for North Korea's nuclear test while 37 percent blamed North Korea and 13.9 percent blamed the Roh administration. An often-cited *Chosun ilbo* poll from 2005 reported that almost two-thirds of South Koreans between the ages of sixteen and twenty-five said that they would side with North Korea in the event of military conflict between North Korea and the United States.[23]

Implementation of the Sunshine Policy in South Korea under Presidents Kim Dae-jung and Roh Moo-hyun created an environment of hope that positively influenced public opinion toward the North. This positive mood enabled many inter-Korean joint cooperation projects, which in turn gave momentum to hope for rapprochement.

However, the positive mood had its limits, especially among a plurality of South Koreans who remained skeptical of North Korea and cautious about its desire to improve the inter-Korean relationship. Adding to the skepticism was the fact that despite an improved mood in the relationship, North Korean cooperation came only in cultural areas and in proportion to compensation received and failed to create tangible improvements in political-military relations. As a result the public's caution over North Korea's reluctance to reciprocate South Korean largesse also kept South Korea from progressing too far. By the end of the Roh administration, the public had wearied of both the costs and apparently the limited results of the engagement policy, and especially the self-censorship in expressing critical assessments of North Korea's manifest failures that seemed to be implicit in the bargain that led to inter-Korean rapprochement. As frustrations with the North built up, the South Korean public grew irritated with the lack of reciprocity in the inter-Korean relationship and less patient with North Korean intransigence on human rights and governance issues.

Following the inter-Korean summit in 2000, South Korean media withheld criticism of North Korea, but by 2007 mounting public frustration with North Korea's human rights record, fed by a stream of stories from a growing number of refugees from the North, led the Seoul government to make policy adjustments in line with major trends in South Korean public opinion. One such adjustment was the South Korean government's decision to facilitate transit of North Korean refugees from Vietnam despite North Korean opposition both to the policy and to its publicization. In a second shift, the Roh administration took a more active role in criticizing North Korean human rights abuses at UN human rights forums after having abstained from such criticism for a number of years.

ROK Ministry of Unification polling during the Roh administration shows relative volatility in South Korean views of policy toward the North. During its first year in office, when President Roh authorized trials of Kim Dae-jung administration figures who had been involved in arranging cash payments in advance of the inter-Korean summit, critics of Roh's policy outnumbered supporters. However, as Roh began to promote engagement with North Korea, South Korean support for Roh's North Korea policy exceeded 50 percent in 2004 and 2005. The first North Korean nuclear test had a big impact on public perceptions, with almost 70 percent of South Koreans holding negative opinions of government policy toward Pyongyang; however, the second inter-Korean summit reversed that trend, with more than 70 percent of South

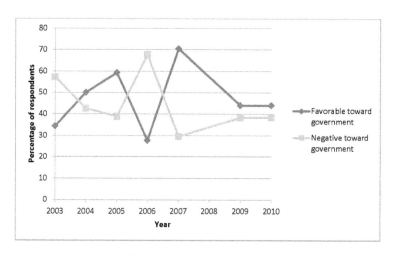

FIGURE 3.1 Views on the Government's Policy Toward North Korea
Source: Ministry of Unification

Korean respondents expressing support for the policy. Figure 3.1 shows wide fluctuations in South Korean public support under Roh Moo-hyun, especially in 2006 and 2007, presumably with North Korea's 2006 nuclear test having a negative effect but bilateral and multilateral efforts to restore dialogue channels with North Korea leading to a rebound. Following the second North Korean nuclear test in 2009, a consistent plurality of the South Korean public supported Lee Myung-bak's tougher policies in 2010.[24]

Lee Myung-bak's tougher policy initially gained support from a plurality of the South Korean public, but there was growing criticism of Lee's handling of inter-Korean relations in the aftermath of North Korean provocations, as shown in figures 3.2 and 3.3. The public's main criticisms of the Lee administration's management of inter-Korean relations appear to be related to perceptions of North Korea's identity, and particularly South Korea's persistent perception that North Korea remained a target for cooperation rather than for hostility throughout 2010, as reflected in the figure. This is testimony to the depth of public desire for inter-Korean relations to be managed in a manner that is conducive to peace and reconciliation.

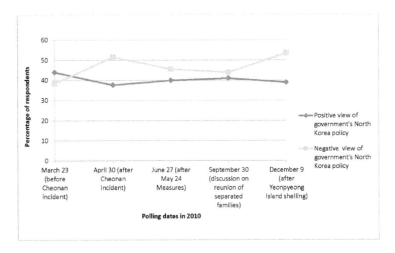

FIGURE 3.2   Views on the South Korean Government's Overall North Korea Policy, 2010
Source: Ministry of Unification

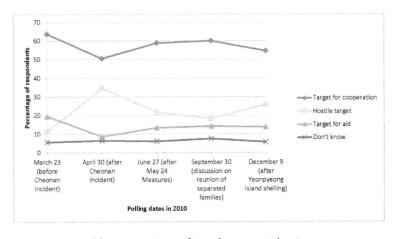

FIGURE 3.3   Public Perceptions of North Korean Identity
Source: Ministry of Unification

South Korean attitudes toward the North hardened following the *Cheonan* and Yeonpyeong provocations. South Korea's EAI polling from 2010 shows a shift in South Korean opinion, especially following the Yeonpyeong artillery shelling. This poll shows attitudes on giving aid to North Korea hardening, as support for "reconciliation and coopera-tion" with the North dropped from 61.5 percent to 55.2 percent between January and December 2010, while support for a "hard-line policy" toward North Korea rose from 37.1 percent to 42.7 percent. The authors of the poll conclude that "the military option, which was unthinkable in the past, is now seriously considered as a reasonable response by the majority of the public."[25]

Notable generational gaps persist when dealing with the North. The lack of direct experience with a unified peninsula and lack of contacts with North Korea have attenuated the emotional attachment of younger Koreans to reunification. The desire to counter this trend is reportedly behind Park Geun-hye's efforts to talk positively about reunification from early 2014, including her description of reunification as a *daebak* (bonanza or jackpot), a term that resonates with South Korean youth. Younger Koreans increasingly see themselves as South Koreans rather than as Koreans and are reported to have less interest in unification issues than their seniors have. One analyst asserts that "for those who do desire unification, the motivation is often derived from South Korea–centered goals: unification for the benefit of South Korea or to prevent China's spreading influence over the North."[26] A striking effect of this more dis-tant view of North Korea is the higher level of anxiety among younger generations in their perceptions of the likelihood of war with North Korea compared with those of their elders, according to the EAI poll in 2010 regarding South Korean views of the North following the *Cheonan* and Yeonpyeong incidents.[27]

South Korean Views of China

South Korean public attitudes toward China were remarkably positive during the 1990s and early 2000s. Credit for this trend goes to a bur-geoning economic relationship that grew on the order of 30 percent annually for a number of years, expanding from $6.37 billion in 1992 to $220.63 billion in 2011. But alongside the harnessing of tremendous economic potential, especially following China's entry into the World Trade Organization (WTO) in 2001, domestic identity issues emerged in 2004 as a drag on the relationship in the context of South Korea's response to China's "Northeast Project" and the so-called Koguryo controversies.[28] This issue emerged as a result of Chinese efforts to promote historical research that would "incorporate" ethnic minority histories into the broader Chinese national narrative. For China, it was an attempt to cut off irredentist claims by Koreans to Chinese territory, while Koreans viewed it as an attempt to geographically annex a slice of their own history. While there is little threat of Korean separatism in China today, the ambiguous history of Korean ethnic activity inside their borders makes Chinese anxious. They worry that an autonomous ethnic minority area on the border of a unified Korea might constitute a pretext for a broader Korean territorial claim.[29] The dispute deeply influenced South Korean public and elite opinions toward China. An April 2004 poll by *Donga ilbo* on the eve of the dispute showed that the majority of National Assembly members of the ruling progressive Uri Party believed that South Korea "should focus more on [aligning with] China than the U.S. in our foreign policy of the future, and that 84 percent of the public agreed that it was important to give 'serious consideration of China.'"[30] However, a January 1, 2005, *Chosun ilbo* survey showed only 40 percent had favorable attitudes toward China, revealing the extent of political damage to China's image that occurred as a result of the Koguryo issue.[31]

Since 2004, South Korean views of China have been conflicted, and doubts about China's political intentions have persisted as a result of clashes between China and South Korea over fishing rights, the emergence of a potential dispute over ownership of Ieo-do, or the Socotra Rocks, and China's continued support for North Korea despite its provocations and aggression toward South Korea.[32] When asked in a Pew poll in 2008 how much influence Koreans want various countries to have in the world, the United States scored 7.35 out of 10, while China scored 5.43. The shift in South Korean opinion toward China is recorded in Pew surveys from spring 2007 and 2008, which showed 52 percent and 48 percent of respondents had positive views of China, respectively, compared with summer 2002, when 66 percent had a positive view of China.[33]

China's shielding of North Korea from international criticism has fanned the flames of negative South Korean public opinion toward China since 2010. The *Cheonan* and Yeonpyeong incidents intensified debates inside South Korea about how to deal with a rising China that continues its current relationship with North Korea and about Seoul's policy orientation toward the United States and China. In the summer following the *Cheonan* sinking, a *Korea Times* editorial noted that "Seoul and Washington have come to a new chapter in their strategic alliance and partnership," to which "no doubt the North's torpedo attack on the South's warship *Cheonan* in the West Sea in March has contributed." But it also argued that "the two countries should be careful not to bring about unnecessary conflicts with neighboring countries, especially China. . . . It would be better for the South to avoid being caught in the rivalry between Beijing and Washington."[34] This is the conventional wisdom among South Korean foreign policy specialists on how to manage relationships with China and the United States.[35]

South Korean analysts appear wary of the long-term risks of U.S.–China tensions that were raised by the *Cheonan* incident and which could threaten a favorable China–ROK partnership; as such, they privately express grave concerns about the weakening of the relationship with China.[36] A May 2010 *JoongAng Daily* editorial argued that "the 'strategic partnership' signed between the two countries last year must not be burned in fiery emotion and rhetoric."[37] A major challenge for South Korean policy is how to build sufficient trust in China–South Korea relations to win more active cooperation with China on political issues, especially as it relates to the future of the Korean Peninsula and possible North Korean instability.[38] An East Asia Institute survey conducted in October 2010 showed that almost two-thirds of South Koreans surveyed were skeptical about the impact of Chinese intervention in the event of inter-Korean conflict, assuming that China would take sides with North Korea. According to that survey, 59 percent of South Koreans believed that China prefers the status quo and holds a negative attitude toward Korean reunification.[39]

Despite negative perceptions of China's intentions to uphold the status quo on the Korean Peninsula, many South Korean analysts also feel that they have no choice but to try to cooperate with China if they hope to achieve reconciliation and eventual reunification with North Korea. Rejecting Lee Myung-bak's management of relations with China as overly confrontational, Park Geun-hye laid out a vision for peace and cooperation in Northeast Asia that places cooperation with China as a high priority. As part of this initiative, Park has proposed a China–South Korea–United States trilateral dialogue, illustrating her hopes that a better China–South Korea relationship will develop in the context of strong China–U.S. relations.

One South Korean has described a rising China in the following terms: "China is behind the tree of North Korea in South Korean eyes; that's why the Chinese military threat is invisible to us because we have an immediate threat from the North, but we have a varying threat perception of China. That view will change. If today Koreans are overconfident when thinking about China, the relationship will shift to one characterized by 'gradual competition' which will become 'a China problem' and then 'a China threat.'" This view is shared by another South Korean observer, who argues that economic cooperation has helped obscure the differences between the two countries. "We should accommodate the increasing economic relationship with China, but . . . China is not a democracy and is very different from the South Korean identity as a democracy and market economy—it is very different from us."[40] These views were once on the margins of South Korea's discussion regarding how to deal with China, but they have gradually become mainstream views. China is looming larger as an essential economic and political partner for South Korea, but South Koreans continue to see their interests and values as more closely aligned with those of the United States. This divergence underscores the diplomatic balancing act that South Korean policy makers face as they reconcile economic interdependence with China with continued dependence on the United States as a guarantor of stability and balance in Northeast Asian regional relations.

Attitudes Toward the U.S.–ROK Alliance

As indicated earlier in this chapter, the decline in positive South Korean attitudes toward the United States in 2002–04 led some analysts to conclude that it was only a matter of time before South Korea moved into China's sphere of influence. During this period of relative turmoil in the U.S.–ROK alliance, American security analysts reportedly began to write off South Korea as a long-term security partner. Yet instead of abandoning the relationship with the United States, South Korean public support for it has rebounded to reach new highs.

An annual global poll conducted by the Pew Research Global Attitudes Project shows a steady increase in favorable South Korean views of the United States, from 46 percent in 2003 to 79 percent in 2010, remaining steady at 78 percent in 2013.[41] This trend parallels results of an EAI poll from 2011 that indicated South Korean favorable views of the United States increased to 74 percent in 2010 (from 57 percent the previous year), a remarkable recovery in a relatively short period of time.[42] This improvement in South Korean public views of the United States is probably best explained by three factors: the effect of North Korean provocations on South Korean perceptions of the security environment, growing concerns about the rise of China, and the improvement in U.S.–ROK relations that occurred under the Lee Myung-bak administration.

Figure 3.4 illustrates the rebound in Korean attitudes toward the United States and suggests that the alliance remains not only durable but essential to the security equation in Northeast Asia. Polls have shown consistent and steady improvement in Korean views of the United States since what was arguably the low point in the relationship following the deaths of the two schoolgirls in 2002. The Pew Global Attitudes project showed a marked increase in positive Korean attitudes toward the United States, from 46 percent in 2003 to 79 percent in 2010.[43]

What accounts for the dramatic improvement in South Korean attitudes toward the United States, and to what extent is South Korean support for the alliance sustainable? A variety of contextual factors help to explain the recovery of South Korean perceptions of the United States.

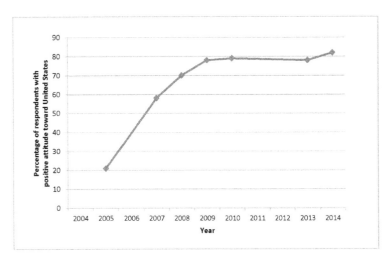

FIGURE 3.4 South Korean Favorability Toward U.S. Influence
Source: Pew Global Attitudes

First, negative perceptions of U.S. policy have ameliorated as it has become clear that the United States was a contributor to stability rather than a source of increased tensions on the Korean Peninsula. As North Korea has played the role of provocateur, the salience of the alliance as a deterrent against North Korean aggression has increased. This does not mean that the United States opposed inter-Korean rapprochement, but the rhetoric toward Iraq and North Korea in the first George W. Bush administration heightened South Korean fears that the United States could drag South Korea into conflict rather than prevent one.

Second, the United States has made extensive efforts to show respect for South Korea's achievements and to treat South Korea as a valued partner not only on the peninsula but also globally. The Lee Myung-bak administration's emphasis on an alliance for peace and its willingness to comprehensively cooperate with the United States on regional and global security issues in the 2009 U.S.–ROK Joint Vision Statement set a framework for the expansion of the alliance and positively influenced American perceptions of South Korea. In a joint press conference with Lee Myung-bak on the sidelines of the G-8 in Toronto in 2010,

President Obama referred to the U.S.–ROK alliance as a lynchpin of stability in the Asia-Pacific.

Third, North Korea's aggression has reinforced the main purposes of the alliance and provided an occasion for extraordinarily close policy coordination to address both security and political aspects of the response to North Korea. As North Korea has pursued its nuclear program, the U.S. willingness to emphasize its commitment to South Korea's security through extended deterrence has deepened institutional cooperation. In addition, both governments have worked together closely to ensure continuity of conventional deterrence despite deferring the transfer of operational control arrangements between the two militaries.

Finally, South Korean support for the alliance with the United States has correlated with a rise in concern about the impact of China on South Korea's security environment. In many respects this development reinforces the primary rationale for ROK support of a strong relationship with the United States: the United States is a powerful external balancer that provides security for South Korea. However, China opposes the expansion of the rationale for the U.S.–ROK alliance precisely because it is worried that it would be the main threat that would propel alliance cooperation.

Sustaining the Alliance

The CCGA/EAI poll from 2008 shows that over 72 percent of Koreans polled think the U.S. military presence increases stability in Asia. The Asan Institute for Policy Studies survey in 2010 indicates that almost three-fifths of respondents perceived the United States and South Korea to have common interests, and over 85 percent of respondents felt that the U.S.–ROK alliance will continue to be necessary. Even among those respondents who described themselves as having an unfavorable attitude toward the United States, 72 percent saw a need for the continuation of the alliance.[44] If current trends hold, there is every reason to think that South Korean support for the alliance would extend beyond Korean reunification, especially given the potential for rising regional tensions and the complexities South Korea faces as it navigates between China and Japan.

Another near-term issue that has become more serious for the alliance is North Korea's effort to establish itself as a nuclear weapon state. Most immediately, this raises questions about how South Koreans view the credibility of U.S. assurances regarding extended deterrence. Following each of North Korea's nuclear tests, the United States has been quick to offer statements of reassurance to Seoul.

But it remains the case that North Korea has a powerful weapon in its arsenal that South Korea does not possess, a difference that pushes South Koreans to believe they should either acquire their own nuclear capability or get the United States to reintroduce tactical nuclear weapons to the peninsula. This is one reason why South Korea pushed the United States—with success—to acquiesce to the extension of South Korean missile capabilities in October 2012. The announcement of new missile guidelines between the United States and South Korea allows South Korea to develop ballistic missiles with a range of up to 1,000 kilometers so that South Korea can reach any target on the peninsula, whereas the prior agreement between Washington and Seoul restricted South Korea to develop missiles with a maximum range of only 150 kilometers.

The Pacific Forum survey in 2007 showed that 22 percent of respondents agreed with the statement that Korea should develop a nuclear weapon capability, while 76 percent disagreed. Half the respondents agreed that Korea should develop an offensive military "strike capability." Following North Korea's second nuclear test in 2009 and its 2010 provocations, South Korean frustration with perceived North Korean efforts to utilize bluster and threats as blackmail and extortion for defensive purposes manifested in growing support for development of a nuclear weapons capability, even while seeking stronger U.S. commitments to defend South Korea, for instance, through calls on the United States to reintroduce tactical nuclear weapons into South Korea. The Asan Institute poll in 2010 showed that 55 percent of respondents agreed with the idea that South Korea should develop its own nuclear weapons in response to North Korea's nuclear threat, while respondents were split down the middle on whether they thought the United States would actually use its nuclear weapons in South Korea's defense. North Korea's third nuclear test in February 2013 pushed South Korean attitudes even further in the direction of desiring its own nuclear deterrent. Immediately following that nuclear test, Asan Institute polling showed that almost 60 percent of South Koreans felt threatened by North Korea's nuclear test, and over two-thirds supported the idea that South Korea should develop nuclear weapons.[45]

South Korea has made remarkable strides in its economic and political development over the past two decades, and this progress is rightfully a source of South Korean confidence. South Korea's economic and political development has transformed it from a consumer to a producer of economic assistance and security resources and has positioned the country to make contributions to international political leadership. However, despite South Korea's growing capacity, it still lives in a neighborhood that severely constrains South Korean accomplishments and leaves it vulnerable to regional tensions and potential aggression. All these factors have an influence on South Korean identity and perceptions both of themselves and their role in the world.

South Korean support for the alliance with the United States has risen steadily over the past decade following a period in which the alliance was arguably remade as a veritable partnership in reflection of South Korea's accomplishments. But despite those accomplishments, South Korean interests remain vulnerable. An increasing sense of threat from both North Korea and China has translated into mounting support for the U.S.–ROK alliance, even among South Koreans who are strongly critical of the United States. A careful analysis of South Korean public opinion since 2007 helps deepen our understanding of these trends and their significance and provides a useful picture of how South Korean public opinion has interacted with foreign policy, both to influence South Korean government positions and to define expectations for what constitutes an effective South Korean government response. South Korean public opinion, as expressed through preferred partners and national priorities, is an increasingly important factor influencing, constraining, and shaping South Korean foreign policy choices and determines how South Korea will apply its growing capabilities and confidence on the regional and international scene.

4

CONVERGENCE AND ALIENATION
IN JAPAN–SOUTH KOREA RELATIONS

IT IS NOT SURPRISING THAT JAPAN–SOUTH KOREA RELATIONS are so complicated, given that Japan invaded and occupied Korea and tried to assimilate Koreans for over three decades during the twentieth century. The psychological scars would be even deeper if not for interceding developments, including the fratricidal Korean War, a bloody fight that relinked Japan and South Korea (from a security perspective) as a result of Japan's logistical support in the war and the establishment of Japan and South Korea's parallel alliances with the United States. Perhaps what is even more remarkable is South Korea's great success by following Japan's developmental path, a path that has created an economic and political partner with shared values and common interests in Northeast Asian stability. Yet in spite of this convergence and repeated efforts to forge a "future-oriented" path in Japan–South Korea relations, historical grievances block the relationship from reaching its full potential.

Despite the common interests and their similar development paths, there is surprisingly little literature on contemporary Korea–Japan relations. The existing literature posits three rationales shaping prospects for cooperation between them. The first is the fact that they share ties with the United States as a common alliance partner. Victor Cha developed this thesis in his landmark study on the ROK–Japan quasi-alliance relationship. He argued that alliance partner evaluations of U.S. commitment to the region have been an important factor in Korean and Japanese calculations of their own relationship, and that perceptions of U.S. distancing from the region during the Cold War were a major factor that enabled South Korea and Japan to set aside history issues and work more closely together.[1]

A second rationale for improved ROK–Japan cooperation is reflected in the "China threat" school, which argues that South Korea and Japan as democratic market economies with shared values should enhance cooperation to thwart the rising influence of a system that remains politically closed to competition under the Chinese Communist Party and poses a challenge to the political, legal, and security status quo. But the relative lack of cooperation between Japan and South Korea during the Cold War, when the common threat from the Soviet bloc was higher, suggests that the emergence of a new threat, such as from China, may not result in enhanced Japan–ROK cooperation. In fact, despite similar threat perceptions related to China's rise, it is increasingly clear that Japan and South Korea have strikingly different preferences when it comes to tactics to manage that rise, stemming from differing geographic conditions and historical experiences.

A third rationale focuses not on the reasons for cooperation but on obstacles to ROK–Japan coordination and joint action. It explores the emergence of identity issues that are powerful factors in domestic politics and ultimately prevent bilateral cooperation between the two countries. Gilbert Rozman has been the most active proponent of an identity-based approach to understanding the limits of cooperation among the countries in Northeast Asia.[2]

After extended observation of the relationship and conversations with many Japanese and South Koreans regarding these differences, we conclude that the threat-based and alliance-based evaluations of conditions for Japan–ROK cooperation cannot overcome the psychological and emotional gaps in perspective on Japan–ROK relations, chasms that are reflected in public opinion in both countries. For this reason, this study has chosen to utilize public opinion data as a way of getting into the heads of the publics on both sides and more deeply understanding the nature and parameters of identity-related issues that have inhibited development of the relationship.

Policy Studies and Prospects for Enhanced U.S.–Japan–ROK Trilateral Coordination

A number of policy studies over the past fifteen years have supported the idea of closer trilateral cooperation among the United States, Japan, and South Korea while recognizing the political constraints that limit such cooperation. One of the earliest such studies of prospects was organized by Ralph Cossa of Pacific Forum CSIS, who argued that "cordial, cooperative relations between the ROK and Japan today, and between a reunified Korea and Japan in the future, are absolutely essential for long-term regional stability." But that work also concluded that a formal three-party alliance is not "advisable, achievable, or necessary."[3] The authors in that volume, published a year after the forward-looking summit between Kim Dae-jung and Obuchi Keizo in 1998, made a strong case for a convergence of strategic interests among the United States, Japan, and South Korea in pursuing coordination to deal with North Korea while also engaging China, but they rarely mention problems in the Japan–ROK relationship related to history. The volume also highlighted the benefits for trilateral cooperation deriving from strengthened Japan–ROK interaction, a point made clear by an early simulation exercise designed to pave the way for closer official Japan–ROK security cooperation.

A subsequent volume from CSIS edited by Kim Tae-hyo and Brad Glosserman delved deeper in an effort to identify clearly the glue that would hold the United States, Japan, and South Korea together. Chapters evaluated strategic factors, economic interdependence, institutionalized cooperation, ideational factors including shared values, and public opinion in each of the three countries as part of a comprehensive examination of what might drive closer trilateral cooperation. That volume also notably failed to explore how to delineate or overcome persistent differences between South Korea and Japan over the historical, territorial, and perception issues that continue to divide them.[4]

James Schoff explored institutionalization of trilateral cooperation as a way to strengthen shared values and interests among the United States, Japan, and South Korea.[5] He concluded that institutionalizing trilateral cooperation clearly faces political limits but also has the virtue of depoliticizing some forms of cooperation and insulating them from the political whirlwinds that derive from flaring tensions over enduring disputes between the two countries.

However, despite the strong rationales for institutionalization of trilateralism that Schoff advocates, powerful constraints prevent the deepening of institutional cooperation. Historically, North Korea has been the primary driver of institutionalized trilateral coordination among the United States, Japan, and South Korea. The two notable achievements in this area in the 1990s are the Korean Peninsula Energy Development Organization (KEDO) and the Trilateral Coordination and Oversight Group (TCOG). However, both mechanisms unraveled during the 2000s, casualties of the rise in bilateral friction over history issues. Their failures weakened the institutional infrastructure that bound the three countries.

North Korea's shelling of Yeonpyeong Island in November 2010 prompted renewed trilateral coordination efforts among the United States, Japan, and South Korea, producing a robust trilateral foreign ministers' statement that stopped just short of endorsing collective action in response to North Korean provocations.[6] This statement affirming that all three countries "share a deep and abiding interest in maintaining peace, prosperity, and stability in the region; expanding the benefits of freer and more open trade; and promoting an protecting freedom, democracy, and human rights worldwide" is notable because it signaled to Pyongyang (and China) that all three nations viewed North Korea's actions as unacceptable and showed that such aggression would have adverse consequences for North Korea (and that North Korean provocations came at a cost to Chinese interests).[7] But it has proven difficult to follow up on as bilateral historical and territorial issues between Japan and South Korea again imposed practical limits on expectations for trilateral coordination.

One clear example of those limits was the failure of Lee Myung-bak and Noda Yoshihiko to conclude defense agreements that would enable sharing of sensitive information and allow the exchange of parts and services between naval services. Military counterparts on both sides recognized the importance and desirability of these agreements, but public outcry based on views of historical issues intervened to prevent the agreements from being concluded in December 2011. A subsequent attempt failed in June 2012, with the Seoul government pulling back only hours prior to the planned signing ceremony as a result of disapproval from influential members of the ROK National Assembly. In this case, differences over history imposed clear limits not only on efforts to strengthen institutional cooperation between Japan and South Korea but also on what the United States, South Korea, and Japan can do together.

Another challenge that has consistently been identified in literature exploring U.S.–Japan–ROK trilateralism is providing assurances that such coordination does not target China. That task has been complicated by these recent forms of trilateral coordination that were designed to signal to Beijing that a failure to restrain North Korea has costs and motivates responses that are adverse to China's security interests. Chinese sensitivities are likely to grow, and as they do, South Korea in particular will find itself under greater pressure from Beijing not to cooperate with the United States and Japan.

Evolution of Japan–ROK Relations in the Post–Cold War Period

The primary framework for managing Japan–South Korea relations since the end of the Korean War has been the parallel Japanese and South Korean security alliances with the United States. The Korean War established a security linkage between Japan and South Korea as a result of Japan's role as a logistical base of support for the United States under the flag of the UN Command in the fight against North Korean aggression. An uneasy relationship characterized by de facto cooperation in the absence of political relations lasted for more than a decade, until the two countries normalized political relations in 1965 under political pressure from the United States. This development was particularly contentious in South Korea but provided important economic assistance to the ROK as Park Chunghee attempted to jumpstart export-led economic growth; Japan's investment and cooperation proved critical to the success of this effort. For the duration of the Cold War, the bilateral relationship improved. Factors explaining the uptick in relations include fear of U.S. withdrawal or reduction of influence in Asia, and Japan's willingness to provide needed economic support to South Korea in support of its own industrialization.[8]

The end of the Cold War, along with South Korea's democratization and continued economic growth, provided the impetus for a gradual shift in South Korea–Japan relations. The two countries moved toward a greater sense of mutuality and equality, supported by South Korea's political and economic development, as well as by growth in cultural relations. By the 1990s South Koreans and Japanese began to know each other in more personal and direct ways, especially as grassroots exchange and interaction grew.

Following the outbreak of the North Korean nuclear crisis in the early 1990s, there was a renewed realization that the threat posed by North Korea's nuclear development was real and could lead to military conflict. As tensions rose and alliance managers thought about the forms of cooperation needed to respond to a contingency on the Korean Peninsula, it was clear that the United States needed stronger coordination with both Japan and South Korea. That need led to the establishment of official trilateral coordination dialogues through which the Japanese and South Korean defense ministries set up direct contacts and built military ties with each other. Despite the inherent sensitivities of the relationship, Japan and South Korea began discussing scenarios for cooperation in humanitarian assistance and disaster relief in the event of a North Korean contingency. A direct Japan–ROK military-to-military relationship began to grow as a result of trilateral track 1.5 discussions (ostensibly unofficial, but involving government officials "in their private capacities") involving the United States. But these contacts were nascent and were constrained by the absence of an updated political framework for the Japan–ROK relationship. The renewal of U.S.–Japan defense guidelines in the mid-1990s strengthened attention to U.S.–Japan cooperation in areas surrounding Japan and resulted in the passage of legislation that would allow Japan to provide greater logistical support to U.S. operations in the event of a regional contingency, including renewed conflict on the Korean Peninsula.

However, tensions over history triggered growing estrangement between South Korea and Japan, and anti-Japanese nationalism proved a ready tool for South Korean politicians. In a newly consolidating democracy, some politicians were quick to capitalize on anti-Japanese sentiment in South Korea to shore up sagging approval ratings. President Kim Young Sam appeared to take advantage of such sentiments, usually in response to insensitive remarks on history-related issues by Japanese cabinet members, comments that negated official efforts by the Japanese government to come to terms with history in the eyes of South Koreans. By all appearances, this was a deeply ingrained cycle in which Japan's awkward and hesitating efforts to come to terms with its past, often in incomplete ways that focused more on the form and wording of apologies than on actions that would convey real contrition, would inevitably clash with South Korean demands for note apologies and compensation from Japan. As South Korean society liberalized, the South Korean public response to Japan's perceived failure to deal with history congealed around several hot-button issues, including comfort women, forced laborers, South Korea's claims to Dokdo/Takeshima, and an international push to rename the Sea of Japan the East Sea.

Since the late 1990s, a pattern has emerged in the South Korea–Japan relationship. Three successive South Korean presidents came into office with the desire to improve relations with Japan, yet each faced setbacks and recurring stumbling blocks to future-oriented cooperation, typically the result of history-related issues. This pattern is the product of two clashing imperatives: a desire to reconcile South Korea's clear interests in maintaining strong economic and political cooperation with

Japan—along with strengthening security cooperation to deal with North Korea through the framework with the United States—and the history issue with Japan, which is both a political issue within South Korea and a source of conflict in its various manifestations between the two governments.

Given the pernicious and deep-rooted cycle of Japanese apology, indiscretion, and inflamed South Korean public reaction, the effort by President Kim and Prime Minister Obuchi to change the cycle by establishing a "future-oriented relationship" in October 1998 is especially notable for both its ambition and its failure. During Kim's 1998 summit with Obuchi, the two leaders agreed to put historical differences behind them in favor of forward-looking relations, setting the stage for a less antagonistic and more cooperative diplomatic relationship and reinforcing an atmosphere of reconciliation in which local-level exchanges would be able to take root and develop. In light of the psychological and emotional gaps between the two publics, this bold approach directly confronted long-standing Korean identity issues in the relationship with Japan.

Starting from Obuchi's expression of "remorseful repentance and heartfelt apology" for Japan's colonial rule of Korea, the leaders focused on building a "future-oriented relationship based on a spirit of reconciliation and friendship" between the two sides in the Joint Korea–Japan Declaration of a New Partnership for the 21st Century. Both leaders agreed to enhanced exchanges, cooperation, and dialogue; to cooperate to secure the post–Cold War world order, promote international economic cooperation, and address various global issues; to encourage North Korea to "take a more constructive posture through dialogues for peace and stability on the Korean Peninsula"; and to cooperate in cohosting the 2002 World Cup.[9] The Japan–Korea joint statement established a framework through which it was possible to promote coordination of issues in the two countries' relations.

But the promise of a new relationship was thwarted even within Kim's term by the emergence of history, textbook, and territorial issues. By the following year, renewed conflicts erupted over Dokdo/Takeshima as the South Korean government permitted tourists to visit the island,

and Shimane Prefecture (the prefecture that would have administrative jurisdiction over the islands if they were Japanese) allowed some Japanese to list the island as their permanent address in census records.

In 2000 the simmering textbook issue was reignited over South Korean civil society calls for their government to object to the publication of Japanese history textbooks that included incorrect or distorted descriptions of Japan's imperial rule. This dispute flared with the approval by Japan's Ministry of Education of a revisionist textbook by the Fusosha Publishing Company for use in Japanese classrooms that challenged or ignored some of the most sensitive aspects of Japan's twentieth-century historical experience in Asia. *Chosun ilbo* criticized the textbook structure as "an idealization of Japan's imperialist past."[10] The Fusosha textbook was only one of several approved by the Ministry of Education for use in secondary schools, and approval did not mean that it would automatically be adopted in the classroom; that decision lay with councils that oversaw secondary education at the local and provincial levels. Nevertheless, mere approval ignited a firestorm among South Koreans who demanded that the South Korean Ministry of Foreign Affairs and Trade take stern measures to protest the approval.

Although the ROK government initially tried to play down the textbook row by expressing disappointment with its Japanese counterpart while attempting to preserve the framework for a positive bilateral relationship, the South Korean public demanded stronger actions, resulting in a cut-off of many local-level and nongovernmental exchanges with Japan. The outcry resulted in the temporary recall of ROK ambassador to Japan Choi Sang-yong in April 2001 and incited public demonstrations in front of the Japanese Embassy in Seoul. This demand for a strong governmental reaction to Japanese provocations pressed Seoul to take more stringent steps than had been anticipated.[11]

To bring tensions under control, South Korea proposed joint history research and teacher exchanges but also announced a variety of sanctions against Japan. In addition, South Korea's National Assembly unanimously passed a resolution calling on the government to make a comprehensive review of ties with Japan, banning Japanese associated with the textbook from entering South Korea, and opposing Japan's efforts to win a permanent seat on the UN Security Council. But the main factor that led to an easing of South Korean views was the fact that many Japanese districts chose not to utilize the controversial textbook.

But there were more troubles to come. The Kim–Obuchi joint statement suffered another blow when Prime Minister Koizumi Junichiro insisted on making official visits to Yasukuni Shrine, where the spirits of convicted Japanese war criminals have been enshrined. For Japanese politicians, especially on the right, Yasukuni Shrine is a symbol of national spirit, sacrifice, and pride, but for South Koreans visits to a shrine where Japanese war criminals are honored suggests a lack of repentance for past bad acts and puts them on guard against revival of an imperialist Japan. While there are few signs that Japan is thinking about changing, much less turning its back on, its peace constitution and embracing an expansionist and militaristic policy toward Asia, the visits incited a vociferous negative public response from China and South Korea. Prime Minister Koizumi's insistence on his right to visit the shrine cast a pall over Japan–South Korea relations and made the relationship more difficult to manage for the duration of his term in office.

Nonetheless, Kim and Koizumi attempted to restabilize the Japan–ROK relationship when they held a summit in October 2001 at which they reached a seven-point accord aimed at resolving disputes between the two nations, establishing the creation of a joint history research forum, and launching negotiations over disputed fisheries. Koizumi also pledged to seek new ways to pay homage to Japan's war dead.

Kim Dae-jung's successor Roh Moo-hyun also sought to place the relationship with Japan on a future-oriented footing when he traveled to Japan in June 2003 despite rising tensions over compensation due to Korean women who were forced to work as sex slaves during World War II. This dispute was triggered by a Japanese Supreme Court ruling that the Japanese government is not obligated to compensate Korean comfort women and that only the Japanese Diet has authority to authorize compensation.

Roh's effort to start on a good footing with Japan was criticized from the outset by the Korean public because he chose a national holiday as the day to travel to Japan. Even as he attempted to strengthen relations with Tokyo, Roh was chastised for skipping "sensitive issues that need to be aired" for the sake of promoting a "future-oriented, transparent partnership." An editorial in the *Chosun ilbo* argued that this approach "will bring nothing but regret," clearly illustrating the political limits and risks in South Korea associated with a future-only approach to improving South Korea–Japan relations.[12] As a result of this pressure, Roh felt compelled to press Japan to be more direct and forthright in its treatment of Japan's imperial history. Tokyo governor Shintaro Ishihara, a conservative nationalist who seemed to delight in roiling the waters, threw fuel onto the fire during this period when he asserted that Koreans chose Japanese rule rather than Chinese or Russian rule at the time of Korea's annexation in 1910.[13]

While textbook and Yasukuni-related issues continued to simmer, the next major crisis in the relationship emerged over the March 2005 decision by Shimane Prefecture to establish Takeshima Day and a recurrence of the textbook controversy that was fed by the Japanese claim to Dokdo. South Korea filed formal protests in a variety of forums over these issues and christened a navy landing vessel with the name *Dokdo*, in turn triggering a Japanese diplomatic protest over the name. South Korea also protested references to Japan's claim to Dokdo that appeared in the Defense White Paper of 2005. The diplomatic crisis threatened to escalate into confrontation the following year as Japan planned to conduct hydrological mapping of the seabed near the Dokdo/Takeshima islands in 2006. This news ramped up tensions, but the matter was ultimately resolved through diplomatic negotiations though which both sides stepped back from unilateral efforts to strengthen their respective claims.

A further complication in the relationship emerged as South Koreans perceived Prime Minister Koizumi's successor, Abe Shinzo, as too close to Japan's right wing. Roh Moo-hyun even expressed his suspicions of Japan's leadership in conversations with President Bush. North Korea's first nuclear test and the subsequent U.S. effort to reengage North Korea diplomatically provided a further backdrop for alienation in South Korea–Japan relations since South Korea supported a more active U.S. approach, including the possibility of establishing a peace treaty with

North Korea, while Japan was deeply frustrated by the Bush administration's outreach and subsequent dropping of sanctions against North Korea, including removal of North Korea from the U.S. list of countries supporting terrorism despite a lack of progress on the issue of North Korean abductions of Japanese citizens, an especially emotional concern of Japanese and some Americans.

Although Prime Minister Abe was known as a rightwing politician, he governed as a pragmatist and effectively removed the Yasukuni Shrine question from the bilateral agenda. But Abe's views on the role of the government of Japan in sexual enslavement of women during World War II continued to be a major preoccupation within the region and even drew the United States into managing the issue. First, the Congress became involved when Representative Michael Honda introduced a resolution calling for the government of Japan to formally acknowledge and accept responsibility for its sexual enslavement of women during World War II, indirectly setting up a lobbying competition between Seoul and Tokyo. South Korean sex slaves testified before Congress at a hearing in February 2007, the issue was fed by an active public lobbying campaign that spring, and the Honda resolution passed the House Foreign Affairs Committee in June, paving the way for consideration of the issue on the floor of the House. Second, the comfort women issue emerged as a quiet issue in U.S.–Japan relations, as the Bush administration undertook efforts behind the scenes to persuade Prime Minister Abe to handle the matter in a manner that would not inflame regional relations. The issue was discussed when Abe met Bush in April 2007. Together, these problems poisoned the relationship between Japan and South Korea under Abe and Roh, particularly as Roh embraced a public campaign that strongly criticized Japan on history issues and fanned the flames of frustration among both the bureaucracy and the public. One of his domestic initiatives, a commission to identify and punish South Koreans who had collaborated during the Japanese colonial period, proved especially damaging.

The December 2007 election of conservative Lee Myung-bak provided a new opportunity for stabilization of Japan–ROK relations, especially since Lee, a former businessman, had many past dealings with Japanese colleagues and was regarded as friendly to Japan. Certainly,

Lee's tougher approach to North Korea and his insistence on denuclear-ization as a precondition for expanded assistance to North Korea elimi-nated one potential obstacle to improved Japan–South Korea relations. However, his election as president did not remove the outstanding his-torical and territorial issues as irritants and obstacles to an improved bilateral relationship, even though it did bring about a less overtly popu-list approach to it.

Under Lee and the DPJ leadership in Tokyo (there were three DPJ prime ministers during Lee's five-year term), the Dokdo/Takeshima dispute took center stage in the relationship. The Lee administration responded strongly to Japanese textbooks that claimed the islands as an integral part of Japanese territory, South Korea took steps to increase its administrative and military structures for asserting actual control over the islands, and a public relations campaign by South Korean nongovernmental organizations extended to high-profile ads in U.S. newspapers. A report that the U.S. Board of Geographic Names had changed its characterization of the islands from "South Korean" to "nondesignated" even had Ambassador Lee Tae-shik buttonholing President Bush in advance of President Lee's inaugural visit to the United States to request that the policy be reversed prior to Lee's sum-mit with Bush.

Shimane prefectural celebrations of Takeshima Day became an annual irritant in the relationship. The victory of the DPJ in the 2009 parliamentary elections offered hope for improved Japan–ROK relations since the DPJ was less likely to be pulled to the right on historical issues. Aside from the Dokdo/Takeshima dispute, the DPJ leadership made a number of conciliatory gestures that markedly improved the atmo-sphere. Foreign Minister Okada Katsuya proposed a joint history text-book with South Korea and China in October 2009, Prime Minister Kan Naoto issued apologies in 2010, and in 2011 Japan returned some South Korean historical archives that had been taken to Japan during colonial rule. Unfortunately, those gestures went unreciprocated and proved to be a missed opportunity for improved Japan–South Korea relations.

Prospects for reconciliation received a boost when South Kore-ans showed great sympathy for Japan following the March 2011 triple disasters. South Korea sent a disaster recovery team to Japan, and many K-pop stars who had gained popularity in Japan were prominent donors to the relief effort. But even as Japan struggled to recover in late March 2011, another round of Japanese textbook revisions that reasserted Japan's claim to Dokdo/Takeshima prompted a sharp downturn in Korean opinion along with a hardening of attitudes on both sides regarding the dispute. Korean Air Lines' overflight of Dokdo on the inauguration of its first A380 jumbo jet and visits by South Korean cabinet minister Paik Hee-young to the island provoked a Japanese response in the form of a monthlong boycott of Korean Air Lines. The establishment of Shimane's Takeshima Day in February, textbook authorizations in March that included assertions to Japan's claim to Takeshima, and the release of Japan's Defense White Paper in July provided seasonal irritants and seemed to institutionalize ritualized protests that easily distracted from (and obscured) constructive cooperation in the relationship.

A South Korean Constitutional Court ruling in fall 2011 concluded that the South Korean government had not done enough to seek redress for comfort women and forced laborers during the Japanese colonial period. That ruling shaped the agenda for a December 2011 summit meeting between President Lee and Prime Minister Noda Yoshihiko at which the two governments were set to agree on an information-sharing agreement and a cross-servicing agreement that would have laid a cornerstone for practical cooperation between the two militaries. A push to sign the agreements occurred in June 2012 following South Korea's legislative elections, but that effort failed owing to negative public opinion, National Assembly opposition, and Lee's decline into lame-duck status in advance of South Korea's December 2012 presidential elections. A long-standing public manifestation of the comfort woman dispute has been a weekly demonstration by comfort women outside the Embassy of Japan in Seoul, which held its thousandth weekly protest by the end of 2011. The dispute was exacerbated by the erection across from the embassy of a statue of a Korean girl in traditional dress sitting on a bench, funded by South Korean citizens' donations; it served as a vivid, tangible permanent reminder of the comfort women issue as a sticking point in the Japan–South Korea relationship.

The low point for Japan–South Korea relations under President Lee occurred with his August 2012 visit to the Dokdo/Takeshima islands and subsequent comments regarding conditions for a hypothetical but unplanned visit to Korea by the Japanese emperor. These events inflamed Japanese opinion toward South Korea and transformed the Dokdo/Takeshima issue from a "mere" territorial dispute to a matter of Japanese national pride. They also indirectly fed heightened tensions surrounding the Senkaku/Diaoyu islands dispute between Japan and China. In turn, South Korean public anxieties regarding Japan's political direction grew as the LDP selected former prime minister Abe Shinzo as its standard-bearer for December national elections. Abe and the party won on a platform that advocated, among other things, Japan's exercise of collective self-defense and seemed to challenge prior statements of apology regarding historical issues by the government of Japan. (In truth, the election result was more of a vote against three years of hapless DPJ rule than a vote for the LDP.)

In contrast to her three immediate predecessors, President Park Geun-hye took office in February 2013 emphasizing that Japan show a "correct understanding of history" and calling on Prime Minister Abe to confront history as the means by which to put Japan–South Korea relations on a more sustainable footing. Park's direct call for Abe to address historical issues as a precondition for a future-oriented relationship is in line with South Korean public frustrations over Japan's seeming inability to put history and the current manifestations of that history that most inflame South Korean attitudes squarely into the past.

Park's insistence that Japan face up to history issues led to a freezing of leadership-level dialogue with Prime Minister Abe during their first year in office. The discomfort in Japan resulting from the cool atmosphere was exacerbated by Park's apparent tilt toward Beijing through the exchange of special envoys with China prior to her inauguration. While Abe sent Deputy Prime Minister Aso to Park's inauguration, their meeting set a cool tone for the relationship. Relations were virtually frozen as South Koreans objected to the sending of Japanese high-level officials to participate in Shimane Prefecture's Takeshima Day, Japan's reiteration of its claim to Takeshima/Dokdo in textbooks and government publications, impolitic remarks by prominent associates of the prime minister denying Japanese government involvement with comfort women, Japanese Diet member visits to Yasukuni Shrine, and Abe's own offerings and eventual visit to Yasukuni on December 26, 2013.

When Defense Secretary Chuck Hagel emphasized the value to the United States of a good Japan–ROK relationship during a meeting with Park in October 2013, the Korean Blue House broke protocol in providing a public release revealing her negative response. This action not only sent a signal of dismay to Japan but also stimulated concern in Washington that Park's hard line toward Abe could be damaging U.S. interests in a stable and cooperative Japan–ROK relationship.

Abe's December 2013 visit to Yasukuni despite U.S. messages from Vice President Joseph Biden discouraging such a visit only weeks earlier further roiled South Korean emotions and drew a rare expression of "disappointment" from the U.S. government. Moreover, Abe's visit to Yasukuni raised questions in Washington about his strategic judgment, as well as concerns about the advisability and conditions under which President Obama should carry out a state visit to Japan scheduled for April that had been postponed the previous fall as a result of budget issues in Washington. Following through with the state visit without also visiting Korea would clearly create a political backlash in Seoul, so the White House adjusted its schedule to include a visit to South Korea as part of the itinerary.

With the visit to Asia in mind, the Obama administration worked to stabilize the estranged relationship between Prime Minister Abe and President Park by brokering a trilateral summit meeting on the sidelines of the Nuclear Security Summit at The Hague. To do so, the United States entered into consultations with both sides regarding the conditions under which such a meeting would be possible. South Korea sought Abe's reaffirmation of the Kono and Murayama statements as the official policy of the government of Japan, which Abe publicly delivered a week prior to the Nuclear Security Summit. This gesture cut short a seeming effort in Japan to undermine the Kono statement through a review of the evidence compiled in support of the statement in the early 1990s.

The trilateral Hague summit proved to be a valuable turning point. It brought Park and Abe together for the first time and catalyzed a director-general dialogue to examine differences between the two governments on the comfort women issue. Thus U.S. intervention helped to stabilize the ROK–Japan relationship in advance of the president's Asia trip and jump-started Japan–ROK bilateral and trilateral contacts. However, both the Park and Abe administrations faced the challenging task of preparing to manage the relationship through a series of delicate anniversaries in 2015, including the seventieth anniversary of the end of World War II and the fiftieth anniversary of Japan–South Korea normalization.

Evolution of ROK–Japan Public Opinion: Attitudes Shift but in Opposing Directions

The establishment of a "future-oriented relationship" on the occasion of the 1998 Kim–Obuchi summit may not have adequately addressed issues of history, but it did mark an important turning point in Japanese attitudes toward South Korea. Polling results from Japan's Cabinet Office (figure 4.1) show a marked positive shift in Japanese attitudes toward

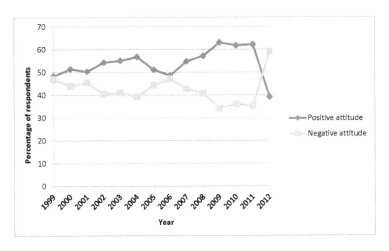

FIGURE 4.1   Japanese Affinity Toward South Korea
Source: Cabinet Office of Japan

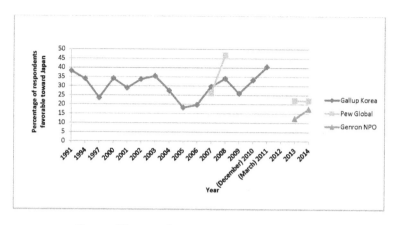

FIGURE 4.2 Korean Views on Japan
Source: Gallup Korea, Pew Global, Genron NPO

South Korea from 1999, a marked turn from long-standing negative feelings toward the ROK. This shift in Japanese perceptions was buttressed during the decade that followed by the increasing popularity of South Korean cultural offerings, including dramas and pop music. However, the shift in positive feelings in Japan toward South Korea was not reciprocated: South Koreans continued to have a predominantly negative attitude toward Japan. Available polling data (figure 4.2) show an upward tick in South Korean attitudes toward Japan that coincided with the coming to power of the DPJ in 2009, but the positive trend peaked in 2011 and never topped 50 percent. Genron NPO and Pew Global polls from 2013 and 2014 show a downturn that coincided with the LDP's return to power under the Abe administration.

A separate BBC Globescan poll of South Korean perceptions of Japan (figure 4.3) shows a similar trend, even though South Korean public attitudes toward Japan were majority positive for the first time in 2010 and 2011. Predictably, the return of textbook issues in late March 2011 soured South Korean public opinion once again following an unprecedented outpouring of sympathy after Japan's triple crisis the same month, and the negative trend was reinforced in 2012 by heightened tensions following President Lee's visit to the Dokdo/Takeshima islands. A series of

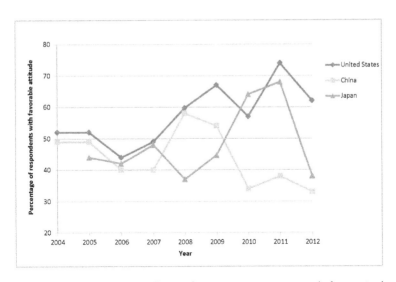

FIGURE 4.3 Globescan Polling of Korean Views Toward the United States, China, and Japan
Source: Globescan

NHK polls conducted in 1991, 1999, and 2010 affirm the positive shift in Japanese attitudes toward Korea but also show that South Korean negative attitudes toward Japan have increased from less than 60 percent in 1991 to 80 percent in 2010. The NHK survey in 2010 also finds a gap in Japanese and Korean perceptions of the quality of the relationship, with over 60 percent of Japanese stating that the relationship is good but less than 40 percent of Koreans responding positively. Moreover, Lee Myung-bak's visit to Dokdo/Takeshima and the subsequent downturn in Japan–South Korea erased the gains made by South Korea over a decade. The Japan Cabinet Office survey from 2012 (fig. 4.1) reflects a dramatic reversal in Japanese perceptions of relations with South Korea for that year.[14] Unfortunately, the mutual negative attitude of Japanese and South Koreans toward each other has persisted. Eighty-five percent of Koreans surveyed in an Asan Institute poll conducted in July 2013 express distrust toward Japan, while a Yomiuri-Gallup poll conducted in December of the same year reports that 72 percent of Japanese polled don't trust South Korea.[15] These results parallel a May 2013 joint poll by the Japanese civil society group Genron NPO and the Seoul-based EAI in which 31.1 percent of Japanese respondents said they have "favorable impression" of South Korea, while just 12.2 percent of South Korean respondents said they feel the same about Japan. A second Genron-EAI poll conducted in July of 2014 shows a worrisome negative trend in Japanese attitudes toward South Korea: only 20.5 percent of Japanese had a "favorable impression" of South Korea in that poll while "unfavorable" responses toward South Korea increased from 37.3 percent to 54.4 percent of respondents. South Korean attitudes toward Japan during this period, on the other hand, showed modest improvement from 12.2 percent to 17.5 percent.[16]

The gap in South Korean and Japanese views of the relationship is persistent and is reflected in multiple polls over time and across a battery of questions regarding prospects for improvement in Korea–Japan relations, affinity toward the other, and assessments of the current state of the relationship. In the case of each question, Japanese respondents have consistently maintained a more positive attitude than have Korean respondents. The NHK poll in 2010 provides some insight into this gap by showing that Japanese respondents are more focused on contemporary matters while South Korean "awareness centered more on historical events." Overall these results suggest that efforts between the two countries to focus on a "future-oriented relationship" provide satisfaction from a Japanese perspective, while a focus on the future at the expense of a resolution of history-related issues appears to be engendering greater discontent and negativity toward Japan in South Korea. The NHK poll suggests that the Dokdo/Takeshima islands dispute has become the primary symbol of South Korea's grievances against Japan and a continuing reminder for South Koreans of their dissatisfaction with the handling of these issues by the government of Japan. The May 2013 Genron NPO/EAI survey also sought to identify the sources of negative impressions that each country has of the other. Among Japanese who have negative impressions of South Korea, 55.8 percent blamed "criticism of Japan on historical issues," while 50.1 percent said the reason was "continued opposition on the issue of Takeshima." Among South Koreans, "the Dokdo issue"

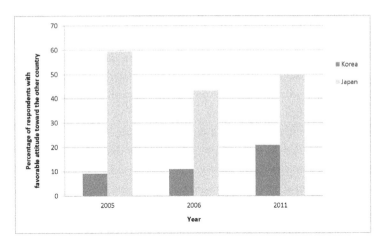

FIGURE 4.4 Relative Trust Between Korea and Japan
Source: *Hankook ilbo*

was blamed by 84.5 percent, along with "inadequate repentance over the history of invasion," findings that parallel other results.

The *Hankook ilbo* and *Yomiuri shimbun* have conducted joint polls on the relative level of trust between South Korea and Japan on three occasions since 2005, the results of which are shown in figure 4.4. Each poll has shown a marked gap in trust levels between the two countries, with Japan showing relative trust toward South Korea in the 46 percent range while South Korea's trust level of Japan has been considerably lower, breaking 20 percent for the first time in 2011 compared with a trust level around 10 percent in 2005 and 2006. The trust gap is consistent with other polls showing that while Japan was relatively satisfied and positive about relations with South Korea, South Koreans have continued to regard Japan with suspicion. In fact, *Seoul shinmun* polls show that the number of South Koreans who consider Japan's efforts to deal with South Korea on historical issues are "satisfactory" shrank between July 2005 and December 2012 from 12.4 percent to 4.7 percent, while the number of those who believe that Japan's efforts have been insufficient grew from 84.3 percent to 94.1 percent.[17] Despite cooperation on future-oriented issues, the history issue and its various manifestations continue to be a major source of discontent toward Japan among South Koreans.

Among the polls that attempted to dig into specific issues in Japan–South Korea relations, there are a number of notable results. A 2005 *Donga ilbo* poll indicates that over 90 percent of South Koreans opposed Prime Minister Koizumi's visits to Yasukuni Shrine, and over 60 percent view Yasukuni primarily as a symbol of Japanese militarism. Over 95 percent of South Korean respondents believe that the question of compensation for victims of Japan's colonial period has not yet been resolved, and two-thirds believe that it will not be possible for Japan and South Korea to overcome problems of history. Over 40 percent see the need for a Japanese apology that is acceptable to Koreans as the primary element needed to solve disputes over history.[18]

A number of joint polls have polled preferences regarding specific issues in the Japan–South Korea relationship. A *Hankook ilbo–Yomiuri shimbun* poll held in April 2010 delved the most deeply into Korean and Japanese attitudes toward specific issues in the relationship. Japanese and South Korean responses regarding whether the relationship will improve, worsen, or stay the same showed virtually identical majorities expecting the relationship to stay the same, but among the rest of respondents, Japanese were more optimistic about the relationship, with 37 percent expecting improvement and only 4 percent expecting the relationship to worsen. Koreans were neatly divided, with 20 percent of respondents expecting improvement in the relationship and another 20 percent expecting the relationship to worsen. Japanese respondents were evenly split over whether the government of Japan has provided a sufficient apology for the colonization of Korea, while South Koreans overwhelmingly viewed Japan as having not sufficiently apologized. The poll shows that South Korean expectations of Japan's efforts to address issues related to history remain unsatisfied; in Japan, views on whether it has done enough to address specific historical issues are split. Genron NPO/EAI surveys from May 2013 and July 2014 underscore the potential for continued difficulties in the relationship. The proportion of Japanese expecting relations to get worse increased during this time period from 18.2 percent to 22.7 percent, while the percentage of

Koreans anticipating a deterioration of relations grew from 26.6 percent to 39.4 percent.

When asked about Korean objections to Japanese textbook treatment of historical rule, 56 percent of Japanese thought the Korean protests were appropriate in certain respects; 29 percent thought that they were inappropriate. This suggests that textbooks are a specific issue on which it might be possible to make progress, although the textbook issue as a whole includes a number of specific items on which South Koreans and Japanese have differing opinions or on which Japanese public opinion itself is divided. Interestingly, 79 percent of Japanese expressed support for a visit by the emperor to South Korea. Fifty-four percent of Koreans favored such a visit, and 35 percent of Koreans opposed it.

The *Hankook ilbo–Yomiuri shimbun* survey from 2010 showed a strong shared sense of threat regarding North Korea's continued nuclear development: 82 percent of Japanese felt extremely or somewhat threatened compared to 68 percent of South Koreans. While 61 percent of Japanese respondents thought that resolving the cases of Japanese citizen abductions was the highest priority for cooperation between Japan and South Korea, only 4 percent of South Koreans prioritized this issue as a matter for cooperation. Fifty-eight percent of South Koreans most strongly supported cooperation with Japan to get North Korea to abandon its nuclear weapons program, a priority shared by 47 percent of Japanese respondents. That convergence dissipated when it came to engaging North Korea: 34 percent of Japanese and 61 percent of South Koreans preferred dialogue, while 58 percent of Japanese and 24 percent of South Koreans preferred pressure.

Prospects for Converging Japan–ROK Interests and Values

There is clearly an asymmetry between South Korean and Japanese views as they think about the past. Yet despite those differences, similarities between the two countries are striking when one drills down to explore values and interests. As can be seen in figure 4.5 from a Pacific Forum CSIS elite opinion poll conducted in 2007 and including Japanese and South Korean respondents, South Korean and Japanese perceptions of

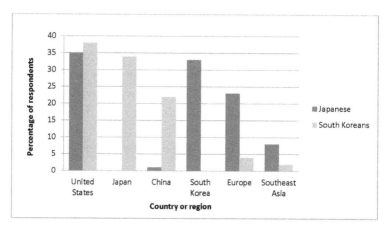

FIGURE 4.5 Similarity of Japanese and Korean Values to Those of Other Countries and Regions
Source: Pacific Forum CSIS

other countries with similar values rank the United States first and each other second, affirming the existence of a set of common values with the United States as an anchor. Japanese placed Europe as a distant third with a plurality of over 20 percent, while South Koreans see China as a distant third with a similar plurality of slightly over 20 percent. These commonalities, when taken together, indicate a strongly rooted similarity of purpose in both South Korean and Japanese worldviews, although the Korean association with China deserves further scrutiny. This suggests that both countries face a common challenge: depending on the United States as a security guarantor while managing the effects of increasing economic interaction with China. China emerged as the number one trading partner of both South Korea and Japan in the 2000s, and the economic relationship with a rapidly growing China has become an important driver of domestic economic growth in both countries. South Korea's economic dependence on China represents about a quarter of South Korea's overall trade, and the Japan–China relationship involves a complicated mix of trade and investment as China has become integrated into both the South Korean and Japanese production supply chains.

Overall, then, there are many ways in which the two countries' identities and world views align. Both are democracies that support the legal and institutional norms and structures that protect human rights and the dignity of the individual. They are both powerful, modern economies, with a commitment to the maintenance of the infrastructure of a liberal trading order: rules, norms and institutions, as well as the security and stability that are the foundation of international exchange. While the Japanese economy is much larger than that of South Korea, the gap is closing and both countries see themselves as underrepresented in international forums; both are looking for ways to maximize their status and influence, as well as play a larger role in international rule making. And finally both are U.S. allies, an identity that creates its own particular costs and benefits.

Threat perceptions also seem to be aligning. Both Japanese and South Koreans see China and North Korea as their biggest security threats. A 2010 *Asahi–Donga ilbo* survey shows that Japanese identified China as posing the biggest threat (57 percent), with North Korea coming second (26 percent). For South Koreans, as in the Pacific Forum survey, North Korea came first (45 percent), and China second (37 percent.)[19] Equally important, discussions with security policy decision makers and analysts reveal that there are differing perceptions of the type of threat each country poses. South Koreans have historically viewed China as an economic rather than a military threat, but Beijing's backing of North Korea during the tumult of 2010, when a South Korean Navy corvette was sunk and a South Korean island was shelled, and its subsequent indifference to South Korean suffering has shifted to some degree perceptions of the utility of the partnership with China and revealed it to be hostile to ROK national interests. For Japan, China is a military threat, a fact revealed by disputes over territory and the ongoing People's Liberation Army military modernization effort that seems aimed at taking on Japan (among other regional challengers). When looking at North Korea, South Koreans feel a physical threat—again made plain during 2010—but they don't fear an imminent invasion. The North Korea threat is real—Tokyo fears being on the receiving end of a ballistic missile—and there is also worry about North Korean proliferation starting a cascade of nuclear dominoes in Northeast Asia.

History: Sticking Points and the Way Forward

The convergence of South Korean and Japanese socioeconomic levels, their democratic development, and the sharing and appreciation of cultural similarities at a popular level are all factors that support improvement in the Japan–South Korea relationship. At the same time, despite several past efforts to put history behind them and to focus on the future, there have been strikingly different responses from the South Korean and Japanese publics. While Japanese public opinion toward South Korea showed a stable positive trend until 2012, South Korean public opinion toward Japan has been worsening, and the intensity of feeling has grown despite efforts to address the major outstanding political differences that are part of the history issue, including treatment of sex slaves, the portrayal of Japan's imperial history, visits to Yasukuni Shrine, and the Dokdo/Takeshima dispute.

But polling trends show that some progress has been made in addressing concerns on these issues, especially on ironing out an understanding of the sensitive historical portrayal of Japanese imperial actions. The focal point for textbook controversies today is centered on ownership of Dokdo/Takeshima. In addition, the South Korean Constitutional Court decision urging the ROK government to continue its efforts on behalf of those who suffered during the Japanese colonial period sharpens the potential for confrontation on the issues of personal compensation and state responsibility because the highest courts in both countries have issued contradictory legal rulings regarding how these issues should be settled. Ultimately it will be necessary to forge a mutually acceptable political solution, supported by the respective publics of the two countries, before it will be possible to reach a final resolution on these issues.

Fortunately, the polling trends on specific issues analyzed in this chapter provide a sound basis for identifying the ingredients that must be addressed to establish a more stable relationship between the two countries. On the basis of this information, we make some bold policy recommendations in the concluding chapter of this book. For now, we simply note that majorities in both countries recognize the importance of the bilateral relationship—over 60 percent in both countries in Genron

NPO/EAI polls. An Asan Institute poll in 2013, however, underscores the extent to which negative sentiment regarding Japan has moved in the wrong direction: 85 percent of South Koreans polled regarded Japan as untrustworthy and 71 percent viewed the relationship as competitive, while only 20 percent viewed the relationship as cooperative.[20]

As one looks at public opinion on the Dokdo/Takeshima issue in greater detail, a *Hankook ilbo–Yomiuri shimbun* in 2010 poll showed stark differences. Just 22 percent of Japanese thought that Japan should consider South Korea's claim, while only 1 percent of Koreans thought that South Korea should consider the Japanese claim. This result underscores the near-universal opposition in South Korea to Japan's claim to the island. The intensity of feeling on the South Korean side is also reflected in a joint *Seoul shinmun–Tokyo shimbun* poll from 2012 that shows 77 percent of South Koreans feel that Japan should concede to resolve the Dokdo/Takeshima territorial dispute, while only 7 percent of Japanese think that South Korea should concede. Instead, 47 percent of Japanese respondents want to take the issue to the International Court of Justice, and 37 percent of Japanese respondents think the two sides should agree on joint management of the islands and its surrounding resources. Clearly South Korean feelings about ownership of the island are very intense, while Japanese respondents overwhelmingly prefer win-win solutions involving joint management or relying on international law to render a final judgment. These polling results frame our thinking regarding possible ways forward, to which we will return in chapter 6.

5

IMPLICATIONS FOR
ALLIANCE MANAGEMENT

SINCE THE END OF THE COLD WAR, U.S. STRATEGISTS AND
policy makers have recognized that alliances—indeed U.S. engagement
with the Asia-Pacific region as a whole—needed to be reevaluated given
a new geopolitical environment. As a result, in the 1990s a series of studies provided ample justification for the continuation of the Cold War
hub-and-spoke security architecture.[1]

While continuity may have made strategic sense, domestic changes
within the United States and its allies challenged the strength and perceived value of alliances, making it more difficult to refurbish and mod-
ernize those institutions. Domestic political debates in an environment
characterized by evolving external threats—initially considered to be
diminishing—demonstrated a willingness to place near-term domestic
political gains ahead of international objectives in ways that appeared
to pit national identity against alliance cooperation. The emergence of

domestic politics as a challenge to the alliances highlighted historical differences between South Korea and Japan, but the ways in which politics asserted itself initially led to a focus in the United States on how to shore up the individual relationships with Japan and South Korea rather than on grappling with the implications of these domestic challenges for their bilateral relationship and prospects for trilateral cooperation. This chapter reviews the rise of domestic political developments and debates in Japan and South Korea, respectively, as challenges to U.S. alliance management.

Japan's Post–Cold War Domestic Politics and the U.S.–Japan Alliance

The U.S.–Japan alliance has been repeatedly tested since the end of the Cold War. The regional security environment has become more difficult to manage, with old threats sharpening and new ones emerging. Economic and political malaise robbed Tokyo of the ability to contribute fundamental elements to the partnership, namely, leadership and the resources to put toward the alliance. Politicians and publics have been more focused on domestic ills than on external challenges. Frequently the mere honoring of commitments has been the benchmark for relations, rather than genuine progress and adjustment to changing circumstances. More recently the United States has had to cope with its own political frustrations, and the ensuing difficulties have been compounded by the budget battles that consume Washington. Alliance modernization is costly and dollars have been tight. At times the two countries have been forced to spend much time and energy dealing with outright crises, such as the 1995 rape of an Okinawan schoolgirl by U.S. Marines, as well as other problems caused by the U.S. presence, such as noise and other forms of pollution. When combined with the long-standing animus between Okinawans and mainland Japanese, this has resulted in a protracted challenge to the form and sustainability of the U.S. troop presence in that part of Japan. When alliance managers did manage to transcend the quotidian, divergent perspectives proved problematic. Americans pressed for out-of-area cooperation while Japanese feared a lack of attention to more proximate threats, including security challenges posed by North Korea.

Against the backdrop of a rising China and a bellicose and threatening North Korea, tightening and strengthening alliance coordination should have been relatively easy. There has been progress with a series of bilateral statements, agreements, and even a road map or two, but developments have been fitful. Frustration follows every breakthrough. It may sound curmudgeonly to begrudge an alliance that has expanded in geographic scope and capability for nearly two decades, but expectations should be higher for a bilateral relationship that is declared critical for each partner and is the proclaimed cornerstone of regional security.

The end of the Cold War loosened ties in Japanese domestic politics, facilitating a split within the ruling LDP that forced it from power in 1993 for the first time since 1955. The LDP returned to the Prime Minister's Office within two years as part of a coalition with the Japan Socialist Party (JSP). It discarded the JSP soon after, a combination of moves that discredited the Left, transformed the political spectrum in Japan, and altered security debates. Yet even while conservatives ruled, political instability in Tokyo and fissures within the LDP prevented a whole-scale shift in policies. The bursting of the economic bubble and the failure to recover invited soul-searching and debates on issues related to national identity. Not only was the country deprived of the resources that financed an international presence, but Japanese certainties about their economic model and the society it created—the starting point for their engagement with the world—eroded as well. The outcome of that debate would have implications for relations with the United States on a variety of levels.

The first crisis was triggered in 1993 by revelations about North Korea's nuclear weapons program. While all preferred a diplomatic solution, Washington and Pyongyang squared off and the prospect of conflict between the two looked real. As the United States and Japan consulted on their response, it quickly became clear that Japan was not prepared—legally or operationally—for the support role it would be called on to play in any U.S. action. Tokyo officials assured the United States that legislation to enable Japan to play that role would be prepared, but public backing for such steps was not assured. The alliance dodged a bullet when the crisis was defused, but alliance managers in both countries were forced to acknowledge new regional security realities and limits on their ability to respond.

The second crisis occurred shortly after, in 1995, when U.S. Marines raped an Okinawa schoolgirl. That crime set off massive protests, endangering the U.S. military presence on the island. At the same time, China demonstrated a readiness to flex its muscles in the aftermath of the visit to the United States by Taiwan president Lee Teng-hui. The subsequent PRC military exercises that threatened Taiwan, the overflight of Japan by a North Korean missile in 1998, and incursions by North Korean spy boats into Japanese waters all contributed to a palpable sense of threat. The need to reaffirm a strong relationship with the United States was plain. President Bill Clinton and Prime Minister Hashimoto Ryutaro signed a Joint Declaration on the Security Alliance for the 21st Century in 1996, which was followed by the revision in 1997 of Defense Guidelines that governed and expanded bilateral security cooperation. An Acquisition and Cross-Servicing Agreement (ACSA) soon followed. Integral to the future of the alliance was the agreement in 1995 to substantially reduce the profile of U.S. forces in Okinawa via the Special Action Committee on Okinawa (SACO) report.

Any comfort that derived from those agreements was short-lived. China's continuing growth and its growing importance to U.S. foreign policy makers alarmed Japanese; the 1998 trip to China by President Bill Clinton, during which he flew over Japan on both legs without stopping, introduced a new phrase—"Japan passing"—to the Japanese foreign policy lexicon and compounded insecurities that only seemed to increase over time. Tokyo felt increasingly reliant on the United States while it seemed that Washington's attention was being drawn away from Asia to regional conflicts in Europe and the Middle East. The Japanese public showed anxiety about global demands placed on them as a result of the relationship with the United States as Washington pursued two land wars and an inchoate "global war on terror." As the United States bogged down in Iraq and Afghanistan, China's rising economic influence was felt even faster than many in Japan had anticipated. This combination threatened a shift in the regional balance of power, stimulating increased calls for greater burden sharing while highlighting Japan's inability to protect itself. Japanese insecurities increased not only because of external threats but because it was increasingly clear to Japanese that they were unable to respond to such threats on their own.

Japan's security policy decision making shifted in the first years of the new century. Following the shock of 9/11, Prime Minister Koizumi Junichiro forged a special relationship with President George Bush and prodded his nation to dispatch Ground Self-Defense Forces to help rebuild Iraq and Maritime Self-Defense Forces to assist refueling efforts in the Indian Ocean as part of the war in Afghanistan. Contrary to expectations, Japan was "showing the flag" and "putting boots on the ground," roles in security affairs previously thought impossible. These shows of support for U.S.-led stabilization efforts boosted the case that Japan could do more as an ally and attempted to shift thinking in Japan about the relative costs and benefits of such action. While Koizumi framed these efforts as part of Japan's responsibility as a global citizen and hoped to shift the way Japanese thought about security contributions, it is unlikely that his thinking took root. To the degree that the public backed Koizumi's initiatives, that support stemmed from the belief among many Japanese that they were the price of continued U.S. commitment to Japan. More significantly, however, Japan's assumption of higher visibility in security affairs and a more forward-leaning role reflected exceptional circumstances—the demands created by the terror attacks of September 11, 2001, and, most important, the George–Jun relationship. The two men held ten summits and many other less formal meetings; by all accounts they knew and understood each other well and had a genuine friendship. But given the deep ambivalence of the Japanese public over U.S. requests for "out-of-area" commitments and the many other concerns closer to home, this era is likely to prove to be the high-water mark for U.S.–Japan relations. According to Pew data, Japanese support for U.S. efforts to fight the war on terrorism peaked in 2002 at 61 percent. Four years later, that figure would plunge to 26 percent. It recovered to 40 percent and has remained at that level ever since, despite the change in the White House and the much more favorable views of the Obama administration more generally.[2]

The trajectory of alliance relations since Koizumi's departure seems to validate the "high-water mark" hypothesis. Of course, there has been progress. No alliance can afford to stand still at a time of regional transformation. The National Defense Program Guidelines were revised in 2004 and again in 2010. In both cases, revisions enlarged the scope of security planning (previously restricted to the defense of Japan narrowly defined) and pushed for more dialogue with the United States on shared concerns, along with more operational defense cooperation. The Security Consultative Committee (the SCC, and usually referred to as the "2+2" since it brings together the secretaries/ministers of foreign affairs and defense from each country) has produced a series of documents that outline the two countries' shared vision; detail new roles, capabilities, and missions; and lay out specific steps to consolidate facilities and better prepare for those responsibilities. The arms export ban of 1967 was relaxed to allow Japan to join joint development and production of military equipment as well as export defense-related equipment for peace-building or humanitarian missions.[3]

The path has not been steady, however, and the pace of change has slowed. When Prime Minister Abe first took office in 2006, he successfully elevated the Japan Defense Agency into a ministry, but he was unable to alter the way that Japan interpreted the exercise of its right of collective self-defense. The United States and Japan struck a series of deals to update the alliance, but successive governments in Tokyo failed to make the hard choices required to move the process forward. The fate of the 2006 roadmap for realignment implementation is illustrative. After years of complaints that the Futenma Marine Air Station in Ginowan, Okinawa, constituted a great danger to nearby residents and the alliance in the event of an accident, the governments in Tokyo and Washington agreed to relocate the facility to an uninhabited site on the north of the main island of Okinawa. This move was part of a larger consolidation of U.S. bases that would reduce the U.S. military footprint without compromising defense capabilities. The United States insisted, however, that moves could only occur when alternative facilities had been identified. Unfortunately, base opponents in Okinawa demanded relocation of facilities off the island; they were not prepared to accept movement elsewhere on Okinawan territory, even if that meant a reduced presence. No Japanese prime minister was prepared to force the issue and override local politicians. As a result, the Futenma facility remained despite the threat it posed to the community—and by extension the alliance—if an accident occurred. Attempts to break the deadlock by permitting the movement of certain facilities without progress on the entire package did not create the goodwill needed for a breakthrough. And recall that the agreement in 2006 was necessitated by the failure to implement the SACO deal from 1995.

Part of the problem resulted from a revolving door in the Prime Minister's Office—six leaders since Koizumi left office in 2006, one of whom, Abe Shinzo, made an unprecedented return to the office at the end of 2012. This prevented Japan's top leader from forging a relationship with either President Bush or President Obama that matched that of Koizumi and using it to push a security agenda. These relationships are critical for dealing with the inevitable tensions that flare within the alliance. In the waning years of the Bush administration, for example, frictions arose between Tokyo and Washington as Japanese worried that American readiness to strike a deal with North Korea would oblige the United States to downplay Japanese concerns with Pyongyang, in particular the fate of abductees kidnapped by North Korea. Those fears were realized in 2008 when the United States dropped North Korea from its list of state sponsors of terrorism, removing one of the sources of leverage that the United States (and by extension, Japan) had to pressure the North to account for its actions. Doubts among the Japanese public about the competence of their prime ministers and the government's failure to appreciate and prioritize the concerns of ordinary Japanese eroded the popularity of those governments and shrunk the political capital prime ministers had to spend on alliance issues.

Alliance modernization became even tougher when the LDP lost power in 2009 and the DPJ took office. While all expected the transition to be a challenge, it proved even more difficult than anticipated. Throughout the fifty-five years of LDP rule, the opposition had been marginalized and excluded from the policy process. Mastering the intricacies of the bureaucracy was always going to be difficult, but that task became exponentially harder when the DPJ platform bashed bureaucrats and pledged to put politicians in the lead in policy making. Hostility went both ways and the new government suffered as a result. The new DPJ government acquired an additional handicap in the form of Prime Minister Hatoyama Yukio, who initially signaled resistance to the new basing plan for Okinawa and was forced to retreat. That was the worst of all possible worlds. He raised—and then dashed—Okinawan hopes and frustrated U.S. alliance managers, looking feckless, ineffectual, and incompetent in the process. His replacement, Kan Naoto, proved little better. Six months into his term, Japan was hit by the triple catastrophe of March 11, 2011, and the government's response was abysmal. Kan was hit for micromanaging the crisis and (unfairly) blamed for a poorly designed crisis management system.

The March 11 catastrophe had two silver linings, however. First, the exceptional U.S. response via *Operation Tomodachi*, which involved 24,000 U.S. service members, 189 aircraft, 24 naval ships, and cost $90 million, convinced Japanese that they had no better friend and ally than the United States. Subsequent public opinion polls showed favorability ratings of the United States among Japanese to have reached record high levels. Second, the response of Self-Defense Forces (SDF) changed Japanese perceptions of the utility of the military, long viewed with disdain. The selfless efforts of SDF personnel demonstrated that the military could be used to promote peace and stability in ways that had nothing to do with war. Many Japanese recognized that the SDF could play a positive role without being involved in an armed conflict.[4] As National Defense Academy professor Kamiya Matake explained, "Japanese have begun to regain the awareness that the role of military force is essential to preserve peace."[5] This latter phenomenon could prove especially important as it shifts a critical perception in Japan—that of the role and utility of the SDF—and reduces a potential conflict between that institution and Japan's identity as a "peace-loving and peace-promoting" society. While Prime Minister Noda ruled as head of a DPJ government, he was at heart a conservative politician and showed no hesitation to exploit shifting public sentiment to press a more traditionally conservative security agenda. He strengthened missile defense cooperation with the United States, passed legislation that loosened restrictions of arms exports, allowed the use of Overseas Development Assistance for security purposes, and changed the overall tenor of alliance discussions to a more positive tone.

Since reclaiming the Prime Minister's Office, Abe Shinzo has built on that foundation to push alliance modernization further still. Many of the policies he has pursued, such as creation of a National Security Council or passage of an Information Security Law, help Japan be more effective in managing its own security and, as a result, a better ally for the United States. He used his political muscle to get LDP politicians from Okinawa to toe the party line on base relocation and back the move of the Futenma Air Base to Nago. The drive to change the interpretation of Japan's exercise of the right of collective self-defense is predicated on permitting Japan to be a better partner of the United States.

Since reaffirmation in 1996, the U.S.–Japan alliance has been consumed for almost two decades with internal challenges, out-of-area distractions, coordination problems on major challenges such as North Korea, and drift resulting from Japanese domestic political weakness. Although the alliance was fortunate for most of this period not to face any truly existential security challenges, alliance managers on both sides have been consumed with operational details rather than the formation of grand strategy and have spent the vast majority of their energies trying to overcome domestic political obstacles to more effective alliance cooperation. The resulting drift in U.S.–Japan coordination, moderated to a certain extent by modest gains in interoperability and the experience of cooperation on stabilization operations in Iraq and Afghanistan, has fed doubts about the capacity and direction of the alliance, even as Japan's sense of vulnerability increases in tandem with China's growing power and regional influence in Asia.

Identity issues have pulled Japan in two directions when Tokyo has been forced to act within the context of its alliance with the United States. The drive for status and recognition, in combination with the demands of Japan's identity as an ally of the United States and a supporter of Western values and interests, pushed Tokyo to respond with military tools when external pressures mounted (and domestic constituencies could be mobilized).[6] At the same time, however, continued aversion to a higher-profile military role and the related preference for a more comprehensive notion of security—a concept that stresses nonmilitary contributions such as development policies, or law enforcement, or environmental protection, and which corresponds to other core elements of Japan's national identity—served as brakes against more active engagement on these issues and made it difficult to implement promises that were made.

South Korea's Post–Cold War Political Transformation and the U.S.–ROK Alliance

Even if the mood and political trajectory of South Korea has moved in a different direction from that of Japan, South Korea's domestic political transformation has been equally challenging for U.S.–ROK alliance management. South Korea's political and economic success bred a confidence that forced a reconsideration of long-standing relationships. In the case of South Korea, the rising influence of domestic politics on alliance management has come in the following forms: First, South Korea's democratization led to an environment where the U.S.–ROK alliance could be subjected to greater scrutiny and more critical evaluation as a result of questions about whether the United States might have delayed democratization through a strong alliance relationship with South Korea's military dictatorship under Chun Doo-hwan. Second, South Korean efforts to reach out to North Korea placed new stresses on alliance management as Seoul perceived its threat environment to be easing. Third, the Bush administration's hard-line policies toward North Korea and the USFK handling of the incident in which two schoolgirls were killed raised doubts among many South Koreans about whether the United States respected and appreciated the extent of South Korea's own political and economic transformation and demanded adjustments in management of the alliance. Fourth, the expansion of South Korea's diplomatic reach—based on an expanded set of political relationships with the postcommunist world following the Cold War and enabled by South Korea's economic modernization—provided South Korea with a wider aperture for considering its foreign policy interests that made South Korea less directly dependent on the alliance with the United States as the focal point of its foreign policy.

South Korea's democratic consolidation resulted in the relative weakening of government authority to control public debate, especially when it came to long-standing taboos such as criticism of the U.S.–ROK alliance. But the alliance was particularly vulnerable to criticism from democracy activists who believed the United States provided support to Chun Doo-hwan and indirectly aided the suppression of a prodemocracy movement in Kwangju that opposed his efforts to usurp power following the assassination of Park Chunghee. Criticism of the U.S. military in South Korea was exacerbated by the fact that, despite many changes in South Korea, the USFK presence and structure had not been substantially updated for decades. In the meantime, South Korea's economic modernization in practical terms meant expanded urbanization, including in areas surrounding U.S. bases, resulting in encroachment and a heightened frequency of conflicts and irritation among Korean neighbors adjoining the bases (a situation not unlike that in Okinawa). As a result, it became important in the 1990s for the USFK to consolidate its presence and return many bases in South Korea for the sake of efficiency and to minimize conflicts with the local community. The first iteration of the Land Partnership Plan (LPP) was negotiated during the 1990s under the Clinton administration. At the same time, democratization opened the door to Korean citizen challenge of past injustices committed by the U.S. military on the peninsula. The most notable of these incidents was a massacre of South Korean civilians that occurred during the Korean War in the village of Nogunri. This incident gained publicity in the late 1990s and was acknowledged with an apology by the U.S. government and the establishment of a scholarship fund for Korean students under the Clinton administration.

A second factor that created stress in the alliance was related to South Korean public perceptions of the Sunshine Policy, and the impact on public perceptions of North Korea resulting from the historic June 13–15, 2000, inter-Korean summit between Kim Dae-jung and Kim Jong-il. On his return to Seoul following the summit, Kim Dae-jung announced that the summit had been a major step toward bringing peace to the Korean Peninsula. In this atmosphere, some South Koreans questioned the need for a continued U.S. security presence on the peninsula, and a number of off-base incidents involving U.S. military personnel served to dramatize the issue further. South Korean public perceptions of U.S. policy in the wake of inter-Korean rapprochement were further eroded by the Bush administration's adoption of a hard-line policy toward North Korea that many South Koreans saw as needlessly creating conditions for conflict on the peninsula rather than as preserving stability. The rise of tensions in the coordination of U.S.–ROK policy toward North Korea had a negative influence on public attitudes toward the USFK.

As South Koreans grappled with these broader concerns, a traffic incident in 2002 involving a U.S. military vehicle and two middle school girls became a flashpoint that set off South Korean public demonstrations regarding the military presence. These demonstrations grew in size and intensity over several months following a U.S. military tribunal decision to acquit the operators of the military vehicle since the accident occurred while they were on duty. The verdict symbolized for South Koreans a failure on the part of the USFK or the U.S. government to recognize the tremendous social and economic changes that had occurred in their country since the security relationship was established in the 1950s. This incident catalyzed efforts by the USFK to readjust the relationship, including a plan to relocate its headquarters out of Yongsan to a base south of Seoul and a considerably more careful approach to managing political aspects of the alliance.

An alliance reaffirmation process had been envisioned in the mid-1990s, but it was not carried out. Instead, in response to the spike in perceived anti-U.S. sentiment among Koreans in 2002–03, the United States and South Korea initiated a round of talks on the Future of the Alliance (FOTA) that were designed to support the reconfiguration of the U.S. footprint on the Korean Peninsula, consolidate U.S. bases, and return bases no longer needed by the United States to the control of the ROK government. That set of talks was followed by the Security Policy Initiative (SPI), which began in 2005 and attempted to establish a joint vision for the alliance and to negotiate a change in command

and control arrangements from a combined command to one in which the ROK government would play a leading role and U.S. forces would play a supporting role in the defense of the peninsula. The Bush and Roh administrations agreed to revise wartime command and control arrangements so that South Korea would lead and the USFK would take a supporting role, with a schedule for implementing new arrangements in April 2012, but that handover was delayed by Presidents Obama and Lee to December 2015 following North Korea's alleged sinking of a South Korean warship in March 2010 and further delayed in October 2012.

A fourth factor that has changed the context and relative importance of the U.S.–ROK alliance in the conduct of South Korea's foreign policy is the expansion and strengthening of South Korea's diplomatic relations, both with former Eastern Bloc countries and most notably with China. Seoul's hosting of the Olympics in 1988 enabled the expansion of South Korean diplomatic relations on a cultural level, but its economic modernization and the "brand" diplomacy of South Korea's largest companies such as LG and Samsung have undergirded an expansion of South Korean diplomatic influence and opportunity that makes the U.S.–ROK alliance relatively less central to the conduct of South Korean foreign policy. Most notably, the rapid growth of the China–South Korean trade relationship from $6.3 billion in 1992 to over $215 billion in 2012 has surpassed the amount of U.S.–ROK and ROK–Japan trade combined.

The broadening of the aperture and reach of South Korea's foreign policy that has been enabled by its economic standing does not diminish the value of the U.S.–ROK alliance or the extent to which the United States and South Korea can work together to promote shared values, but it does mean that there is a range of contending interests that South Korea must manage alongside the U.S.–ROK alliance. Notably, Lee Myung-bak made it his objective to restore the U.S.–ROK alliance as a central element in South Korea's national security policy, enabling strategic level dialogue that built on prior agreements to settle specific operational issues in the relationship. President Lee's approach led to a positive joint statement in his initial meeting with President Bush in the summer of 2008 and eventually to a June 2009 Joint Vision Statement at the White House between Presidents Lee and Obama. The Joint Vision Statement was notable because it provided a vision for expanded alliance cooperation off the peninsula at regional and global levels in addition to envisioning a comprehensive and multifaceted approach to both parties' alliance coordination toward North Korea that extended to a range of opportunities for cooperation in nontraditional security areas.[7] As noted in chapter 3, the number of South Koreans who supported the alliance with the United States jumped from the mid-40 percent range in 2004 to the mid-70s in 2012.

The U.S. Rebalance: Implications for Alliances in Northeast Asia

"Rebalancing" to the Asia-Pacific has come to be identified as a signature policy initiative of the first Obama administration.[8] Since President Obama was born in Hawaii, lived several years as a child in Indonesia, and regards himself as a Pacific president, an Asia-Pacific orientation might seem natural for him. But the rebalance reflects far more than the president's biography. As Secretary of State Hillary Clinton explained, "rebalancing" to Asia is a framework for U.S. foreign policy in the aftermath of the Iraq withdrawal and the Afghanistan drawdown.[9] It is intended to reassure U.S. allies, friends, and partners of an ongoing commitment to the region at a time of geopolitical transformation. Rebalancing begins by recognizing the shift in the world's economic and strategic center of gravity toward the Pacific. The Asia-Pacific region now generates some 50 percent of world trade and its growth outpaces that of all other regions.[10] This "rise of Asia" demands a structured and comprehensive response. Rebalancing is strategy in the purest sense: an attempt to more tightly couple national security and economic prosperity in U.S. policy. This linkage was first laid out in President Obama's *National Security Strategy*, itself an attempt to establish a conceptual framework for policy in the aftermath of the Global War on Terror.[11] In this world, it is common sense to devote more U.S. resources to a region that is larger and potentially more unstable, and where the impact of that instability could be global in scope, given its centrality to supply chains.

This new policy is framed, first and foremost, in terms of the "soft" elements of U.S. power. Secretary Clinton argued that "it starts with forward deployed *diplomacy*," and her colleagues emphasize the need to develop diplomatic, economic, and security architecture to keep pace with the extraordinary changes in Asia. A hallmark of this policy is the call for more comprehensive engagement of Asia, an echo of the "smart power" approach that launched Clinton's tenure at the State Department. References to a policy that "spans the entire U.S. government" imply that engagement to date has overly focused on the military. Clinton's enumeration of the six elements of the U.S. policy illustrate its scope: deepening working relationships with emerging powers (including China); engaging regional multilateral institutions; expanding trade and investment; advancing democracy and human rights; maintaining a foreign broad-based military presence; and strengthening bilateral security alliances. Specific goals include opening new markets, curbing nuclear proliferation, and keeping sea lanes free and open.

The need for a coherent and structured approach to U.S. alliances is underscored by the fiscal constraints that have emerged in the United States and affect all its allies in Asia. Government finances are tight, and defense budgets are not immune from demands for cuts. The recognition of new security challenges and spiraling hardware and program costs does not drown out the call for smaller defense budgets. Cuts are inevitable, but their impact can be minimized by the realization of efficiencies across defense bureaucracies. Cooperation, coordination, and integration across the alliance system can distribute and reduce costs without undermining security.

The rising influence of public opinion on foreign policy in Korea and Japan and the interaction between public opinion and the politics of national identity within each country's domestic politics means that increasing public participation in and the growing influence of public opinion on security and foreign policy have forced alliance managers in the United States, South Korea, and Japan to accommodate a broader range of stakeholders. In both alliances with the United States, this adjustment has not been easy. Threat perceptions in all three countries have been changing, and the responses have not been consistent among the three either on their own—they prioritize different threats and prefer different responses—or over time. Domestic politics in each country has been volatile since the end of the Cold War (or to some degree, because of the end of the Cold War), and security and foreign policies have been a principal divide within each country. And finally, relations with the United States have been a key element of domestic political debates in Japan and South Korea, both within the context of the alliance and on their own. The U.S. decision to cast trade deals with key partners as "strategic"—the primary argument made on behalf of the Korea–U.S. Free Trade Agreement—extends the reach of alliance issues to new areas in bilateral relations, although this is a deliberate part of the rebalancing strategy and aims to demonstrate U.S. commitment in nonmilitary ways.

As previous chapters have shown, public opinion in Japan and South Korea is shaped in similar ways but imposes differing political constraints, reflecting the peculiarities of each country's history, economic, political, and strategic situation and perception of national objectives. For all the similarity in values, historical trajectories, political and economic systems, and even threat perceptions, the two countries are quick to see each other as antagonists that have not reconciled over the past. At times, such as when President Roh declared a "diplomatic war" against Japan in 2005, when Prime Minister Koizumi insisted on visiting Yasukuni Shrine in 2006, or at the beginning of 2014 when tensions between Japan and Korea were inflamed by a range of issues, identity politics has threatened to drive South Korea and Japan into conflict, challenging the U.S.-led alliance structure that has implicitly relied on—and, to a certain extent, imposed a congruence of national interests on—Seoul and Tokyo in response to a shared external threat. This new dynamic has enhanced security dilemmas, the prospect of regional arms races, and even conflict over territory, history, and resources, requiring the United States to consider the relationship between alliances and regional security.

Future Potential Prospects and Constraints Facing U.S. Alliance Strategy in the Asia-Pacific

Thus far alliance adjustment, adaptation, and modernization have proceeded along discrete paths for each alliance. There has been little effort to integrate or coordinate the efforts. But the time has come to reconsider the wisdom of that approach and to explore the merits of a more closely integrated and integrative approach to U.S. alliances in Asia.

In theory there are six possible configurations that could develop as the security environment in Asia evolves and the United States attempts to redefine its role and relationship to the region: (1) regionalizing alliance cooperation with Japan and South Korea into a multilateral structure; (2) maintaining the status quo, including the idea of a "virtual alliance" in which the United States is the pole for parallel bilateral alliances with South Korea and Japan; (3) passive delinking and independent treatment of the two alliances; (4) maintaining alliances and bases but without forward-deployed forces; (5) focusing on one alliance at the expense of the other; and (6) dismantling of the U.S.-led alliance structure in favor of independence and autonomy for alliance partners. Although the Obama administration's rebalancing strategy means that the United States has rejected the latter three choices, and the challenges associated with the rise of China appear to preclude those options as realistic possibilities, we include them here given that long-term fiscal considerations might require the United States to make hard choices about its role as a global power and the level of financial investment it is willing to make to underwrite Asia's security.

Regionalization of Alliances

The Obama administration's rebalancing policy appears to broaden the U.S. approach to maintaining security in the Asia-Pacific. As a starting point, Washington is intent on strengthening the long-standing investments that it has made in the region. With a half century of success in maintaining the peace, the U.S.-led alliance structure is a ready-made framework for a broader multilateral effort. It has helped build confidence among partners, facilitated the integration of militaries, and stimulated habits of cooperation among allies. It is common sense to put this history, experience, and familiarity to work. The U.S. *National Security Strategy* declares alliances "the bedrock of security in Asia and a foundation of prosperity." Secretary Clinton identified "strengthening U.S. bilateral alliances" as a core component of the U.S. rebalance.[12] Secretary of Defense Robert Gates noted in 2008 that U.S. security is better served by "more multilateral ties rather than hubs and spokes,"[13] although Gates and like-minded thinkers usually seek the inclusion of security partners like Singapore, Indonesia, Vietnam, and India with allies. This approach is often referred to as "minilateral" cooperation because it remains restricted in terms of partners and scope; that is, it is piecemeal and is not institutionalized. But an implicit assumption of the rebalance is that U.S. alliances can form the core of a multilateral security structure in which those allies work more closely with each other. At the same time, the Obama administration is hesitant to drive toward full-bore regionalization of alliance networks for fear of feeding Chinese anxieties that the rebalance is intended to be a China containment policy. As reflected in our review of South Korean and Japanese public opinion, allies are reluctant to be seen as part of such a design, regardless of U.S. intent.

To achieve enhanced multilateral security cooperation with the United States at its center, the United States could seek to bind Japan and South Korea more closely as the central players in a multilateral security alliance network that would play a stabilizing and socializing role in Asia similar to that of NATO in Europe. Ideally America's other three Asian allies (Australia, the Philippines, and Thailand) would join the Northeast Asian pair to create an East Asian alliance network. This is an ambitious goal; most would dismiss it as sheer fantasy, arguing that several factors make the notion of "a NATO in Asia" impossible.[14] While there are as yet no initiatives that span all the alliances, one—the Trilateral Strategic Dialogue (TSD)—could provide a cornerstone for future developments. Launched in 2002, the TSD includes the United States, Japan, and Australia. It was elevated to the ministerial level in 2005 and has served as a benchmark for trilateral security dialogues among security partners. The success of the "Core Group," the quadrilateral initiative that included the United States, Australia, Japan, and India and formed the nucleus of the response to the December 26, 2004, tsunami, made abundantly clear the benefits that could be achieved from cooperation among security partners.[15] Another option is an "alliance caucus" at which the United States and its allies would meet informally on the fringe of other multilateral meetings to discuss issues and develop positions.[16]

Sadly, the constraints on cooperation among the United States and its Asian allies are formidable, making the dream of a formal, six-nation organization seem like, well . . . a dream. While supporting the TSD, Kevin Rudd, twice prime minister and once foreign minister of Australia, has been explicit about its limits. He emphasized in a speech in November 2010 that "the dialogue is not an alliance" and that he "was not attracted to the idea of growing the TSD."[17] That could reflect the failure of earlier efforts to engage India in a quadrilateral dialogue or concerns about China's reaction to such an initiative. South Korea has also stood outside these forms of cooperation for a variety of reasons, but the biggest obstacles to South Korean participation are related to ongoing difficulties in Japan–South Korea relations and South Korea's caution about how China might view such cooperation. Other obstacles are readily apparent. The six countries have vastly different military capabilities, and their ability to make meaningful contributions to a regionally based effort is sorely constrained. While they share broadly defined interests in the protection of peace and prosperity, the maintenance of stability, and open sea lanes, consensus quickly dissipates when they are asked to identify priorities and to define specific threats. In Japan's case, legal constraints ban collective security efforts, and while the country is debating a change in those limits, they will be eased, not eliminated.

Finally, there is China. Beijing sees U.S.-led alliances as "Cold War relics," legacies of a bygone era that have outlived their use and purpose. Chinese officials, security planners, and analysts believe that those arrangements are ultimately intended to contain China, reduce its room for maneuver, and thwart its efforts to reclaim its rightful place as the leading nation of Asia.[18] They oppose multilateral arrangements that focus on collective defense on grounds that they conflict with the need for cooperative security arrangements that are inclusive rather than divisive. They fear that modernization will rearm China's neighbors and undermine Beijing's attempts to extend its influence. They worry that strengthened alliance ties embed the United States more deeply in the region and strengthen the U.S. position in Asia as the balance of power is shifting in Beijing's favor. Chinese also fear that a more credible military instrument will undermine diplomatic efforts to resolve crises, encouraging countries to take a firmer stand and raising the risk of war.

As a result, China is not prepared to embrace or endorse a multilateral framework that starts from those alliances. Instead, Chinese insist that multilateral institutions—especially security initiatives—should be inclusive and aimed at no specific country. Moreover, the mere hint of Chinese objections is sometimes sufficient to get other countries to back away from such efforts. No country wants to be forced to take sides in a division of the Asia-Pacific region. Nor are regional governments likely to risk antagonizing Beijing when they look to it for cooperation on other regional initiatives, particularly in the areas of economics and trade. As a result, a U.S.-led multilateral collective defense arrangement faces inherent limits as the foundation for NATO-style regional security cooperation because Beijing would not join and would oppose its establishment without China's participation as inimical to Chinese interests.

If an East Asian alliance network is untenable, this does not necessarily preclude the institutionalization of trilateral United States–Japan–South Korea security cooperation. There are sufficient common interests, threat perceptions, or sense of shared values to motivate the three governments to act in concert on many issues, as suggested in the trilateral statement the three countries issued in December 2010 following the North Korean shelling of South Korea's Yeonpyong Island. President Obama in his approach to Japan and South Korea has emphasized common values as a basis for continued close partnership with both countries, and that thinking appears to represent a bipartisan consensus on cooperation with these countries since it builds on ideas of previous leaders in each country.[19] During his April 2008 visit to the United States, Lee Myung-bak hit a similar note, saying, "The days of ideology are over. The politicization of alliance relations shall be behind us. We shall not let ideology and politics blind us to common interests, values, and norms."[20]

Deepened institutional cooperation among these three countries might serve as a buffer or hedge against domestic political volatility deriving from nationalist sentiment by anchoring security cooperation in the service of a clearly defined set of common aims. Fortunately the data from the previous chapter show a convergence in perceptions in each country about threats, interests, and values. Japan and South Korea, like the United States, see North Korea as a threat and worry about whether China's rising power will reinforce or challenge existing global norms. Both countries believe their national interests most closely align with those of the United States; there is similar agreement when it comes to values, but there is less coherence on which to build in this area, particularly given that common threat perceptions seem to be a stronger motivator for cooperation than are common values. Moreover, the establishment of the Trilateral Coordination Secretariat among Japan, South Korea, and China in 2010 sets a precedent for institutionalization of trilateral cooperation in the region, and there is no reason why others should object to strengthened mechanisms for coordinating among the United States, Japan, and South Korea.

In addition, tightened finances in all three countries are likely to put a premium on burden sharing and the need for a collective approach to the provision of public goods. Despite hesitancy and public opposition in South Korea and Japan, greater burden sharing is also desirable insofar as it promotes greater equality among partners. It gives each country important insight into the thinking of its partners, as well as some influence over policy formulation. On the downside, this might impose new stresses and raise expectations of both the United States and alliance partners regarding what the other side will contribute. Great respect and responsibility could result, but so too could heightened tension and disappointment.

Significantly, the security policies of Japan and South Korea are already linked in many ways. The UN Command arrangements for implementing the Korean Peninsula armistice of 1953 still designate certain U.S. bases in Japan as UN-flagged, and Japanese security analysts clearly perceive the stability and diplomatic orientation of the Korean Peninsula as critical to Japan's security.[21] The impetus for such cooperation has strengthened given growing South Korean and Japanese concerns about China and North Korea; by the end of 2010 South Korea and Japan were considering formal agreements on acquisitions and cross-servicing and on intelligence sharing, steps that would tie the two countries operationally in ways that would also lay the groundwork for enhanced alliance-based trilateral coordination. Ultimately, those efforts proved premature, however. They were mishandled by the Seoul government and were shelved after furious opposition in the Korean National Assembly.

The fate of those two agreements confirmed that obstacles to enhanced and institutionalized cooperation remain formidable. The first problem is the legal restriction imposed on Japan by its constitution and Article 9. The signing of an Acquisition and Cross-Servicing Agreement with Australia suggests, however, that the legal barrier is not insurmountable. In addition, coordination on peacekeeping operations or humanitarian assistance/disaster relief operations could also prove possible despite Article 9 constraints. And while the agreement on intelligence sharing[22] with the ROK was shelved in June 2012, it was not the result of Japanese legal constraints. Second, despite data that make a case for Japan–ROK cooperation, powerful undercurrents work against stronger ties. Historical legacies, textbook issues, and territorial disputes over the Dokdo/Takeshima islands intermittently poison bilateral cooperation despite an apparent desire on both sides to contain and manage these disputes. The readiness of Korean politicians to play the "Japan card" and the ease with which they whip up nationalist sentiment against Japan suggests that Korean feeling and thinking prevents cooperation.

Chinese objections to larger forms of alliance-based cooperation do not disappear when the objective is smaller arrangements among allies. Among U.S. allies, Japan and the ROK would theoretically make the largest contributions in the event of a Taiwan contingency, one of China's top national security concerns. Beijing sees Seoul as the least resolute—or the one most inclined to go its own way—of the three actors on many issues and would therefore try to block any mechanism that would minimize chances of South Korean defection from U.S. and Japanese positions. China has started to put down clear markers to Seoul regarding enhanced trilateral cooperation with Japan as a component of the U.S.–ROK alliance and is on guard against any hint of expansion of the objectives of the alliance beyond dealing with the North Korea threat to take on issues concerning China. Moreover, China sees Japan as its principal antagonist among Asian nations. While it once accepted the U.S.–Japan alliance as a way to ensure that Japan would not rise again to threaten China, Chinese officials and analysts increasingly see the United States as promoting if not facilitating Japan's remilitarization.[23] A revitalized alliance structure that supported Japanese efforts to assume a larger regional security role would be tarred with the same brush.

De Facto Trilateral Alliance

In this option, the United States would continue to manage alliances with Japan and South Korea bilaterally but will encourage greater cooperation and consultation to stimulate greater mutual understanding of the core objectives of security cooperation in a regional context. This scenario sidesteps the constitutional objections to alliance regionalization and minimizes domestic political objections in both countries by playing down formal linkages among the three countries—especially between Seoul and Tokyo.

Essentially this option comes closest to representing the current situation, in which the U.S.–Japan and U.S.–South Korea alliances provide the glue for limited forms of trilateral coordination within a political environment that circumscribes full-scale trilateral cooperation. It is what a group of experts proposed as a "virtual alliance" in 1999. According to one participant in that effort, such an alliance "can be achieved through the maintenance of a reinvigorated U.S.–Japan alliance, the continuation of a solid U.S.–Korea security relationship post-unification, and the strengthening of bilateral security cooperation between Tokyo and Seoul."[24] Hopes were high for this option at the turn of the century. Relations between Japan and South Korea, always fraught, seemed to enjoy great possibilities as Prime Minister Obuchi Keizo and President Kim Dae-jung forged a relationship that would look forward, not back. The strengthening of that always problematic bilateral facilitated operation of the Trilateral Coordination and Oversight Group, which was born of the "Perry Process," the congressional-mandated review of U.S. policy toward North Korea that was led by former secretary of defense William Perry in 1999. TCOG brought the three allies together at a relatively high level to develop and then implement policy recommendations. TCOG was a success: quarterly reviews became monthly meetings and management devolved to more junior participants. The group became less formal and ultimately dissolved as the Roh government in South Korea sought more distance between itself and the United States and proved ready to use Japan as a scapegoat for its domestic political difficulties—a decision made easier by the insistence of Prime Minister Koizumi to visit Yasukuni Shrine in defiance of Korean and Chinese protests.

The return to power of conservatives in Seoul, the coming to power of governments in Tokyo determined to build stronger relations with Asian neighbors, and a U.S. administration convinced that alliances needed tending rejuvenated the trilateral coordination process. Security planners in Japan and South Korea recognized that their futures are intertwined. Few governments were as concerned as was South Korea about the difficulties in the U.S.–Japan alliance that followed the inauguration of the DPJ government in Japan. The prospect of the removal of U.S. Marines from Okinawa, first responders in the event of a contingency on the peninsula, troubles security planners and analysts in Seoul.[25] Similarly, few countries were as staunch in their support of South Korea as was Japan after the North Korean provocations in 2010—the sinking of the ROK Navy Corvette *Cheonan* and the shelling of Yeonpyeong Island. Japan knows that it too is threatened by North Korea and wants Pyongyang to know that it will face fierce and united opposition in the event of a crisis.

In December 2010 Secretary of State Hillary Clinton hosted her counterparts from Japan and South Korea, Foreign Ministers Maehara Seiji and Kim Sung-hwan, respectively, for a "historic" meeting where they "jointly affirmed the importance of unity and ways to enhance policy coordination on myriad issues from ASEAN to North Korea."[26] Washington has since worked to institutionalize this cooperation.[27] The three foreign ministers met on the sidelines of the July 2011 ASEAN Regional Forum (ARF) meeting in Bali, Indonesia, where they reaffirmed their commitment to trilateral cooperation both regionally and globally. They met a year later in Phnom Penh, Cambodia, again at the ARF ministerial, and repeated their pledge to work together and to "strengthen their cooperation to reinforce regional cooperation mechanisms, including ASEAN, ARF, and EAS (the East Asia Summit), as a foundation for multilateralism in the region."[28] The three also pledged to form a working-level Steering Group, based in Washington, to facilitate trilateral cooperation.[29] When the three foreign ministers met in New York City in September 2012, on the sidelines of the annual meeting of the United Nations General Assembly—marking the fourth trilateral ministerial meeting in three years—they could take satisfaction from their continuing dialogue, the establishment of the Steering Group, and the inauguration of assistant secretary–level discussions as well.[30]

While this option seems desirable—it is always good to promote security cooperation and integration among the three countries to the extent possible—it is likely to demand a much more active commitment on the part of the United States to facilitate closer South Korea–Japan relations and to encourage the resolution—or at least the submergence—of disputes over territory and history. Historically the United States has refused to shoulder that role, especially since the odds are high that either Seoul or Tokyo would consider U.S. mediation as less than "even handed" when it did not get the outcome it sought.[31] In the September 2012 meeting of the three foreign ministers, Secretary Clinton explicitly stated that "the US has no intention in any of those disputes . . . we have no intention of playing a mediating role."[32] Victor Cha has argued that this made sense in the past since an active U.S. role relieves the pressure on the two countries to make their bilateral relationship work themselves.[33] That may no longer be the case, however, as the issues in the relationship have metastasized and are now being contested within the United States.[34] While it is not yet a majority view, there is increasing interest in Washington in finding ways for the United States to take a more active role in promoting cooperation between its two Northeast Asian allies, even if that means becoming directly involved in the disputes that divide them.[35] A trilateral summit at The Hague in March 2014 on the sidelines of the Nuclear Security Summit was possible only because the United States brokered the understandings necessary to make the meeting politically feasible for President Obama and his Japanese and South Korean counterparts.

Status Quo (Transformation) or "Passive Delinking"

A dynamic security environment requires more flexibility and options for the United States. For some strategists, the structure and formality of alliances limit their effectiveness, tying down assets and limiting their availability in the event of crises. The Rumsfeld-era Global Posture Review emphasized the need for flexibility and implied the devaluation of fixed alliance commitments because they could operate as potential constraints on a flexible U.S. response, especially to out-of-area conflicts. For example, there are fears that commitments to Korean Peninsular security could deprive the United States of troops and materiel that it might need in the event of a contingency elsewhere. In response, the United States has developed the concept of "strategic flexibility" for precisely that goal. Transformation to adapt to those new realities is not abandonment (as some allies might fear). Rather, it means that the United States would focus on its own needs in the context of global security trends and work with alliance partners in Asia as needed to maintain maximum flexibility to respond to both conventional and nonconventional threats. In this option, alliance cooperation would be based on the assets and support alliance partners can offer, but little concern is given to the extent to which alliances work together, and little coordination is necessary to promote cooperation among alliance partners. This option allows the United States to avoid entanglement in the difficult South Korea–Japan relationship because the focus is on making the two alliances work. This approach is the result of the application of a template that attempts to respond to global threats with little regard for the particulars of the context in which it is applied. This has been the default option during times of tension in the South Korea–Japan relationship, for instance, during most of the Bush administration.

Focus on One Alliance, Accept Decline of the Other

Alliances are difficult to maintain. They require constant tending in the best of times and can absorb considerable time and attention when things sour. In the mid-2000s political developments in South Korea suggested that a rupture between the United States and South Korea was likely, if not inevitable. The political ascendance of progressives in Seoul raised fears that the alliance had outlived its usefulness. The ROK looked to be capable of defending itself against its nemesis to the north, and the administration in Seoul seemed ready to look to China rather than the United States to protect vital important security interests. In contrast, U.S. strategists felt the alliance with Japan continued to have real strategic value for long-term U.S. interests—especially if ties to South Korea were being loosened. They argued that U.S. efforts should focus on ensuring that the U.S.–Japan security alliance would remain the bulwark for ensuring Asian stability. Little effort would be made to maintain the alliance with Korea given the likelihood that pressure from China would decrease Korean incentives for strategic cooperation with the United States in the long-term.[36]

Compelling though that logic may have sounded in 2003–04, it quickly evaporated. The prospect of a reconsideration of the U.S.–ROK alliance contributed to the political reversal in Korea. South Korea remains committed to the alliance with the United States, and public support for the U.S.–ROK alliance has dramatically and steadily increased since its most recent low point in 2003–04. There may be periodic spikes of anti-U.S. sentiment in Korea, but there is a large reservoir of goodwill that supports the alliance and sees it as serving Korean national interests and promoting regional security.

Second, this approach undervalues the significance of the Korean Peninsula in Japanese security. When the United States decided to reduce troop levels on the peninsula in June 2004, Japanese were alarmed. An *Asahi shimbun* editorial noted that the realignment of U.S. forces in Korea "directly affects Japan's security and military base issues." On the other side of the political spectrum, the *Sankei shimbun* agreed: "There is no doubt that a change in the US forces in South Korea will have an impact on the security of Japan and East Asia."[37] The prospect of a China–South Korea alignment, which would allow China to dominate the Korean Peninsula, would likely raise Japanese insecurities to acute levels—especially if the United States was seen as acquiescing to such a development. Finally, any withdrawal of U.S. forces from the region, and especially given uncertainties on the Korean Peninsula, would raise questions about the U.S. commitment to providing regional security more generally.

After U.S.–ROK relations settled down and the alliance regained its footing, U.S.–Japan relations were rattled. There were many reasons for the political chaos that followed the DPJ historic election victory in 2009: the novelty of a political transition, the DPJ's lack of political experience and naïveté, its proclivity for bureaucrat bashing, and its internal chaos, to name just a few. But as Prime Minister Hatoyama talked about a new Asia policy that recalibrated relations between the United States and Japan's regional partners, security and foreign policy officials in Washington had an unnerving feeling of déjà vu. Hatoyama's decision to question a painstakingly negotiated agreement to reconfigure the U.S. presence in Japan confirmed for many fears that the pendulum had swung.

It was ironic then when President Obama and President Lee met in Toronto in July 2010 and declared that their alliance "is the lynchpin of not only security for the Republic of Korea and the United States but also for the Pacific as a whole."[38] That flew in the face of the diplomatic boilerplate that the U.S.–Japan relationship was the most important bilateral relationship, "bar none." (Japanese officials were reportedly checking dictionaries to see if there could be multiple lynchpins.)

But like South Korea, the Japanese government quickly reaffirmed its commitment to its alliance with the United States. After the missteps of the Hatoyama government, Prime Ministers Kan and Noda of the DPJ proved to be stalwart defenders of the U.S.–Japan alliance. The pendulum completed its swing with the return to power of the LDP in December 2012. No surprise there. As in the ROK case, our data show overwhelming public support for the alliance, agreement that it serves Japan's national interest, as well as considerable identification with U.S. values and interests. Indeed, Since the LDP return to power, Japan has had more direct threats to its security that have underscored the central role the alliance plays in protecting Japan and its national interests.

The idea of playing up one alliance at the expense of the other makes sense in a Machiavellian way—if it is possible to channel the competitiveness constructively. In fact, Japanese and South Korean commitments to "burden sharing" in the context of the alliances have historically increased when alliance partners are fearful of U.S. withdrawal.[39] If such a dynamic could be managed effectively, the two allies could be prodded to be "the better partner." A South Korean progressive explained in an interview, "In devising its Northeast Asia policy, the United States needs to assure South Koreans that the strengthening of the U.S.–Japan alliance is not at the cost of the U.S.–Korea alliance; otherwise, public opinion within Korea could be unstable on this issue and could result in a loss of the balance of power within Northeast Asia." Many South Koreans do not desire to distance themselves from the United States to get closer to China. Rather, they are frustrated with the United States: in their eyes, Washington does not value the alliance with South Korea to the same extent that it values the alliance with Japan. Similarly, the Japanese desire for status and "uniqueness" explains some of its focus on the mantra of the singular importance of the U.S.–Japan alliance.

The problem of course is that such a competition requires a diplomatic deftness and strategic cold-bloodedness that few strategists have or are ready to practice. And such an approach goes against the spirit of the alliances, which is presumably based on underpinnings of mutual interests and mutual trust. Playing on national insecurities is a risky and dangerous course. There is the very real danger that such a strategy would backfire, undermining either or both alliances.

If the costs to communities that host U.S. troops were thought to be too high, the regional threat environment were to be seen as relatively benign, or the U.S. presence were to become disadvantageous to its national interests, the United States could maintain a residual or symbolic commitment to political and security cooperation with South Korea and/or Japan and maintain bases or other facilities to equip forces in the event they were forward deployed, while limiting or eliminating the need for a semipermanent U.S. troop presence. In addition, U.S. budget imperatives may create a situation in which U.S. national security planners must take a cold, hard look at the costs of the U.S. military presence in Asia and whether U.S. commitments are sustainable. If the United States were to pull back, an option for reducing costs while maintaining residual commitments might be to maintain access to facilities while ending or drastically reducing overseas deployments of U.S. military personnel. Maintenance of bases would allow for the stationing of U.S. troops in response to ad hoc crises but would not presume the permanent use of such facilities for the purpose of maintaining forward-deployed forces. This option is already in practice elsewhere: the United States maintains alliance relationships with Australia, the Philippines, and Thailand but does not maintain a permanent troop presence in any of them. During his second term as secretary of defense, Donald Rumsfeld promoted the doctrine of "places, not bases" to maximize U.S. flexibility, reduce the U.S. footprint—and the resulting political sensitivities—on some communities, as well as reduce costs. In an era of increasing vulnerability to over-the-horizon attacks, the dispersal of forces makes strategic sense. The high incidence of natural disasters in the Asia-Pacific region—the 1991 Mount Pinatubo eruption was instrumental in bringing about the end of the U.S. troop presence in the Philippines, and the March 11, 2011, tsunami submerged an ASDF air base and a GSDF camp—also encourages use of a smaller, more flexible presence.

While this option would diminish frictions with local communities, eliminating a source of opposition to the alliances, there are real downsides. The first and most important is the degree to which such a move would be seen not as a rationalization of alliances to make them more durable and enduring but as a wavering of the U.S. commitment to regional security and each country's defense. Doubts about the credibility of the U.S. commitment could encourage Seoul and/or Tokyo to take self-help measures that might be destabilizing. Other governments might be tempted to exploit this shift, alter the regional balance of power to their advantage, or test the U.S. commitment to regional security or that of its allies. Finally, while arrangements would be made to ensure U.S. access to local facilities in the event of an emergency, there is no guarantee that access would be available: there is a big difference in locally deployed forces responding and U.S. forces moving into or through local positions in a crisis. In short, uncertainty about the U.S. response in a crisis would be greatly magnified.

Independence/Autonomy

Consideration of this option can be seen as the combined result of two ongoing trends: technological advances that provide new capabilities and encourage flexibility in force deployments, and U.S. frustrations created by domestic politics in allied nations that limit the use of U.S. forces deployed there, compromise the strength of the relationships, and oblige the United States to spend disproportionate amounts of time responding to local issues. This view sees a reduced need for institutionalized relationships and views alliances as a drag on U.S. freedom of action to pursue its national interests. The intellectual center of gravity for this argument is the concept of "offshore balancing," promoted by Christopher Layne, John Mearsheimer, and Stephen Walt, which argues that the United States should eschew commitments of large numbers of forward deployed forces and instead use other regional powers to maintain a balance of power within a given theater, intervening only when that balance seems threatened. Layne argues that the 2012 Defense Strategic Guidance "reflects the reality that offshore balancing has jumped from the cloistered walls of academe to the real world of Washington policy making."[40] Some see the decision to transfer operational control of wartime command of coalition forces from the United States to South Korea

("OpCon transfer") as a U.S. preference for this option. Similarly, some observers see the letter to Defense Secretary Leon Panetta from U.S. senators Levin, McCain, and Webb in 2012, expressing concern about moving U.S. forces from Japan to Guam, as a first step in the revision of the agreement by the two countries to realign U.S. forces in Japan.[41] While all three men still favor forward deployment of U.S. forces, there are concerns that they could be laying the groundwork for a different U.S. posture.

In the absence of a firm U.S. commitment and a local presence, Washington would rely instead on "coalitions of the willing" in which countries join the United States based on perceived self-interest rather than because of alliance commitments. In addition to reducing U.S. commitments and those associated burdens, this policy promotes autonomy for former alliance partners, reduces security burdens on the United States, and eliminates "free riding."

A variant of this scenario envisions the development of a multilateral security mechanism that replaces U.S.-led alliances as the main force promoting stability in East Asia. In recent years security multilateralism has picked up the pace in Asia. In 1994 the ASEAN Regional Forum was launched, and today it includes twenty-seven participants and is considered the premier multilateral security dialogue in Asia. While the ARF is sometimes dismissed as "toothless" or a mere talk shop, attendance at the forum is now considered indicative of a government's commitment to Asian regionalism. More recently ASEAN has launched the ASEAN Defense Ministers Meeting Plus (ADMM+), which includes ASEAN and its eight dialogue partners—Australia, China, India, Japan, South Korea, New Zealand, Russia, and the United States—in focused discussions of defense issues. It seeks to provide a platform for countries to seek common points in security cooperation, focusing on nontraditional security threats. The ADMM+ has six working groups and the plenary meets every two years.[42] There is also the East Asia Summit, at which leaders of those same governments meet to discuss political issues of regional significance.

The rapid development of China-led economic interdependence in East Asia has strengthened the constructivist case that economic interconnections could eventually become the source of regional stability, thereby replacing the alliances. However, any structure would have to prove itself reliable and capable of addressing regional security challenges before alliance partners would be willing to dissolve the long-standing bilateral security arrangements that have provided stability and prosperity in recent decades. And, as is plainly the case, alliances are not necessarily incompatible with other security mechanisms, much less regional economic mechanisms. They can all coexist.

While some in the United States yearn for the freedom and reduced commitments that follow from the end of its alliance commitments, there are powerful arguments against cutting those ties. The most powerful is the uncertainty about how allies might react. With four Northeast Asian actors—China, North Korea, Russia, and the United States—possessing nuclear weapons, South Korea and Japan would be pressed to follow suit. Both countries have the materials and lack only the will to proceed and some of the technology; both are considered "virtual" or "latent" nuclear states.[43] Survey results show that the Japanese do not seek a nuclear capability, but the ending of the U.S. nuclear umbrella could force Tokyo's hand. As Satoh Yukio, one of Japan's premier strategic thinkers, has noted, "U.S. extended deterrence is essential for Japan's commitment to and efforts for global nuclear disarmament."[44] In South Korea as well, the nuclear temptation would grow without the U.S. alliance to backstop ROK defenses.[45] Seoul developed a clandestine nuclear program in the 1970s when the United States contemplated withdrawing its forces from the Korean Peninsula.[46] Termination of U.S. alliances would also reduce if not eliminate the influence that the United States has over the policies of its allies. That would reverse a half century of U.S. foreign policy if Victor Cha is correct when he argues that the U.S. alliance system in Asia was designed to help Washington control its "rogue" allies in the region.[47] Moreover, U.S. allies and other nations in Asia looked to U.S. alliances as a means of constraining those allies as well, Japan in particular. So while the end of the U.S.–Japan alliance would free Tokyo from restraints imposed by the United States, it would also increase suspicions or heighten the possibility of conflict with Japan, especially in South Korea and China. Instability could result from

Japanese behavior as well as fears of that behavior regardless of what Japan actually does.[48]

Evaluation of the Six Options

The Obama administration's rebalance to Asia bolsters efforts to replace a bilateral hub-and-spokes approach to Asian security with a networked approach in which alliance cooperation occurs both multilaterally and among allies of the United States regardless of U.S. involvement. The renewed focus on Asia has created pressures for increased cooperation between Japan and South Korea, but it is clear that political constraints in that relationship over history continue to limit the potential for bilateral security cooperation between the two countries, and in turn those limits make the prospect of a regionalized U.S.-led alliance network untenable. Identity politics will influence the scope of what is possible, in terms of both the form and function of each alliance and whether the two alliances might be integrated more deeply to provide a more powerful and effective platform for maintaining security in East Asia.

The rebalance counters the potential effects of fiscal constraints on U.S. forward presence. While disengagement seems the most farfetched scenario, a combination of fiscal restraints, fatigue with playing the role of global policeman, and renewed nationalism within the region could push the United States to downsize its military presence in Asia in the longer term. In the Chicago Council on Global Affairs poll in 2012, only 53 percent of respondents agreed that maintaining superior power is a very important U.S. foreign policy goal (a 14-point drop from its peak), a growing number (38 percent) want the United States to reduce its overseas bases, and 68 percent endorse defense budget cuts.[49] Those numbers are cautionary but not yet alarming. On the other end of the spectrum, a regionwide, institutionalized alliance network seems even more unlikely.

Therefore the most likely developments are variations on the status quo. This is to be expected, given policy makers' proclivity for incremental change and the idea that current arrangements correspond to external threat perceptions. But there is reason to be optimistic.

There is a convergence among the United States, Japan, and South Korea around common values and interests, and this may provide a basis for deepening and regionalizing security cooperation in Northeast Asia. There is also evidence that the United States, South Korea, and Japan have overlapping threat perceptions stemming from unease about the future of North Korea and China (although the views of China are considerably more diverse). In addition, there will be an increasing need to pool resources, both in response to budgetary pressures in each country and to respond to ever-increasing investments in military capabilities throughout the region generally, but especially given China's defense modernization program.

There are significant practical obstacles, particularly in managing the Japan–ROK relationship, that must be addressed before it would be possible to deepen trilateral security cooperation. Even if threat perceptions coincide, priorities and preferred responses may not. There is a deep-rooted emotional element of this relationship—the history question—that must be addressed satisfactorily to open the full potential for Japan–ROK cooperation and thus for regionalization of U.S. alliances in Northeast Asia. Equally important is the need to ensure that any enhanced trilateral cooperation avoids inciting a negative Chinese reaction or is not "misread" as an attempt to "contain" China or cast China as a threat. Unless Japan and South Korea agree to put history behind them, however, constraints on the potential for Japan–South Korea cooperation will persist in an environment where U.S. capacities face fiscal constraints and China's power continues to grow.

6

REINVIGORATING TRILATERALISM

NORTHEAST ASIA IS A REGION OF EXTRAORDINARY VITALITY and change. It is a locus of economic energy and technological dynamism, the place where the top three economies in the world intersect with each other; its democracies are vibrant and evolving; its societies among the most wired in the world, early adapters, and the place where technology and culture are interacting in ways that influence the rest of the world. But while the changes are mesmerizing, it is important to remember that the region enjoys great continuity as well. The Cold War lingers in Northeast Asia: two countries remain divided. The U.S. alliance system continues to be the cornerstone of regional peace and security, deterring enemies and reassuring allies, partners, and friends.

But the framework that has provided continuity is undergoing transition, given new threats, new capabilities, China's rise, and a new sense of what is required and what is possible. These developments could introduce greater volatility in the region and could undermine the stability that has provided the foundation for Northeast Asia's—East Asia's— peace and prosperity. But despite new developments, long-standing tensions in the region may become a battleground for clashing national interests or may reflect fundamentally different political systems and values. Sharpening those divisions are historical memories that shape, if not define, national perceptions of countries and their neighbors. Those memories are powerful manifestations of national identity, the glue that holds these communities together, and which has a powerful influence on public opinion and decision making. But if they help define national communities, they also sharpen the conflicts between nations, often obscuring, if not bulldozing, the concerns and characteristics that Japan and South Korea may share.

Historically, decision making on foreign and national security policy is the province of elites; in the case of Japan and South Korea, the key actors have been bureaucrats who manage those countries' alliances with the United States. While Cold War legacies linger in Northeast Asia, the end of the superpower standoff "unfroze" domestic politics in the region, transforming national political debates as well as creating new possibilities in foreign policies. Old enemies disappeared. New relationships became possible. The U.S. alliance system, once thought indispensable to regional peace and security, was susceptible to challenge by newly empowered publics who decided to reexamine conventional wisdom in light of a seemingly new environment. At various times during the past two decades—in Japan in the mid-1990s, in South Korea from 2002 to 2004, and again in Japan in 2009 and 2010—the U.S. alliances with Japan and South Korea appeared to be in danger. In each case, however, the alliance survived and emerged even stronger.

This study provides evidence for the durability of these alliances. Equally important, it interprets the impact of changing public views in Japan and South Korea of the U.S.–Japan, U.S.–South Korea, and Japan–South Korea relationships. This information is necessary to gain an accurate understanding of how our partners see themselves, conceive of their national identity, and understand their role in the region and the world.

Understanding Japan

The portrait of Japan that emerges from an analysis of Japanese public views of themselves and their security environment is one of a people who are proud of their country, but that pride should not be equated with assertive nationalism. Instead it comes from membership in a distinct group—an island nation that has stood apart from its neighbors for centuries. This sense of separateness facilitated the forging of a national spirit and sense of unity. It also privileged homegrown solutions that created the world's second largest economy out of the rubble of World War II.

Yet the Japanese model of capitalism, once so successful, has sputtered during the past two decades. Japan discovered that it is not inoculated from the ills of Western society—suicide, homelessness, terrorism, anomie. The quiet confidence that previously animated Japanese public attitudes has dissipated. In its place there is doubt and confusion about the country's future and place in Asia and the wider world. Despite being part of "the most important bilateral relationship, bar none," Japan feared being eclipsed as a U.S. partner by China, a fear that become palpable when China overtook Japan as the world's second largest economy. Anxiety was magnified by political confusion and immobility in Tokyo. The catastrophic events of March 11, 2011, and their aftermath provided an exclamation point for Japanese concern. Japanese resilience in the face of that crisis underscored a core feature of Japanese character and identity. Ironically, however, that same trait has become a hindrance to the reform that many believe is essential to Japan's future: the readiness to "endure" hardship blunts the impulse to bring about needed change.

Just as disturbing for Japanese was the deterioration of the security environment. Dreams of a peaceful post–Cold War world evaporated in the wake of attacks by a millenary terrorist group, a shoddy crisis management system, and the twin menaces posed by a provocative North Korea and an increasingly assertive China. Mounting external challenges have forced the country to ask basic questions about its security posture and, in the process, look hard at the meaning of its conception of itself as a "peace-loving nation."

Japan's preferred policy response, not surprisingly, has been to strengthen relations with the United States. The United States is seen as the country's most important security partner; when compared with other countries, its interests and values are most like those of Japan. Japanese show the most warmth for Americans among all countries surveyed, and there is high support for a world in which the United States has considerable international influence. While there are frictions in the relationship—Japan's pride creates demands for more equality in the relationship; tension is inevitable when those status concerns are not met—that does not mean that Japan seeks new security partners. This was most evident in 2009–10 when the first Democratic Party of Japan government under Prime Minister Hatoyama Yukio flirted with a "more balanced" approach to foreign policy that would seemingly put more distance between Tokyo and its ally. That orientation was decisively rejected. China is acknowledged to be Japan's most important economic partner, but that relationship enjoys little trust. Since the September 2010 incident in which a Chinese fishing boat rammed two Japanese Coast Guard vessels near the disputed Senkaku/Diaoyu islands, relations between the two countries have plummeted. In a poll taken days after the incident, a record 84 percent of respondents said they didn't trust China.[1] Nearly three years later, 90.1 percent of respondents in one authoritative poll said that they had an "unfavorable impression of China," and 80 percent characterized the bilateral relationship as "bad."[2]

Public opinion polling reveals a country that is focused on itself. Japan does not seek to project power. Even as the LDP government contemplated "new" defense and security policies in 2013, the emphasis remained on homeland defense.[3] Attempts to push more ambitious policies, such as constitutional revision that focuses on Article 9, garnered considerable pushback and have been delayed. Japan's international contributions are a function of its successes at home. Japan does not seek to lead but rather to export its good behavior and successes. Japan is not indifferent to the world beyond its borders—it is acutely aware of its vulnerability—but the public is little prepared to do much to change that world. These tendencies have been magnified by the March 2011 earthquake.

Understanding South Korea

Like Japan, South Korea enjoyed extraordinary success in the second half of the twentieth century. It too developed a modern, world-beating economy out of the destruction of war. At the same time, it emerged from the long shadow of colonialism and military dictatorship to propagate a thriving and energetic democracy. South Korea recovered from crippling economic crises with barely a stumble. Economic vitality, political success, and a shared sense of confidence are three components of South Korea's postwar development experience that are contributing to the emergence of a positive South Korean national identity.

Yet South Koreans also remain acutely aware of their vulnerability, manifested today most clearly by history and geography. Despite all their accomplishments, it takes little for South Koreans to confess to feeling like "a shrimp among whales"—a small country very much at the mercy of its larger neighbors, subject to forces beyond its control. A ferry accident involving the deaths of over three hundred people in April 2014 brought these feelings of fragility to the fore, stimulating reflection among Koreans over the durability of their achievements. This sense of vulnerability is particularly striking when one considers that the size of South Korea's economy now rivals that of some of the larger countries in Europe.

South Korean public opinion surveys reveal a country that is optimistic about the future and takes great pride in "being Korean." When Koreans look at the world around them, they have the greatest affinity with the United States: Koreans perceive their values and interests as most similar to those of the United States. Consistent with that, the United States is considered to be the country's most important security partner. Fortunately, the overwhelming majority of Koreans see the United States as a reliable security partner and the most important contributor to their country's national security.

China looms large in the Korean mind. It is generally considered to be the country's most important economic partner, but China's economic successes have led many Koreans to view it as a ruthless competitor and perhaps even a threat. Koreans have turned increasingly cautious about China, with issues such as tainted products, Beijing's support for North Korea, and the "Northeast Project," which rewrites history to incorporate ancient fiefdoms on the Korean Peninsula long seen as Korean and declares them Chinese (and to effectively eliminate irredentist claims in the event of Korean unification), all increasing distrust of China. Nevertheless, Beijing is seen as an important channel in efforts to engage Pyongyang as well as a nation equally inclined toward skepticism of Japan.

As in Japan, the top priorities of Koreans are domestic—economic reform and promoting growth. The focus on domestic affairs is partly a response to the presence of an implacable foe just miles from the nation's capital. There are signs that an internationalist Korean mindset is evolving beyond a preoccupation with long-standing security challenges on the peninsula, however, prodded by President Lee Myung-bak's notion of "Global Korea" and the international support that concept has garnered. This process is still in its early stages, but President Park Geun-hye seems to have embraced it as well.

South Koreans see the North as a threat, even while they still feel a kinship tie. That tie is dissipating among a younger generation that has had no direct experience with the North and sees the potential for South Korea to move beyond the North to play a role on a bigger stage, however. That distance is widened by a growing sense of superiority toward the North felt by most South Koreans, a feeling produced by the country's economic performance, its rising international stature, and North Korea's accumulated failure—even the heights of South and North Koreans now differ as a result of the economic disparity between the two countries. Northern provocations, oddly enough, confirm this feeling, even while generating a sense of threat.

There is little emotional connection between the two halves of the Korean Peninsula. Most young Koreans identify themselves as South Koreans, and they have little inclination to make sacrifices for kin they have never known. For this generation, dealing with North Korea is a security imperative, not a familial one.

The Weakest Leg: Japan–South Korea Relations

The relationship between these Northeast Asian neighbors is perplexing. Japan and South Korea share geographic circumstances and geopolitical outlook. Threat perceptions generally track closely with each other. Both publics share values and interests, closely identify with the United States, and increasingly share a cultural affinity as political and economic barriers to such interchange have declined, especially among the younger generation. Rising numbers of South Koreans travel to Japan as Japanese flock to Korea. The economic gap between the two countries has closed as a result of Korea's modernization, enabling both sides to see each other on more equal terms. Both see the United States as their most important security partner and want to maintain closer ties with the United States in security affairs. Both see North Korea as a threat, and while Japanese are more open in their hostility toward China, South Koreans evince mounting concern about China and its behavior.

Nevertheless, suspicion that quickly edges into animosity dominates the bilateral relationship. Long-standing disputes over history and territory are inflamed by regular, more recent provocations. High levels of mistrust generate cycles of rapprochement and rupture. In many cases raw political calculations prevail over considerations of the national interest, but those gambits are successful because they mine a deep vein of ill will. Two events at the end of 2013 illuminate the state of the bilateral relationship. In November South Korea announced that it planned to build a statue to honor Ahn Jung-geun, an independence activist who in 1909 assassinated Ito Hirobumi, the Japanese colonial governor of Korea, which was then a Japanese protectorate. Ahn is revered in Korea as the man who struck at the embodiment of a hated imperial power that had subjugated his country and for which he was prepared to make the ultimate sacrifice. He is, for Korean nationalists, the quintessential "freedom fighter." For Japanese, however, he was not just "a criminal" who killed a ranking official but the murderer of a seminal figure in Japanese national history, a four-time prime minister who was instrumental in modernizing Japan. These competing conceptions of Ahn go beyond historical "facts": they reflect foundational views of each country and cannot be contested without doing real damage to the other nation's conception of itself.

The second incident occurred a few weeks later when it was revealed that the government of Japan had provided ten thousand rounds of ammunition to South Korean peacekeepers serving in South Sudan. When the news broke, ROK officials denied that they had requested assistance from Japan, saying that they had asked the United Nations for help (the troops were part of a UN force), and that Japan was using the incident to make Korea look weak, as well as to help erode Japanese constraints on security assistance to other nations and score political points.[4] Lost in the furor was the fact that Seoul and Tokyo had convergent interests and, by virtue of their alliances with the United States, used similar, hence interchangeable, ammunition. For ROK troops on the ground in a dangerous deployment, the Japanese gesture was much appreciated; for politicians and pundits in Seoul, political overtones mattered more. In this context it is hard to disagree with the ROK analyst who characterized the bilateral relationship as one of "mutual abandonment," in which both countries "have different strategic calculations," "political parties and civil society on each side lost interest in taking initiatives to improve bilateral ties," and "political cooperation is not a top priority."[5]

Prospects for Trilateralism

Historically, U.S. foreign policy in Asia has focused on bilateralism, primarily through its alliances, and pursuing multilateralism, primarily through international institutions when it seemed to pay dividends. In recent years a combination of new security threats and challenges, opportunities created by a fluid international system, and tightening fiscal constraints have encouraged more creativity in U.S. foreign policy: one intriguing manifestation of this new thinking is the search for "minilateral" solutions to problems. This approach favors flexible arrangements, often temporary, that bring together like-minded countries for fast and focused action.[6]

This approach has renewed attention on trilateralism. The United States–Japan–South Korea trilateral would seem to be a natural grouping, but historical constraints have been a powerful brake on cooperation and coordination. Some change is occurring. Foreign ministers from the three countries have met regularly, as have lower-level officials; a trilateral Steering Group has been established. This is no ad hoc arrangement; the U.S. State Department's *Quadrennial Diplomacy and Development Review* (*QDDR*) from 2010 calls for "a more systematic trilateral process, including . . . the US–Japan–South Korea trilateral."[7] This is a promising development, but it should be expanded. Notably, despite historical tensions, Japan, China, and South Korea successfully established a Trilateral Coordination Secretariat (TCS) in 2010; despite the U.S.–Japan and U.S.–ROK alliances and shared values and political systems among the three countries, no such administrative mechanism exists to promote common cause among Seoul, Tokyo, and Washington.

There is a compelling basis for alliance-based cooperation to meet new security challenges. The nature of many of those threats requires new approaches—they are too big and too diffuse for any single nation to tackle on its own. Moreover, the growing capabilities of allies and partners allows for a more distributed division of labor. Burden sharing is always important in alliances, but it has become even more pressing amid complaints by "junior partners" that alliance structures are unequal and allies want more status, and the United States, like those allies, faces increasingly straitened fiscal circumstances. Increased cooperation with allies is more efficient, results in a more effective use of resources, consolidates ties among partners, and builds the confidence and capabilities needed to respond to crises. A forward-leaning U.S. strategy that transforms the terms of its Asian engagement also helps rewrite the prevailing narrative, shifting perceptions of actors and their roles. The focus on alliances also reminds observers that the balance of power is not determined by the United States and China alone; instead the United States has an entire network of security partners and relationships that should be taken into account as well.

These benefits are usually seen from the U.S. perspective, but partner governments enjoy them too, along with other advantages.

Most significantly, those ties ensure that the United States remains engaged in the region. There is always fear of U.S. abandonment or withdrawal, and the more institutionalized the arrangements, the less likely that possibility. At the same time, heightened cooperation gives allies more insight into and impact on U.S. decision making. Allies often complain about American unilateralism; stronger ties with more institutionalized linkages between bureaucracies ensure that allies know what Washington is thinking and give them some leverage over outcomes.

Consistent with this logic, a central component of U.S. discussions with Northeast Asian allies following the Nuclear Posture Review (NPR) in 2010, in which the United States reiterated its commitment to reducing its reliance on nuclear weapons without diminishing its deterrent, has been an attempt to explain to allies that other ties can bind the United States and its allies besides "a nuclear tripwire" and to develop those alternative means of reassurance and deterrence.[8] Deeper integration of conventional defense structures or expanded ties to other nations could do the trick. Strong ties also ensure that allies have privileged access to intelligence and technology. For Japan, stronger ties with the United States and its allies reduce suspicions of Japanese intentions and facilitate Tokyo's integration into regional security planning. For other allies, South Korea in particular, expanded forms of cooperation provide a window into Tokyo's thinking and afford them some influence over Japanese security policy and planning. This opportunity has taken on additional importance as Japan reviews constraints on its exercise of the right of collective self-defense and contemplates a revitalized regional security role, along with new defense policies to make it possible. Likewise, Japanese security officials and analysts complain that changes in ROK security policy, and the workings of its alliance with the United States, are similarly opaque.[9]

Finally, the deepening of trilateral cooperation and regionalization of the alliances in an organic fashion provides a benchmark for expansion of security cooperation among like-minded governments beyond the three countries. It may also serve to develop standards that can be used to deepen and broaden security cooperation in Northeast Asia.

This would set a high requirement for like-mindedness as a basis for strengthening the effectiveness of collective action against regional threats. Such cooperation would challenge others to consider, respect, and perhaps eventually adopt like-mindedness based on converging values, reinforced by strong coordination in the service of collective security in Northeast Asia.

There are two primary arguments against the pursuit of vigorous trilateral cooperation in Northeast Asia. The first is that it risks offending China. There is no doubt that Chinese analysts will see enhanced trilateral coordination as a device to constrain its behavior and a potential means of containing its influence. Chinese security planners and analysts routinely dismiss U.S. alliances and the U.S.-led alliance system as "Cold War relics" that should be abandoned. But Chinese perceptions should not be confused with reality. All three countries—the United States, Japan, and South Korea—have strong relationships with China, ranging from the "strategic partnership" that Seoul and Beijing enjoy to the "positive, constructive and candid U.S.–China relationship." While Japan's relations with China have been deteriorating in recent years, both sides recognize that this state of affairs cannot continue. All three have intimate and robust economic relations: the United States is China's top trade partner, Japan is number two, and South Korea is number four (after Hong Kong).[10] Economic interdependence, salted with intense competition, is the norm, not hostility or containment. The three nations should be sensitive to Chinese concerns, but that does not mean they should give China a veto—especially when the interests of the three countries and China may conflict.

The second argument centers on the well-known historical obstacles to an enduring cooperative Japan–South Korea relationship. Despite long-standing animosities, bilateral cooperation has improved. Few countries were as supportive of South Korea as Japan as Seoul dealt with provocations from the North during 2010. That year also marked the centennial of the annexation of the Korean Peninsula by Japan, and the DPJ government worked to overcome the lingering anger and resentment. In August 2010 Prime Minister Kan Naoto, with cabinet endorsement, conveyed an official apology to South Korea expressing feelings of "deep remorse and heartfelt apology" for the suffering caused by colonial rule. This was accompanied by a pledge to return more than 1,200 royal books seized during Japanese colonial rule, a promise that was honored by the end of the year. Also in December that year, Seoul and Tokyo signed a civilian nuclear pact to promote the peaceful use of nuclear power and agreed to jointly develop rare earths mined in third countries. Discussions began on an Acquisition and Cross-Servicing Agreement that would allow reciprocal provisioning of supplies and administrative support between the SDF and ROK military and a General Security of Military Information Agreement (GSOMIA) that would allow the two sides to share confidential information gained momentum.[11] South Korea sent observers to U.S.–Japan naval exercises and Japan reciprocated a few months later. While the ACSA and GSOMIA initiatives were later derailed, the breadth of discussions suggests that there is a powerful demonstration effect at work; success breeds a willingness to extend cooperation in other areas. Efforts to lay the foundation for functional cooperation should be a priority.[12]

Progress has been fitful, however, as irritants too often resurface. Prime Minister Kan's suggestion that the SDF troops could be used to evacuate Japanese nationals from South Korea in the aftermath of the shelling of Yeonpyeong Island prompted angry pushback from Seoul. South Korea showed great sympathy for Japan in the aftermath of the March 11, 2011, events and provided emergency relief. But that goodwill quickly evaporated when Japan's Ministry of Education approved new textbooks that claimed the Dokdo/Takeshima islands are Japanese.[13] All is not lost, however. Even as Japan–South Korea relations plunged to new depths, opinion surveys showed that the Korean public sought to put a floor to the relationship. Polling data at the end of 2013 indicated "clear support for President Park to take steps to repair the relationship with Japan." Those steps include a summit between Park and Prime Minister Abe and the signing of a GSOMIA. Significantly, the support was "bipartisan and includes all age cohorts."[14]

There is space for strengthened trilateralism. We recommend two courses of action. The first is bold by current standards but is nevertheless a lowest common denominator approach to trilateralism that operates within the constraints imposed by ongoing Japan–South Korea tensions over history. The second is a "Grand Bargain" among the three countries. It is extremely ambitious and requires courage and calculation by leaders in all three capitals. Both require political leaders in Tokyo and Seoul to reject the temptation to use the other to score domestic political points. Instead they must demonstrate real leadership to lay the foundations for a more enduring framework of institutionalized trilateral cooperation that would benefit all three countries.[15]

The first strategy tries to capitalize on the existing move toward trilateralism through a two-pronged approach that pursues bottom-up and top-down methods to strengthen existing cooperation among foreign ministries. It begins with a leader-level trilateral statement that makes the case for trilateral cooperation and indicates their readiness to focus on contributions to regional and global security. In fact, foreign ministers from the three countries issued such a statement in December 2010 following the North Korean shelling of Yeonpyeong Island, but such a statement bears repeating. The important thing is to frame trilateral cooperation in ways that benefit all three countries and indicate that it is being done as part of the international responsibilities of each country. This is intended to shape the context in which the inevitable intense national debates about cooperation will occur. Such a statement would send a signal to their publics, as well as their bureaucracies, of top-level support for increased trilateralism. Those leaders would reinforce that message by meeting regularly, both as stand-alone events and on the sidelines of multilateral gatherings such as the UN General Assembly, the G20, or the East Asia Summit, as they currently do bilaterally. Such meetings need to become routine. A trilateral foreign and defense ministers meeting, a "2+2+2," should also be implemented.

The second level is at the other end of the bureaucracy, the working level.[16] Thus far, security and foreign policy planners have limited their ambitions in light of ever-shifting political winds. That is understandable. But threat perceptions are aligned: North Korea is considered a menace, and there is significant and growing concern about Chinese behavior among the three. U.S. plans to reconfigure its deterrent strategy—the 2010 Nuclear Posture Review continues the effort to reduce the role of nuclear weapons in defense planning—mean that all U.S. allies need to work with Washington to ensure that deterrence is not compromised in the process, especially in light of North Korea's growing nuclear threat.

The similar geographic and geopolitical settings that Japan and South Korea share make a trilateral extended deterrence dialogue, one that examines questions of both alliance renovation and reassurance, an obvious first step.[17] Similarly, the three policy-planning staffs should be meeting regularly to assess regional contingencies. As part of its emphasis on "smart power," the *QDDR* seeks to better coordinate activity across the interagency process; that effort should be extended to the trilateral realm. All three countries should be identifying shared concerns and pushing the relevant bureaucratic constituencies together. Those discussions should be extensive, involving a wide range of institutional interests and addressing a broad agenda. Topics could include alliance interests, security cooperation, nontraditional security threats, trade and economic concerns, financial stabilization, North Korea, and China, to start just a short list. We are gratified to see that this discussion is underway in the trilateral Steering Group, and we hope that its scope will remain expansive and that participants will ensure that it maintains a global perspective. The tension between the regional focus of Japan and South Korea and the global focus of the United States is notable, but there are signs of change. Former president Lee's pursuit of "Global Korea" has transformed perceptions in his country of its appropriate role. In many of our discussions, Koreans and Japanese suggest that out-of-area cooperation might prove more fruitful than endeavors close to home.

Hard security cooperation will be difficult, but it is not impossible. The defense ministers from the three countries held trilateral meetings in 2013 and 2014 at the annual Shangri-la Dialogue. The three militaries have held annual Defense Trilateral Talks (DTT) since 2008. Japan was an observer in U.S.–South Korean naval exercises in 2008 and 2010 after the Rim of the Pacific (RIMPAC) exercises were completed. In 2012 and again in 2013, the three countries held trilateral naval exercises that focused on interoperability and preparation for various contingencies.[18]

The Pacific Command's multilateral security exercises could serve as the basis for an initial consideration of opportunities for more systematic operational cooperation. There should be a careful examination of what the three militaries are doing and what more they can do together to combat specific regional threats. Again, out-of-area activities could explore ways to enhance cooperation and maximize the efficient use of assets. Humanitarian assistance and disaster relief is another potentially fruitful focus. Another option is cooperation among a larger group of U.S. allies, perhaps in a quadrilateral format that includes Australia, to provide cover for the more politically sensitive coordination between Seoul and Tokyo.

The apparent need for political cover underscores a basic question for advocates of trilateralism: should attention be drawn to successful examples of cooperation? In theory, success writes its own narrative, creating momentum and reminding skeptics both of the value of cooperation and that current difficulties have not proven insurmountable. At the same time, there is fear that drawing attention to such activities will make them targets the next time there is a problem between Seoul and Tokyo. Invisibility may deprive proponents of trilateralism of examples to help them make their case, but it also insulates those efforts from political retribution when circumstances deteriorate.

Strengthened trilateral cooperation could help buttress modest international contributions by South Korea and Japan to global security needs while addressing in a more direct way the prospects for regional security cooperation. While domestic politics will continue to represent a threat to enhanced trilateralism, institutionalization of cooperation may serve as a hedge against politicization of such cooperation and against the effects of domestic political volatility on the alliance relationships.

One important potential divergence concerns the scope of the alliances: are Japan and South Korea on the same page when it comes to cooperation on out-of-area operations designed to ensure global stability? During the Bush administration, both alliances were framed as global and based on shared values, but Japan and South Korea appear to have responded differently to this framework. Interestingly, that parallel framing for the alliances with Japan and South Korea reemerged in the

U.S.–Japan Joint Statement and U.S.–ROK Joint Fact Sheets released in conjunction with President Obama's April 2014 visit to the region. Although Japan under Prime Minister Koizumi made unprecedented contributions to U.S. and international operations in Afghanistan and Iraq, domestic support for such military contributions ultimately proved to be unsustainable, a reality that became painfully clear when the DPJ came to power and the government slowly reduced the geographic scope of its security commitments. South Korea under Roh Moo-hyun had a vigorous debate on these issues, and, despite fears of its "anti-American" tilt, it ultimately was the third largest contributor of troops to Iraq. South Korea has expanded its security contributions off the Korean Peninsula, built a modest peacekeeping capacity, and gained practical experience through participation in multilateral antipiracy campaigns in the Gulf of Aden and postconflict stabilization efforts in Afghanistan. Seoul has elevated the objective of contributing to global stability operations as one of its top three objectives in South Korea's 2010 Defense White Paper along with providing for South Korea's security and preparing for Korean reunification.

Much remains to be worked out in the respective bilateral relationships to lay the groundwork for strengthened trilateralism. The U.S.–ROK defense relationship has been focused primarily on working out new command and control arrangements to replace the current Combined Forces Command (CFC) arrangements. This transition has provided an opportunity for the United States and South Korea to review in detail roles and missions in the event of conflict on the peninsula, but there has not yet been a deep analysis of how the United States and South Korea might cooperate in a regional context, and that conversation has foundered over South Korean entrapment concerns over the old concept of "strategic flexibility," especially as it relates to whether the United States might drag South Korea into a conflict with China. The "realignment" of U.S. forces in Japan continues to be a work in progress, with the Tokyo government—whether LDP or DPJ—unwilling to spend political capital to make hard choices and push past existing hurdles. There are also the constitutional constraints on a more energetic

Japanese security role, the most significant of which is the renunciation of the right of collective self-defense. This may not be insurmountable, however: while surveys show little desire to abandon Article 9, there is some support for permitting Japan to join collective action if authorized by some institution. The issue of authorization—legitimacy—is crucial to Japanese readiness to act.

A more energetic Japanese security policy may raise alarms, although given the constraints above we believe they are overstated. Not only is there little inclination among Japanese to embrace a more aggressive security role, but the structure of Japanese politics will restrain military adventurism. Both the Komeito, a Buddhist party that is a key coalition partner of the LDP, and the U.S. government play outsized roles in Tokyo. Both will blunt the sharp edges of Japanese nationalism and assertiveness. Also, nesting Japan's higher profile within a trilateral framework, especially one that includes South Korea, should help reduce concern at home and abroad. But if trilateral security cooperation is an assurance measure to keep South Korea from being alarmed by the prospect of a more active security role for Japan, a more tightly coupled security relationship with South Korea and the United States can help counter isolationist tendencies in Tokyo and ensure that the world's third largest economy continues to do its share in the provision of public goods. And finally, South Korea would stand to benefit from enhanced collective security capabilities in the service of joint regional defense operations. In this sense, trilateral defense cooperation is simply following the pattern of swap arrangements that has been established in responding to financial crises.

Go Big, Be Bold

A second, more ambitious, option is the "Grand Bargain." This consists of a series of moves by each government that would attempt to reconstitute the historical, psychological, and emotional context in which Japan, South Korea, and the United States interact. The agreements would have to be detailed and carefully orchestrated, and the particulars are best left to the three governments involved, but the three pillars of such a gesture, or series of gestures, would include the following:

1. A U.S. commitment to acknowledge that it too has been deeply involved in the historical events at the end of World War II that now serve as flashpoints for identity-related wounds between Japan and South Korea that have yet to heal. A first step toward acknowledging the past while also enabling the establishment of a new framework for future-oriented relations among the three countries would include a U.S. acknowledgment of the suffering of Japanese civilians that accompanied the atomic bombings of Japan. This might be accomplished through a presidential statement acknowledging Japan's atomic bomb victims and pledging to continue efforts to roll back nuclear weapon stockpiles around the world. In addition, the U.S. government should grapple more directly with its failure to tie up the loose ends surrounding the postwar settlement, especially as it relates to questions of disputed sovereignty and conflicting maritime claims. A stronger U.S. effort to address these issues as part of the San Francisco Treaty might have kept them from becoming flashpoints. A review of U.S. handling of these issues might assist in formulating a policy on these disputes. These steps would be undertaken so as to enable Japanese and South Korean responses to effectively address historical grievances and lay the framework for a stable and productive Japan–ROK relationship.

2. A Japanese commitment to acknowledge state responsibility for the crimes and injustices perpetrated by the imperial government, military, and soldiers during the occupation of Korea. To demonstrate its sincerity and provide a symbol of reassurance to Koreans that renewed military aggression is impossible, Japan would give up its claim to the Dokdo/Takeshima islands and make financial payments from the government of Japan to individual Koreans who suffered as sex slaves or forced laborers under Japanese colonial rule; leading politicians would abandon historical revisionism so as to avoid antagonizing Korean sensitivities and promote a zero-tolerance policy among Cabinet members and top party officials.

3. A Korean commitment to accept the Japanese offer, pledging to acknowledge Japan's efforts as a final gesture in settling issues of history and commence a forward-looking relationship with Japan. Korea would provide a definitive indication of the steps Japan must take to "wipe the slate clean."

We recommend a new Japan–ROK Treaty of Friendship and Partnership, which would contain several key provisions that would help transform perceptions of each country and blunt the sharp edges of identity that drive the two nations into conflict. First, it would contain a "no-war clause" that would declare that the two countries would never use force to settle any dispute between them. This would put a cap on tensions and deflate charges and suspicions that frictions might be resolved by force. Second, the treaty would declare Japanese support for the unification of the Korean Peninsula under the Seoul government, a statement that would end speculation about long-term intentions in Tokyo about the fate of the peninsula. Third, it would delineate the shared values and interests that unite the two countries and would declare them a basis for cooperative action by the two governments. Fourth, it would explicitly recognize and back Japan's regional security role in East Asia. Fifth, it would establish a day for joint commemoration by the two countries of the history of the twentieth century, a day that would signal the meshing of the two countries' history and future.

Plainly this is the sort of bold approach that will generate controversy and pushback in each country. There are real, practical questions about buy-in, implementation, and ultimate success. Nevertheless, we feel it is important and useful to identify such an option and make the case for it, regardless of those challenges. It would unshackle the potential for closer South Korea–Japan relations. It would surmount the historical and territorial issues that have constrained relations between the two countries. It would put history in the past and open the door to a true future-oriented relationship that has stood in the way of better South Korea–Japan relations for so long.

Our data, interviews, and the flows (not the ebbs) of Japan–South Korea relations show reconciliation is possible, that there is an intellectual understanding of the need for a new approach that, properly done, would create the framework for a more stable and sustainable South Korea–Japan relationship. Ultimately it seems that it is the perceived commitment to reconciliation that is problematic, not reconciliation itself. In other words, success depends on a belief that the attempt to overcome the past is sincere, not merely a political gesture or one that is capable of being rescinded or undone. That is why we urge Japanese leaders to make concrete gestures that will demonstrate their sincerity and their readiness to move forward; giving up the claim to Dokdo/Takeshima is hard to top in this regard. Specific gestures, however, must occur within a larger context. A grand bargain must eventually accommodate an entire range of actions and issues, creating a new framework for interpretation that forces a reconsideration of the entire relationship. This reinterpretation will be facilitated by the boldness of the particular steps taken: a willingness to do big things helps shift the context in which each nation frames its views of the other—and its views of itself.

Practically, a grand bargain would enable both countries to focus on real security problems and avoid wasting resources (time and money) on concerns that are emotionally satisfying but largely tangential to national security, such as shoring up Dokdo's defenses against a Japanese attack. It will end the "one step forward, two steps back" process that has consumed both countries' politics and their publics. It will signal that Tokyo and Seoul are prepared to build a platform that allows them to take a larger role in the region and the world. It could create a new leadership axis in Northeast Asia, one that has the potential to refashion security relations and multilateral dynamics in Northeast Asia and beyond.

The key question is whether Japan, and its conservatives in particular, can be persuaded to act accordingly. It will be tough sell, but there is a long list of reasons why it is in Japan's best interest. For a start, anything that reduces hostility and suspicion toward Japan is good. Virtually all trends—demographic, financial, political, military—are working to Japan's disadvantage; that is a poor position from which to contemplate the future. Putting a floor under Japan–South Korea relations will permit the two countries to work together to substantively address future challenges that both countries will face, bilaterally and with the United States. Moreover, this relationship can become a platform for Japan, both alone and working with security partners, to take a larger role in the region. The theorists can call it realpolitik, fatalism, realism, or whatever they like, but all those perspectives push Japan to promote reconciliation with its neighbor.

A conservative prime minister's ideology might press him or her to resist this approach, but the prospect of a historical rapprochement with Korea along with the certainty of better protecting Japan's national security should overwhelm that reluctance. The idea of Japan playing a larger security role in the region, which would be enabled by cooperation with Korea and the United States, corresponds with a conservative vision of Japan's international role. It goes almost without saying that it will demand a farsighted prime minister with impeccable conservative credentials to take a step that would parallel Richard Nixon's trip to China. To those who argue that few Japanese politicians fit the bill, we counter that there only has to be one, and he or she could draw inspiration from former prime minister Nakasone Yasuhiro, a genuine conservative who understood the need for Japan to put relations with Asian neighbors on a new footing.[19] Indeed, the Japanese leader who forges an enduring reconciliation with South Korea (and his or her Korean counterpart) will be remembered not just as a great leader but as a world historical figure.

We recognize that renouncing the claim to Dokdo/Takeshima will be especially controversial, but it makes sense. South Korea has effective control of the islands and will not be giving them up. Retaking control may be a dream of Japanese nationalists, but it is not going to happen. As one authoritative U.S. analysis concludes, "the only way the South Koreans will relinquish control is if military force is used to eject them. . . . It is hard to imagine that Japan would ever be willing to attempt this or could amass the capability to actually sustain control if it ever did seize the islets. This suggests that the use of force by Japan is out of the question. In effect, South Korea's de facto control is permanent."[20] Continuing to claim the islands only inflames bilateral relations and creates an ugly and unnecessary obstacle to their improvement. In renouncing its claim, Japan wins the moral high ground. And it can renounce that claim without prejudicing its position in other territorial disputes.[21]

If we are correct and trends are working against Japan, why then should the ROK embrace this arrangement? If time is on its side, it might wait for a better deal or eventually be able to impose one on its own terms. That calculation overlooks the cost of alienating the United States, antagonizing Japan, and depriving itself of a partner in addressing pressing security challenges. Closer relations with Seoul should help minimize doubts about Tokyo's intentions, a benefit for Japanese and South Koreans, as it provides the ROK with insight into Japanese decisions and an opportunity to bind Japan in cooperative relations so as to effectively foreclose the possibility of a return in Tokyo to policies that might threaten South Korean national security interests.

While we have discussed its advantages in strategic terms, the most important dimension of this grand bargain may be the moral aspect. The grand bargain would transform the Northeast Asian regional dynamic politically, but it will not stick unless the change is built on a "moral" foundation. Governments have to be seen taking responsibility for the past—and, in the ROK's case, for the future. This larger context lifts the problem out of the realm of politics and strategy and infuses it into the grassroots level. As long as the Japan–South Korea relationship and its attendant problems are addressed primarily at the political level, ordinary citizens will not see it as a concern of theirs and will not engage. Moral decisions are for each citizen to make; framing the relationship on this level gives them—ordinary Koreans and Japanese—a stake in the future of the relationship and a role to play in setting its course.

Considering this as a moral decision has other implications. It means that the grand bargain cannot be seen simply as a transaction. It has to be based on principles, not an exchange or a political deal involving quid pro quos. All three countries participate but for their own reasons; each is doing "the right thing" on its own merits, not for some particular benefit.

It also means that the United States has to be a participant and a catalyst for reframing the terms of interaction among the three countries. Alexis Dudden argues that "any study of these countries' post-1945 relations fails without substantially considering the role of the United States in the matter."[22] Historically, Washington has kept its distance from the inner workings of the Japan–ROK relationship and has kept arm's-length from any proposals or efforts to cast the United States as a mediator in managing difficulties in Japan–South Korea relations. Victor Cha has argued that this once made sense since the threat of U.S. disengagement propelled Seoul and Tokyo to fashion their own solutions to their inner frictions. In addition, there was always a fear that the United States would be forced to take sides, antagonizing one of its partners. Vice President Joseph Biden laid out long-standing U.S. policy during his December 2013 visit to Asia when he told a Korean audience, "We welcome mutually acceptable solutions to historical and territorial disputes and support dialogue and diplomacy that can lead to such solutions. But let me be clear: the United States does not intend to act as a mediator."[23]

The conventional wisdom has run its course, however. In truth the United States has long played a critical role in Northeast Asian politics—it is, in Dudden's memorable phrase, "the proverbial elephant in the middle of the room"[24]—going all the way back to the opening of the twentieth century, when President Theodore Roosevelt brokered the Portsmouth Treaty that ended the Russo-Japanese War. South Korean nationalists still brandish the Taft–Katsura Agreement, in which the United States acquiesced to Japanese control of the Korean Peninsula, as a sign of U.S. perfidy. Forty years later U.S. officials drew the line that divided the Korean Peninsula in half, creating two states that uneasily coexist to this day. Stanford Sociologist Shin Gi-wook points to the Tokyo War Trials, the San Francisco Treaty that officially ended World War II, and U.S. "crimes against humanity" to make the case that the United States is already deeply involved in Northeast Asian politics.[25] Japanese might add the occupation, the writing of their constitution, and the failure of the United States to definitively settle territorial questions before it handed sovereignty back over to Japan after the war. Given U.S. willingness to mediate the Israeli–Palestinian dispute and the Northern Ireland imbroglio, and to offer to mediate South China Sea disputes, its refusal to get involved in Northeast Asia seems arbitrary. U.S. interests are certainly as high and as strategic. Moreover, the inclination to see the U.S. hand in whatever develops—apparently Prime

Minister Abe thought he had U.S. acquiescence to a Yasukuni visit at the end of 2013, while South Koreans see the U.S. as enabling the conservatives and their agenda in Tokyo—means that Washington gets no credit for keeping its distance.[26] And finally, the United States is finding that it cannot avoid involvement in challenging revisionist nationalist interpretations in Japan over history just to keep Japan's current relationships in Asia stable: it has direct and indirect stakes in the consequences of that narrative being accepted or rejected by Japanese. Indeed, the most compelling argument is that the costs of noninvolvement are mounting. The strategic and economic significance of Northeast Asia is rising, and the failure of Seoul and Tokyo to establish a durable and lasting relationship is increasingly detrimental to U.S. interests. Not only are threats more pressing, but the contributions the three countries can make together are ever more essential to countering those threats. The United States went to considerable effort—staving off crises up to the last minute—to get a trilateral meeting of the three heads of state at the Nuclear Security Summit held in The Hague in March 2014. Plainly Washington sees the stakes involved and will expend considerable effort to push trilateralism.

A U.S. statement acknowledging the civilian suffering and loss of life associated with the atomic bombings, even as it brought an early end to the war, would respond to the Japanese sense of victimization that has dominated the country's consciousness in the postwar era while underscoring the international taboo on nuclear use that has held in the international community from the Cold War to the present. At the same time, U.S. readiness to recognize the extraordinary suffering resulting from the use of the atomic bomb, perhaps in the context of President Obama's reiteration of his commitment to implementing a Global Zero policy of ridding the world of nuclear weapons, would oblige Japan to make a gesture with regard to its own imperialistic excesses across the Asia-Pacific. If Japan were to pocket a statement of this nature without a reciprocal commitment to examine and provide redress for victims of its own state behavior, it would undermine Japan's own moral standing. Formal American acknowledgment of Japan's victimization as the only country to have suffered civilian casualties from use of an atomic weapon would drive up the cost for the government of Japan of a refusal to acknowledge its own actions during the war and would deal a blow to Japan's international authority and legitimacy.

That shift in international perception should encourage South Korea to join the grand bargain. If the United States were also to more aggressively support redress for wrongs done to women in conflict, a position that should be framed generally—but with very specific implications for Korea—Seoul would likely be even more enthusiastic. President Obama has already stated, at his press conference in Seoul in April 2014, his desire to see a "fair and just" approach to these historical issues. But, and this is critical, Seoul must reciprocate by spelling out specifically what it expects from Japan and by taking Japan's "yes" for an answer. This provides Tokyo with precise benchmarks for a positive relationship—a test of its intentions—and binds Seoul as well.

Many will still argue against U.S. action or even the need for a grand bargain. The United States risks a lot by inserting itself into this process. Previous U.S. attempts to look at its own history have been corrosive and did damage to the U.S. image and its cause. While Japan–ROK relations are not great, they are not bad. There is more going on in that bilateral relationship than often meets the eye and relations—even trilateralism—are moving forward, albeit at their own pace. Moreover, as Jennifer Lind has argued, apologies can trigger a backlash that makes relations even worse.[27] But the failure of Japan and South Korea to come to terms with history, especially in the run-up to the fiftieth anniversary of the normalization of their relationship, creates real limits on their security cooperation. The stubborn refusal to move on may ultimately impose high costs for both sides if they don't make a more active effort to place their relationship on a more fundamentally sustainable path today.

We believe that the upside is too great to settle for "safe" inaction, and ultimately the costs will weigh heavily on U.S. relationships with both Northeast Asian allies as Washington is continually thrust by one side or another into the center of controversy. A conservative backlash in Japan is possible, but that risk is reduced when such a statement is made by a conservative leader and is part of a package of gestures that reinforce its value and meaning. Moreover, the pragmatic calculation is just that: a practical assessment. We have outlined equally compelling reasons why the ledger could be a net positive.

The chances of success in this effort can be increased because the grand bargain approach we advocate is framed by the identity issues we have focused on in this study. Bold gestures will be "a shock to the system," forcing each country to reassess its image of the other and to reconfigure the preconceived identity it has of its partner and, at the same time, itself. A grand bargain appeals to the Japanese sense of themselves as a "peace-loving" nation and people. It offers them the opportunity to seize the moral high ground and use that as a platform for a larger international profile, without actually having to physically do something. Even abandoning the claim to Takeshima is less an action than recognition of the inability to change reality on the ground. It is a self-motivated, self-actualized moral gesture. In each dimension, Japan is compensating for the larger forces diminishing its international presence. It is a counter to its shrinking national confidence.

A similar logic works for South Korea. Moving forward with Japan should appeal to Korea's new sense of confidence and its readiness to step up its international engagement. It builds a forward-looking relationship with its closest regional partner, and its military ally, that permits more cooperation and coordination based on shared values, concerns, interests and threat perceptions.

Indeed, one of the most significant conclusions of this study is that Japan and South Korea should be working together to tackle shared problems and to protect their national interests—and those of the United States. Together, Tokyo and Seoul can do far more than they can alone. Working with the United States provides extraordinary opportunities to reach beyond their grasp and enhance their security and their influence in Northeast Asia and beyond.

NOTES

1. The Japan–South Korea Divide

1. Brett Ashley Leeds and Burcu Savun, "Terminating Alliances: Why Do States Abrogate Agreements?" *Journal of Politics* 69, no. 4 (2007): 1125.

2. See, for example, Moises Naim, *The End of Power: From Boardrooms to Battlefields, from Churches to States, Why Being in Power Isn't What It Used to Be* (New York: Basic Books, 2013).

3. Speech delivered by Deputy Secretary of Defense Ashton B. Carter, "The U.S. Strategic Rebalance to Asia: A Defense Perspective," U.S. Department of Defense, August 1, 2012, New York.

4. To add to a lengthy list of studies, see Carl Baker and Brad Glosserman, "Doing More and Expecting Less: The Future of U.S. Alliances in the Asia Pacific," *Pacific Forum CSIS Issues & Insights* 13, no.1 (February 2013), which explores the prospects of those alliances. (That project is much different from this one in scope and methodology.)

5. Howard French, "Japan Rediscovers Its Korean Past," *New York Times*, March 11, 2002.

6. Peter Katzenstein and Nobuo Okawara, "Japan, Asian-Pacific Security, and the Case for Analytical Eclecticism," *International Security* 26, no. 3 (Winter 2001/02): 154.

7. See, for example, Yosef Lapid and Friedrich Kratochwil, eds., *The Return of Culture and Identity in IR Theory* (Boulder: Lynne Rienner, 1996).

8. For an example of constructivist arguments for norms, identity, and culture in national security, see Peter J. Katzenstein, ed., *The Culture of National Security: Norms and Identity in World Politics* (New York: Columbia University Press, 1996).

9. Martha Finnemore, *National Interests in International Society* (Ithaca: Cornell University Press, 1996).

10. Kenneth Pyle, *Japan Rising: The Resurgence of Japanese Power and Purpose* (New York: PublicAffairs Books, 2009), 100.

11. Gilbert Rozman ed., *East Asian National Identities: Common Roots and Chinese Exceptionalism* (Stanford: Stanford University Press, 2012), 9.

12. Ibid., 17.

13. Gilbert Rozman, "A National Identity Approach to Japan's Late 2013 Foreign Policy Thinking," *Asan Forum* Special Forum, January, 25, 2014. http://www.theasanforum.org/a-national-identity-approach-to-japans-late-2013-foreign-policy-thinking/

14. Kim Jiyoon, "National Identity Under Transformation: New Challenges to South Korea, *Asan Forum* Special Forum, January 25, 2014. http://www.theasanforum.org/national-identity-under-transformation-new-challenges-to-south-korea/#.

15. Kuniko Ashizawa, "When Identity Matters: State Identity, Regional Institution Building, and Japanese Foreign Policy," *International Studies Review* 10 (2008): 571–72.

16. Michael Horowitz, "Research Report on the Use of Identity Concept in International Relations," Weatherhead Center for International Relations and the Harvard Identity Project (2002), 1.

17. Ibid., 16.

18. Ibid., 1.

19. Astrid Von Busekist, "Uses and Misuses of the Concept of Identity," *Security Dialogue* 35, no. 1 (2004): 81.

20. Rogers Brubaker and Frederick Cooper, "Beyond Identity," *Theory and Society* 29 (2000): 2

21. Ashizawa, "When Identity Matters," 573n6.

22. For examples of this viewpoint, see Samuel P. Huntington, "The Clash of Civilizations?" *Foreign Affairs* 72, no. 3 (1993): 22–49; and Jonathan Mercer,

"Anarchy and Identity," *International Organization* 49, no. 2 (Spring 1995): 229–52.

23. Peter Hays Gries, "Social Psychology and the Identity-Conflict Debate: Is a 'China Threat' Inevitable?" *European Journal of International Relations* 11, no. 2 (2005): 235–65.

24. Erik Gartzke and Kristian Skrede Gleditsch, "Identity and Conflict: Ties That Bind and Differences That Divide," *European Journal of International Relations* 12, no. 1 (2006): 53–87.

25. Andrew Oros, *Normalizing Japan: Politics, Identity, and the Evolution of Security Practice* (Stanford: Stanford University Press, 2008), 28.

26. Scott Snyder and Brad Glosserman, survey conducted December 2007–April 2008.

27. Pyle, *Japan Rising*, 127.

2. Japan's Identity Crisis

1. "Japan's Lost Decade," *Economist*, September 26, 2002.

2. Paul Sheard, "The Bull's Eye of the Third Arrow of Abenomics," *S&P Global Research*, November 8, 2013, 2.

3. Pew Global Attitudes Project Question Database, "Question: Are You Satisfied or Dissatisfied with the Way Things Are Headed in Our Country Today?" http://www.pewglobal.org/question-search/?qid=784&cntIDs=@25-&stdIDs=.

4. Jeff Kingston provides a lengthy and depressing catalog of concerns in *Japan's Quiet Transformation: Social Change and Civil Society in the Twenty-First Century* (London: RoutledgeCurzon, 2004), 1–35. David Leheny documents the rise of "a vague anxiety" in *Think Global, Fear Local: Sex, Violence, and Anxiety in Contemporary Japan* (Ithaca: Cornell University Press, 2006), 27–47.

5. For a more complete summary of this process, see Ralph Cossa and Brad Glosserman, "U.S.–Japan Defense Cooperation: Has Japan Become the Great Britain of Asia?" Pacific Forum CSIS *Issues & Insights* 3, no. 5 (March 2005).

6. There has been a flood of studies on the impact of the Tohoku earthquake, with both official (Diet) and unofficial (private organization) analyses. Tokyo Electric Power (TEPCO) also produced a detailed assessment. None are pretty. Richard Samuels of MIT, one of the leading analysts of Japan's energy industry and one of the keenest U.S. observers of Japan, published his analysis "3.11: Disaster and Change in Japan" in spring 2013. Glosserman's assessment, "The Choice: Japan After March 11," is forthcoming.

7. While Japanese foreign policy was consistent throughout the Cold War era, not all Japanese shared a single view. As Richard Samuels makes clear, Japanese thinking about foreign policy and grand strategy has been a rich weave of divergent approaches and outlooks. The differences were largely muted and the direction steady, despite loud voices on either fringe, because of the success of the Yoshida doctrine (which prioritized economic development over defense and diplomacy to facilitate Japan's reconstruction) and the conservative nature of Japanese society. See Richard Samuels, *Securing Japan: Tokyo's Grand Strategy and the Future of East Asia* (Ithaca: Cornell University Press, 2007); and Mike M. Mochizuki, "Neo-Revisionist History and Japan's Security Normalization," paper prepared for the OSC online discussion of Japanese nationalism, January 28–February 8, 2008.

8. Soeya Yoshihide, "A Normal Middle Power: Interpreting Changes in Japanese Security Policy in the 1990s and After," in *Japan as a Normal Country: A Nation in Search of Its Place in the World*, ed. Yoshihide Soeya, David A. Welch, and Masayaki Tadokoro (Toronto: University of Toronto, 2013), 79.

9. The best articulation of this view is Michael J. Green, *Japan's Reluctant Realism: Foreign Policy Challenges in an Era of Uncertain Power* (Basingstoke, UK: Palgrave Macmillan, 2001).

10. Paul Midford, *Rethinking Japanese Public Opinion and Security: From Pacifism to Realism? Studies in Asian Security* (Stanford: Stanford University Press, January 21, 2011), Kindle edition, loc. 317–31.

11. Ibid., loc. 317.

12. Soeya Yoshihide is the foremost proponent of this view. See for example, "A Normal Middle Power."

13. Ibid., 76.

14. Hirata Keiko, "Who Shapes the National Security Debate? Divergent Interpretations of Japan's Security Role," *Asian Affairs: An American Review 35*, no. 3 (Fall 2008): 123–51.

15. Unless otherwise indicated, all quotes are from author interviews in Tokyo in October and December 2007.

16. Author interview, Kyoto, November 9, 2012.

17. Cabinet Office, Government of Japan, "Public Poll on Japanese Society, 1980–2013," http://www8.cao.go.jp/survey/index-sha.html.

18. Cited in Juan Diez-Nicolas, "Cultural Differences in Values in Conflict, War and Peace," *World Values Research* 3, no. 1 (2010): 6.

19. See Glosserman, "The Choice," chap. 7.

20. Pew Global Attitudes Project, "Japanese Public's Mood Rebounding, Abe Highly Popular," July 11, 2013.

21. Author interview, Tokyo, December 1, 2012.

22. "After 60 Years of Peace, Japan's Future Lies in Global Cooperation," *Mainichi*, April 28, 2012.

23. Pew Global Attitudes Project, "Japanese Public's Mood Rebounding, Abe Highly Popular."

24. Pew Global Attitudes Project, "Economies of Emerging Better Rated During Difficult Times," May 13, 2013.

25. See, for example, Sugimoto Yoshio, "Class and Work in Cultural Capitalism: Japanese Trends," *Asia-Pacific Journal*, October 4, 2010. The OECD reckons some 12 percent of the Japanese population lived in poverty in the mid-1980s at the height of Japan's success, and that figure has been climbing ever since. But the important thing here is the belief of Japanese that their society is overwhelming middle class. Sugimoto also notes that the data show that this belief is not uniquely Japanese.

26. U.S. Department of State Office of Research, Opinion Analysis, "Abe's Job Jar: the Public's Priorities for a 'Beautiful' Japan," November 17, 2006.

27. A national poll by Hokkaido University professor Yamaguchi Jiro, cited in "Japan Struggles with Decisions on Foreign Investment," OSC Analysis, April 7, 2008.

28. Author interview, Sapporo, December 5, 2011.

29. *Yomiuri shimbun*, January 2008 opinion poll, Mansfield Opinion Poll Database. http://www.mansfieldfdn.org/polls/2008/poll-08–04-htm.

30. Ibid.

31. Pew Global Attitudes Project Question Database, "Question: What's More Important, a Society Where Everyone Is Free to Pursue Their Life's Goals Without Interference from the State or That the State Play an Active Role in Society to Guarantee That Nobody Is in Need?" http://www.pewglobal.org /question-search/?qid=1030&cntIDs=@25-&stdIDs=.

32. Pew Global Attitudes Project, "Pervasive Gloom About the World Economy," July 12, 2012.

33. See, for example, Christian Caryl and Akiko Kashiwagi, "The Gap Society," *Newsweek*, November 12, 2007.

34. Hoshi Takeo, "Will Abenomics Restore Japan's Economic Growth?" October 12, 2013. http://www.nomurafoundation.or.jp/data/20130911_T_Hoshi_000 .pdf.

35. David Pilling and Jonathan Soble, "Shinzo Abe Interview: I Am Convinced Our Road Is the Only Way," *Financial Times*, October 7, 2013.

36. See, for example, "Forward Progress Amidst Frustration: Report of the 20th Japan–US Security Seminar," Pacific Forum CSIS *Issues & Insights* (2014) (forthcoming).

37. Pew Global Attitudes Project Question Database, "Question: Our People Are Not Perfect, but Our Culture Is Superior to Others." http://www.pewglobal .org/question-search/?qid=50&cntIDs=@25-&stdIDs=.

38. Ibid.

39. Glosserman gives this issue considerable space in "The Choice," chaps. 4 and 7. The Tokyo government's thinking is evident in the strategy for Abenomics; see "Japan Revitalization Strategy: Japan Is Back," Prime Minister's Office, June 14, 2013.

40. Sawa Takamitsu, "Abe Set to Overturn Legacies of Koizumi and Nakasone," *Japan Times*, October 13, 2013.

41. U.S. Embassy in Japan, "Trends in Japanese Study Abroad and Visa Issuance." See also Institute of International Education, "Open Doors 2013 Fast Facts."

42. Author interview, Tokyo, July 23, 2012.

43. Cabinet Office of Japan, Survey on Foreign Relations 2012, November 26, 2012.

44. Dentsu Institute of Human Studies, "The Era of Competition: The Fourth Comparative Analysis of Global Values," March 2000, 8.

45. "Poll on Japan's Constitution," *Yomiuri shimbun*, April 8, 2008.

46. "ASAHI Poll: 59% Against Moves to Allow Collective Self-Defense," *Asahi shimbun*, August 26, 2013. http://ajw.asahi.com/article/behind_news/politics /AJ201308260110.

47. *Kyodo News*, "69 Percent Say Abe Should Heed Fallout from Yasukuni: Poll," *Japan Times*, December 29, 2013.

48. The official translation of Article 9 reads: "ARTICLE 9. Aspiring sincerely to an international peace based on justice and order, the Japanese people forever renounce war as a sovereign right of the nation and the threat or use of force as means of settling international disputes. (2) In order to accomplish the aim of the preceding paragraph, land, sea, and air forces, as well as other war potential, will never be maintained. The right of belligerency of the state will not be recognized."

49. For an excellent analysis of the foreign policy dimensions of this debate, see Soeya, *Japan as a Normal Country*. Soeya's conclusions match many of those outlined here.

50. Linus Hagstrom, "The 'Abnormal' State: Identity, Norm/Exception and Japan," *European Journal of International Relations* 20, no. 2 (2014): 2.

51. Ibid., 9.

52. *Nikkei shimbun*, April 2009 Opinion Poll, April 18–20, 2008, Mansfield Opinion Poll Database. http://mansfieldfdn.org/program/research-education-and -communication/asian-opinion-poll-database/listofpolls/2008-polls/nikkei -shimbun-april-2008-telephone-opinion-polls-08-11/.

53. Takashi Mochizuki, "Most Japanese Support Change to Postwar Charter," *Wall Street Journal*, May 5, 2013.

54. "Poll on Japan's Constitution," *Yomiuri shimbun*, April 8, 2008.

55. "Opinion Poll and Results," *Sankei shimbun*, September 17, 2013.

56. "Poll on Japan's Constitution," *Mainichi shimbun*, September 15, 2012.

57. "54% Against, 38% for Easing Constitutional Amendment Procedures," *Asahi shimbun*, May 2, 2013.

58. Pew Global Attitudes Project Question Database. http://www.pewglobal .org/question-search/?qid=904&cntIDs=@25-&stdIDs=.

59. Cabinet Office of Japan, Outline of "Public Opinion Survey on the Self Defense Forces (SDF) and Defense Issues," March 2012.

60. "Abe on Historical Mission to Amend Constitution," *Asahi shimbun*, August 13, 2013. http://ajw.asahi.com/article/behind_news/politics/AJ201308130045.

61. Yamashita Go, "Survey: More than Two-thirds of Upper House Members Now Favor Constitutional Revision," *Asahi shimbun*, July 24, 2013.

62. See, for example, Advisory Panel on Reconstruction of the Legal Basis for Security, "Report of the Advisory Panel on Reconstruction of the Legal Basis for Security," May 14, 2014. http://www.kantei.go.jp/jp/singi/anzenhosyou2 /dai7/houkoku_en.pdf.

63. Quote and poll figures from Toko Sekiguchi, "Abe's Collective Self Defense Pitch Faces Uphill Battle," *Wall Street Journal*, May 27, 2014. http://blogs .wsj.com/japanrealtime/2014/05/27/abes-collective-self-defense-pitch -faces-uphill-battle/.

64. Pyle, *Japan Rising*, 35

65. Hagstrom, "The 'Abnormal' State," 13n73.

66. Some date problems in the relationship to when then Chinese president Jiang Zemin visited Japan in 1998 and spent much of the tour offending his hosts. Most attribute his behavior to anger over the fact that Japan was not prepared to extend China the same apology South Korean president Kim Dae-jung received on an earlier visit.

67. Ministry of Defense, *Defense of Japan 2008*, 3.

68. A depressing catalog can be found in Jim Przystup's analysis of China–Japan relations in *Comparative Connections*, a quarterly journal on Asia-Pacific bilateral relations published by Pacific Forum CSIS (and coedited by Glosserman). http://csis.org/program/comparative-connections.

69. For details of the controversy, see ibid.

70. Chicago Council on Global Affairs, "Soft Power in East Asia," *Comparative Topline Reports*, June 2008.

71. Pew Global Research Project, "America's Global Image Remains More Positive than China's," July 13, 2013.

72. Survey on Foreign Relations, November 26, 2012.

73. Genron NPO, "The 9th Japan–China Public Opinion Poll," August 13, 2013. http://www.genron-npo.net/english/index.php?option=com_content&view=article&id=59:the-9th-japan-china-public-opinion-poll&catid=2:research&Itemid=4.

74. Toru Fujioka, "Japan's Exports Rebound, China Becomes No. 1 Customer," *Bloomberg News*, August 21, 2008.

75. Another poll offers slightly different conclusions. In a national survey in November 2007, a similar overwhelming majority (81 percent) identified the United States as Japan's closest security and diplomatic/political partner, and a plurality (40 percent) said the United States was the most important economic partner. That still bests China (36 percent), but the gap is closing: 56 percent of respondents identified the United States as the most important economic partner a year earlier. Department of State Office of Research, Opinion Analysis, "Security Issues Losing Traction with the Japanese Public?" December 13, 2007, 3.

76. *Asahi shimbun*, "Japan–China Joint Poll," September 24, 2012, 13.

77. Genron NPO, "The 9th Japan–China Public Opinion Poll."

78. Ibid.

79. Pew Global Research Project, "America's Global Image Remains More Positive than China's," chap. 4, "The Global Balance of Power." http://www.pewglobal.org/2013/07/18/chapter-4-global-balance-of-power/.

80. See, for example, Brad Glosserman, "Japan-U.S. Security Relations: Alliance Under Strain: A Conference Report," Pacific Forum CSIS *Issue & Insights* 8, no. 13 (March 2008); and Brad Glosserman, "The China Challenge and the US–Japan Alliance," *PacNet* 83, November 21, 2013.

81. This is consistent with other polls; see note 86.

82. Pew Global Research Project, "America's Global Image Remains More Positive Than China's," chap. 1, "Attitudes Toward the United States." http://www .pewglobal.org/2013/07/18/chapter-1-attitudes-toward-the-united-states/.

83. Survey on Foreign Relations, November 26, 2012.

84. This too is consistent with other surveys of the broader public versus elites. In a December 2007 poll, 64 percent of respondents believed the U.S. military presence in East Asia helps regional stability; 62 percent credited the bases in Japan for playing that role. Sixty-seven percent say U.S. forces in Japan are important for Japan's defense, just below the record 71 percent that agreed with that statement in 2006. "Security Issues Losing Traction with the Japanese Public?" Department of State Office of Research, Opinion Analysis, December 13, 2007, 3.

85. Cabinet Office of Japan, Outline of "Public Opinion Survey on the Self Defense Forces (SDF) and Defense Issues."

86. Department of State, Office of Research Opinion Analysis, "Alliance Transformation and Public Opinion in Japan," June 19, 2006.

87. Ibid.

88. Author conversations with U.S. Department of Defense officials, February 2013.

89. "What Is Abe's Real Motive for Collective Self-defense?" *Asahi shimbun*, February 9, 2013.http://ajw.asahi.com/article/views/editorial/AJ201302090056. Also see Ikejiri Kazuo, "Shinichi Kitaoka: Abe Advisor to Recommend Lifting Ban on Collective Self-Defense," *Asahi shimbun*, August 10, 2013. http://ajw .asahi.com/article/behind_news/politics/AJ201308100058.

90. Pew Global Research Project, "America's Global Image Remains More Positive than China's," chap. 1.

91. Glosserman, "The Choice," chap. 7.

92. Japan Ministry of Foreign Affairs, "Statement by the Minister of Foreign Affairs of Japan on Adoption of the 'National Security Strategy,'" December 17, 2013. http://www.mofa.go.jp/press/release/press4e_000141.html.

93. Kitaoka Shinichi, "Japan's New National Security Policy Based on 'Proactive Pacifism,'" *Nikkei Asian Review*, February 6, 2014.

94. Michael Green, "Normalizing Japan: Politics, Identity and the Evolution of Security Practice (Review)," *Journal of Japanese Studies* 36, no. 2 (Summer 2010): 486.

95. Kato Yoichi, "SDF's New Antipiracy Base Creates a Dilemma," *Asahi shimbun*, August 5, 2011. http://ajw.asahi.com/article/behind_news/politics /AJ201108055418.

96. Murakami Haruki, "As an Unrealistic Dreamer: Catalunya International Prize Speech, June 10." http://www.senrinomichi.com/?p=2541.

97. The TPP is a U.S.-led trade initiative that is designed to set a new standard for regional trade deals, inject new momentum into multilateral trade talks, and bind the United States more tightly to Asian economic partners.

98. Ben McLannahan, "Japan on Brink of Recession," *Financial Times*, November 12, 2012.

99. Sigma1, "Japanese Elections: Least Hated Rather than Popularity Contests," December 19, 2012. http://sigma1.wordpress.com/. In an NHK poll ten days before the election, only 6 percent of voters identified foreign policy as their top concern.

100. Linda Sieg, "Japan's Abe Set for Second Term, to Tap Allies for Cabinet," *Reuters*, December 25, 2012. http://news.yahoo.com/japans-abe-set-second -term-tap-allies-cabinet-005235524—business.html.

101. Andrew Oros, one of the leading scholars of identity and Japanese national security decision making, makes this same point in *Normalizing Japan*, 32.

3. South Korea's Growing Confidence

1. Shin Gi-wook, *Ethnic Nationalism in Korea: Genealogy, Politics, and Legacy* (Stanford: Stanford University Press, 2006), 1–2.

2. Kim Jiyoon, "National Identity Under Transformation: New Challenges to South Korea," *Asan Forum Special Forum*, January 25, 2015. http://www.theasanforum .org/national-identity-under-transformation-new-challenges-to-south-korea/#.

3. Andre Schmid, *Korea Between Empires, 1895–1919* (New York: Columbia University Press, 2002).

4. B. R. Myers, *The Cleanest Race: How North Koreans See Themselves and Why It Matters* (New York: Melville House, 2011).

5. Nicholas Eberstadt, Aaron L. Friedberg, and Geun Lee, "Introduction: What If? A World Without the US–ROK Alliance," *Asia Policy* 5 (January 2008): 2–5.

6. Secretariat of the National Security Council, "Theory on Balancer in Northeast Asia: A Strategy to Become a Respected State in International Cooperation," April 27, 2005. Accessed via Open Source Center, Doc #KPP20050428000225. http://www.opensource.gov.

7. "Lee Presents Three Objectives for US–Korea Alliance," *Korea Times*, April 16, 2008.

8. "Global Korea: The National Security Strategy of the Republic of Korea," Chongwadae, South Korea, June 2009.

9. Patrick M. Cronin, "Vital Venture: Economic Engagement of North Korea and the Kaesong Industrial Complex," Center for New American Security, February 2012. http://www.cnas.org/files/documents/publications/CNAS _VitalVenture_Cronin_0.pdf.

10. Park Geun-hye, "A New Kind of Korea: Building Trust Between Seoul and Pyongyang," *Foreign Affairs* (September/October 2011). http://www .foreignaffairs.com/articles/68136/park-geun-hye/a-new-kind-of-korea.

11. Steven Denney and Karl Friedhoff, "South Korea and a New Nationalism in an Era of Strength and Prosperity," *PacNet* 75, October 7, 2013. http://csis.org /files/publication/Pac1375_0.pdf.

12. Institute of International Education, "Open Doors Data." http://www .iie.org/en/Research-and-Publications/Open-Doors/Data/International -Students/Leading-Places-of-Origin/2008–10, and http://www.iie.org /en/Research-and-Publications/Open-Doors/Data/International-Students /Leading-Places-of-Origin/2000–02.

13. Ministry of Education, Science, and Technology. http://er.asiae.co.kr/erview .htm?idxno=2010101209340570586.

14. 2012 Edelman Trust Barometer. http://trust.edelman.com/trust-download /global-results/.

15. Asan Institute for Policy Studies and German Marshall Fund of the United States, "International Trends: Korea, Key Findings 2012." http://trends .gmfus.org/files/2012/10/1347995244Korea2012_web1.pdf.

16. Chicago Council on Global Affairs, "The United States and the Rise of China and India; Results of a 2006 Multination Survey of Public Opinion" (2006). https://www.thechicagocouncil.org/UserFiles/File/POS_Topline%20 Reports/POS%202006/2006%20Full%20POS%20Report.pdf.

17. Chicago Council on Global Affairs, "Foreign Policy in the New Millennium: Results of the 2012 Chicago Council Survey of American Public Opinion and U.S. Foreign Policy." http://www.thechicagocouncil.org/UserFiles/File /Task%20Force%20Reports/2012_CCS_Report.pdf. Also Scott Snyder, "American Support for the U.S.–ROK Alliance: Steady as She Goes," Chicago Council on Global Affairs, September 12, 2012. http://www.thechicagocouncil.org /UserFiles/File/Task%20Force%20Reports/2012_CCS_ROKEssay.pdf.

18. Asan Institute for Policy Studies and German Marshall Fund of the United States, "International Trends: Korea, Key Findings 2012."

19. *Donga ilbo*, May 31, June 15, as cited in Lee Geun, "Political and Economic Consequences of the Inter-Korean Summit," paper presented at the 2001 KAIS International Conference, June 22–23, 2001, 11.

20. Han Mann Gil, "Role of Education in National Unification," *Korea Focus* 9, no. 2 (March–April 2001): 134.

21. Yi Tong-hyon, "Reporter's Note: North Korea Policy Should Stick to Principles," *JoongAng ilbo* (Internet version in Korean), January 2, 2001, FBIS Document no. KPP20010102000094; Gallup Poll Survey on Political Support, December 26, 2000.

22. *Donga ilbo*, May 31, June 15.

23. Referenced in Sheila Miyoshi Jager, "Time to End the Korean War: The Korean Nuclear Crisis in the Era of Unification," *Nautilus Institute Policy Forum Online* 06–93A, November 2, 2006. http://www.nautilus.org/fora/security/0693MiyoshiJager.html. The KBS poll was published in *OhmyNews* on October 17, 2008.

24. Various polls conducted on behalf of the Ministry of Unification, 2003–2010.

25. Nae-young Lee and Han-wool Jeong. "EAI Issue Briefing on Public Opinion No. 91: The Impact of North Korea's Artillery Strike on Public Opinion in South Korea," East Asia Institute, December 2, 2010.

26. Emma Campbell, "South Korea's G-Generation: A Nation Within a Nation, Detached from Unification," April 13, 2010. http://www.eastasiaforum.org/2010/04/13/south-koreas-g-generation-a-nation-within-a-nation-detached-from-unification/.

27. Lee and Jeong. "EAI Issue Briefing on Public Opinion No. 91."

28. Peter Hays Gries, "The Koguryo Controversy, National Identity, and Sino-Korean Relations Today," *East Asia* 22, no. 4 (Winter 2005): 17.

29. These concerns are not unfounded: a small number of Koreans do make that type of claim. It is highly unlikely that such issues would gain traction in Korea as a matter of government policy—unless the Chinese create grounds for Korean suspicion of interference on the peninsula itself. There is a "Kando" claim that Korea has apparently given up that includes some Chinese territory; when China gets too heavy-handed, there are temptations on the part of South Korean scholars to recommend revival of that claim.

30. "Public Polls About China," *Donga ilbo*, May 4, 2004, accessed via Open Source Center, Doc. #KPP20040503000103. http://www.opensource.gov.

31. Chung Jae-ho, "Dragon in the Eyes of South Korea: Analyzing Korean Perceptions of China," in *Korea: The East Asian Pivot*, ed. Jonathan D. Pollack (Newport, R.I.: Naval War College Press, 2004): 253–67.

32. Scott Snyder, "Korea Between China and the United States," paper presented at Shorenstein APARC conference on "Korea and Vietnam: The National Experiences of Foreign Policies of Middle Powers," March 2012.

33. Pew Global Attitudes Project. http://pewglobal.org/reports/pdf/260.pdf, 92.

34. "Closer Alliance," *Korea Times*, July 21, 2010.

35. Chung Jae-ho, *Between Ally and Partner: Korea–China Relations and the United States* (New York: Columbia University Press, 2008).

36. Author conversations in Seoul, December 2010.

37. "Let's Cool Off over China," *JoongAng Daily*, May 8, 2010.

38. Bonnie Glaser and Scott Snyder with David Szerlip and See-Won Byun, *Responding to Change on the Korean Peninsula: Impediments to US–South Korea–China Coordination*, Center for Strategic and International Studies, May 2010.

39. Han Sukhee, "South Korea Seeks to Balance Relations with China and the United States," November 2012, Council on Foreign Relations. http://www.cfr.org/south-korea/south-korea-seeks-balance-relations-china-united-states/p29447.

40. Author interviews in Seoul, October 2008.

41. Pew Research Global Attitudes Project: South Korean Opinion of the United States. http://www.pewglobal.org/database/?indicator=1&country=116.

42. *EAI Issue Briefing* 95, March 7, 2011. http://www.eai.or.kr/data/bbs/kor_report/2011030815542638.pdf.

43. Pew Research Global Attitudes Project: South Korean Opinion of the United States.

44. Asan Institute for Policy Studies. "South Korea in a Changing World: Foreign Affairs," April 17, 2013. http://en.asaninst.org/contents/2012-asan-annual-survey-2/.

45. "South Korean Public Opinion on North Korea, Nuclear Weapons, and Defense," Public Opinion Studies Center, Asan Institute for Policy Studies, February 2013.

4. Convergence and Alienation in Japan–South Korea Relations

1. Victor D. Cha, *Alignment Despite Antagonism: The US–Korea–Japan Security Triangle* (Stanford: Stanford University Press, 1999).

2. Gilbert Rozman, ed., *National Identities and Bilateral Relations: Widening Gaps in East Asia and Chinese Demonization of the United States* (Princeton: Woodrow Wilson Center Press and Stanford: Stanford University Press, 2013).

3. Ralph A. Cossa, ed., *US–Japan–ROK Relations, Building Toward a "Virtual Alliance"* (Washington, D.C.: Center for Strategic and International Studies, 1999).

4. Tae-hyo Kim and Brad Glosserman, eds., *The Future of US–Korea–Japan Relations: Balancing Values and Interests* (Washington, D.C.: Center for Strategic and International Studies, 2004).

5. James Schoff, *Building on the Trilateral Coordination and Oversight Group (TCOG): Exploring the Prospects for Expanding the TCOG Process as a Key US–South Korea and US–Japan Alliance Management Tool* (Herndon, Va.: Institute for Foreign Policy Analysis, 2005).

6. U.S. Department of State, Trilateral Joint Statement, July 12, 2012.

7. Office of the Spokesman, U.S. Department of State, "Trilateral Statement Japan, Republic of Korea, and the United States," December 6, 2010. http://www.state.gov/r/pa/prs/ps/2010/12/152431.htm.

8. Cha, *Alignment Despite Antagonism*.

9. "Unofficial 'Text' of Joint Declaration," *Korea Times*, October 8, 1998. Accessed via Open Source Center. http://www.opensource.gov.

10. "A History of Lies," *Chosun ilbo*, April 4, 2001. http://english.chosun.com/site/data/html_dir/2001/04/03/2001040361399.html.

11. "ROK Envoy to Japan Notes Japanese Government Cannot Avert Responsibility for Textbooks," *Yonhap News Agency*, April 13, 2001; "Anti-Japanese Sentiment Revived by Japan's Approval of Textbook," April 15, 2001. Accessed via Open Source Center. http://www.opensource.gov.

12. "Roh's Tack in Tokyo," *Chosun ilbo*, June 9, 2003. http://english.chosun.com/site/data/html_dir/2003/06/08/2003060861001.html.

13. "Japan Must Not Distort Past," November 1, 2003. http://koreajoongangdaily.joinsmsn.com/news/article/Article.aspx?aid=2054198.

14. Kei Kono and Miwako Hara, "Japan-Korea Past, Present, and Future: From a Public Awareness Survey," Japan Broadcasting Corporation (NHK), Broadcasting Culture Research Institute. http://www.nhk.or.jp/bunken/english/reports/pdf/report_111201-1.pdf.

15. Asan Institute for Policy Studies, "South Koreans and Their Neighbors," November 28, 2013; and Yomiuri-Gallup poll, "Record 55 Percent See Japan–U.S. Ties as "in Good Shape," 87 Percent See Japan–China Ties as 'Bad,'" *Yomiuri shimbun*, December 16, 2013.

16. Genron NPO and East Asia Institute, "The First Joint Japan–Korea Public Opinion Poll: Analysis Report on the Comparative Data," May 2013, and "The Second Joint Japan-Korea Public Opinion Poll: Analysis Report on the Comparative Data," July 2014. "Favorable" includes "favorable impression" and "relatively favorable impression."

17. "Results of *Seoul shinmun–Tokyo shimbun* Joint Poll: Number of Koreans Who Think Japan Is Responding Well Is Only 4.7 Percent, Considerably Lower than in 2005." http://www.seoul.co.kr/news/newsView.php?id=20130104003001.

18. "*Donga ilbo* Opinion Poll on South Korean Attitudes Toward Japan and Other Nations," Mansfield Public Opinion Polling Database. http://mansfieldfdn.org/program/research-education-and-communication/asian-opinion-poll-database/listofpolls/2005-polls/march-2005-dong-a-ilbo-opinion-poll-on-south-korean-attitudes-toward-japan-and-other-nations/.

19. Data are from the *Asahi shimbum/Donga ilbo* June 2010 Joint Public Opinion Poll. http://mansfieldfdn.org/program/research-education-and-communication/asian-opinion-poll-database/listofpolls/2010-polls/.

20. Kim Jiyoon, Kang Chungku, Lee Eui Cheol, and Karl Friedhoff, "Public Opinion on Korea/Japan Relations/Tax Reform," Asan Institute, August 1–15, 2013; and "South Koreans and Their Neighbors," Asan Institute, November 28, 2013.

5. Implications for Alliance Management

1. Studies of the U.S.–Japan alliance include Ralph Cossa, ed., *Restructuring the U.S.–Japan Alliance: Toward a More Equal Partnership*, CSIS Significant Issues series (Washington, D.C.: Center for Strategic and International Studies, October 1997); Mike Mochizuki, ed., *Toward a True Alliance: Restructuring U.S.–Japan Security Relations* (Washington, D.C.: Brookings Institution Press, 1997); Michael Green and Patrick Cronin, eds., *The U.S.–Japan Alliance, Past, Present and Future* (New York: Council on Foreign Relations, 1999); Nishihara Masashi, ed., *The Japan–U.S. Alliance: New Challenges for the 21st Century* (Tokyo: Japan Center for International Exchange, 2000); and Gerald Curtis, ed., *New Perspectives on U.S.–Japan Relations* (Tokyo: Japan Center for International Exchange, 2000). There was considerably less work on the U.S.–ROK alliance. See, for example, Jonathan D. Pollack, Young Koo Cha, and Changsu Kim, *A New Alliance for the Next Century: The Future of U.S.–Korean Security Cooperation* (Santa Monica, Calif.: Rand Corporation, 1995).

2. Pew Research Global Attitudes Project, "Question: Do You Favor or Oppose U.S.-Led Antiterrorism Efforts?" http://www.pewglobal.org/database/?indicator=8&country=109.

3. Jeffrey Hornung, "Assessing the DPJ's Stewardship of the Alliance," CSIS Japan Chair Platform, March 15, 2013.

4. See "Outline of Public Opinion Survey of the Self Defense Forces and Defense Issues," Cabinet Office, March 2012, in particular questions 2 ("Impressions toward the SDF") and 3 ("Evaluation toward SDF disaster relief activities related to the Great East Japan Earthquake,"). http://www.mod.go.jp/e/d _act/others/pdf/public_opinion.pdf.

5. Matake Kamiya, "Role of the SDF Reappraised," *Japan Journal*, April 2012, 23.

6. A summary of this response is provided in Cossa and Glosserman, "U.S.– Japan Defense Cooperation," and in the chapters on U.S.–Japan relations in *Comparative Connections*, the Pacific Forum's triennial electronic journal of bilateral relations. See also Toby Dalton and Scott Snyder, "The Ties That Bind? Culture, Values, and Ideation in US–ROK–Japan Security Cooperation," in Kim and Glosserman, *The Future of US–Korea–Japan Relations*, 116–18.

7. Scott Snyder, ed., *The U.S.–South Korea Alliance* (Boulder: Lynne Rienner, 2012).

8. This analysis draws on Brad Glosserman, "Stressing the Linchpin: The US– ROK Alliance and 'Rebalancing' to Asia," *Asan Issue Brief* 27, September 19, 2012.

9. Hillary Clinton, "America's Pacific Century," *Foreign Policy* (November 2011).

10. Pacific Economic Cooperation Council, "Asia Pacific Economic Output: Chapter 1." http://www.pecc.org/research/state-of-the-region/412-chapter-1-asia -pacific-economic-outlook.

11. Office of the White House, *National Security Strategy*, May 2010.

12. Ibid., 42.

13. "Speech by Defense Secretary Gates in Jakarta, Indonesia Discusses a Range of Security Issues on East Asia," February 25, 2008. http://www.america.gov /st/texttrans-english/2008/February/20080225130031eaifaso.2525141.html

14. Amitav Acharya blames a regional norm against collective self-defense in "Why Is There No NATO in Asia? The Normative Origins of Asian Multilateralism," Weatherhead Center for International Affairs, Harvard University, Paper no. 05–05, July 2005. Christopher Hemmer and Peter Katzenstein identify several factors, one of which is the U.S. failure to see its identity as similar to that of Southeast Asia, in "Why Is There No NATO in Asia? Collective Identity, Regionalism and the Origins of Multilateralism," *International Organization*, 56, no. 3 (Summer 2002): 575–607.

15. While the Core Group is an example of ad hoc multilateralism, discussed below, it can also be put here in our typology: it plainly demonstrates the benefits of institutionalized cooperation.

16. Nicole Forrester, "Time for an Alliance Caucus," *PacNet* 21, March 27, 2012. The Pacific Forum CSIS explored options for U.S. alliances in Asia in Baker and Glosserman, eds., "Doing More and Expecting Less."

17. Foreign Minister Kevin Rudd, "Australian Perspectives on Trilateral Security Cooperation in the Asia Pacific," Canberra, November 18, 2010.

18. Major General Pan Zhenqiang, "Elements of a Long-Term Stable and Cooperative China-U.S. Relationship," in *Building Toward a Stable and Cooperative Long-term US–China Strategic Relationship*, ed. Lewis Dunn, Ralph Cossa, Brad Glosserman, and Li Hong, Pacific Forum CSIS *Issues & Insights*, 13, no. 2 (December 2012); Ralph Cossa, Brad Glosserman, and David Santoro, "Progress Continues but Disagreements Remain: The Seventh US–China Strategic Dialogue on Strategic Nuclear Dynamics," Pacific Forum CSIS *Issues & Insights* 13, no. 6 (January 2013).

19. Remarks of President Barack Obama at Suntory Hall, Tokyo Japan, November 14, 2009. President Bush spoke of the need for democracies to work more closely together. Prime Minister Aso Taro put "values-based diplomacy" at the rhetorical center of his foreign policy but showed little inclination to back his words with action when Southeast Asian democrats were challenged.

20. Lee Myung-bak, speech to the Korea Society Annual Dinner, April 15, 2008.

21. David Santoro and Brad Glosserman, "Building Toward Trilateral Cooperation on Extended Deterrence in Northeast Asia: The First US–ROK–Japan Extended Deterrence Trilateral Dialogue," Pacific Forum CSIS *Issues & Insights* 13, no. 14 (September 2013).

22. General Security of Military Intelligence Agreement (GSOMIA).

23. Wu Xinbo, "The End of the Silver Lining: A Chinese View of the US–Japan Alliance," *Washington Quarterly* 29, no. 1 (Winter 2005–06): 119–30.

24. Ralph Cossa, "US–Japan–Korea: Creating a Virtual Alliance," *PacNet* 47, December 3, 1999.

25. Author conversations in Seoul, fall 2010.

26. Remarks of Kurt Campbell, assistant secretary of state for East Asia and the Pacific, before the Senate Foreign Relations Committee, March 1, 2011.

27. Ibid.

28. U.S. Department of State, Trilateral Joint Statement, July 12, 2012.

29. Ibid.

30. U.S. Department of State, "Background Briefing: Readout of the Secretary's Meeting with Japanese Foreign Minister Koichiro Gemba and Korean Foreign Minister Kim Sung-hwan," September 28, 2012.

31. Gilbert Rozman, ed., *U.S. Leadership, History, and Bilateral Relations in Northeast Asia* (Cambridge: Cambridge University Press, 2011).

32. Ibid.

33. Cha, *Alignment Despite Antagonism.*

34. "In New Jersey, Memorial for Comfort Women Deepens Old Animosity," *New York Times*, May 18, 2012. See also Santoro and Glosserman, "Building Toward Trilateral Cooperation."

35. Author conversations with State Department officials, Washington, D.C., October 2013.

36. While some observers feared the worst, the portrait of a progressive ROK government ready to turn its back on the alliance was an exaggeration. Even under Roh Moo-hyun, South Korea remained a solid partner of the United States, contributing forces to overseas missions. Nonetheless, the perception that the ROK was swinging into China's orbit was pervasive, and views in the Pentagon contributed to the conclusion that the alliance was heading for a rupture.

37. From "Highlights: Japanese Editorials on U.S. Decision to Reduce Troops in ROK 9 June 04," *FBIS Report* JPP20040609000012 Japan, June 9, 2004.

38. "Obama Says There Must Be Consequences for Korean Ship Sinking," Reuters. http://www.reuters.com/article/2010/06/27/us-g20-northkorea-usa-idUSTRE65Q00I20100627.

39. Cha, *Alliance Despite Antagonism.*

40. Christopher Layne, "The (Almost) Triumph of Offshore Balancing," *National Interest*, January 27, 2012.

41. "Senators Levin, McCain and Webb Express Concern to Secretary Panetta Regarding Asia-Pacific Basing," Office of Senator James Webb, April 24, 2012. http://www.webb.senate.gov/newsroom/pressreleases/2012–04–24.cfm?renderforprint=1.

42. Bonnie Glaser and Denise Der, "American Reassurance and Rebalance Encourages Cooperation and Progress at ADMM+," CSIS *CogitASIA*, September 5, 2013. http://cogitasia.com/american-reassurance-of-rebalance-encourages-cooperation-progress-at-admm/.

43. For Japan, an authoritative assessment is available at *GlobalSecurity.org*. http://www.globalsecurity.org/wmd/world/japan/nuke.htm.

44. Yukio Satoh, "Agenda for Japan–US Strategic Consultations," National Institute for Defense Studies, Tokyo, 21. http://www.nids.go.jp/english/event/symposium/pdf/2009/e_02.pdf.

45. Lee Byong Chul, "South Korea's Nuclear Weapons Temptation," *Yale Global Online*, October 14, 2011. http://yaleglobal.yale.edu/content/south-koreas -nuclear-weapons-temptation.

46. "South Korea Special Weapons," *GlobalSecurity.org*. http://www.globalsecurity .org/wmd/world/rok/index.html.

47. Victor Cha, "Powerplay: Origins of the U.S. Alliance System in Asia," *International Security*, 34, no. 3 (Winter 2009–10): 158–96.

48. Bill Tow notes that the United States is "underwriting the defense normalization of Japan in ways that would benefit allied and regional collective security without unduly alarming China and other regional actors." "The Trilateral Strategic Dialogue: Facilitating Community Building or Revisiting Containment," *National Bureau of Asian Research Special Report* (December 2008): 3.

49. Chicago Council on Global Affairs, "Foreign Policy in the New Millennium," *Chicago Council Survey* (2012): 14–15.

6. Reinvigorating Trilateralism

1. Ethan Epstein, "Japan's New Islands? Nationalism Makes a Comeback," *Weekly Standard* 17, no. 43 (July 30, 2012). http://www.weeklystandard.com /articles/japan-s-new-islands_648833.html.

2. Genron NPO, *The Ninth Japan–China Public Opinion Poll*, Analysis Report on the Comparative Data, August 12, 2013, 4, 10. http://www.genron-npo.net /english/opinionpoll_9thjc.pdf.

3. The policies are "new" because they continue trends in place prior to the return to power of the Liberal Democratic Party in 2012.

4. Max Fisher, "Japan and South Korea Can't Even Cooperate over Peacekeeping in South Sudan," *Washington Post*, December 26, 2013. http://www .washingtonpost.com/blogs/worldviews/wp/2013/12/26/japan-and-south -korea-cant-even-cooperate-over-peacekeeping-in-south-sudan/.

5. Bong Youngshik, "ROK and US Views on the Foreign Policy of the Abe Administration," *Asan Forum*, November 6, 2013.

6. Clinton, "America's Pacific Century."

7. U.S. State Department, *Quadrennial Diplomacy and Development Review* (December 2010), 73.

8. This has been a staple of bilateral U.S.–Japan and U.S.–ROK strategic dialogues that Pacific Forum CSIS has held. The reports for those meetings are on the Pacific Forum website.

9. Both Japan and South Korea complained of a lack of transparency in the other's alliance with the United States during trilateral discussions. See Santoro and Glosserman, "Building Toward Trilateral Cooperation."

10. See "China's Top Trade Partners 2009." http://www.uschina.org/statistics/tradetable.html.

11. David Kang and Ji-Young Lee, "Japan-Korea Relations: The New Cold War in Asia?" in *Comparative Connections* 12, no. 4 (January 2011): 134; and "Japan, ROK Said Eyeing Defense Ties," *Yomiuri shimbun*, January 5, 2011. http://www.yomiuri.co.jp/dy/national/T110104004658.htm.

12. An impressive list is laid out in the joint statement released by the three foreign ministers in their December 2010 meeting. It includes such items as dealing with North Korea and engaging China and Russia within the Six-Party Talks framework as well as in general, coordinating development efforts in Southeast Asia and the Lower Mekong River area—in particular, addressing global challenges such as terrorism, proliferation of weapons of mass destruction, piracy, and climate change.

13. Park Cheol hee, "The Great East Japan Earthquake and Coordinating Army U.S. Allies," Center for U.S.–Korea Policy, Asia Foundation, April 27, 2011.

14. Karl Friedhoff and Kang Chungku, "Rethinking Public Opinion on Korea–Japan Relations," *Asan Issue Brief* 73, October 15, 2013.

15. Genuine reconciliation is a long-term process that at some point must address education and by extension textbooks. We focus on defense and security policy and the future of U.S. alliances, and we acknowledge the need for work in this area. Readers should explore other efforts already underway, such as the Divided Memories and Reconciliation Project at Stanford University's Shorenstein Asia Pacific Research Center.

16. Of course grassroots efforts are needed as well, but those are difficult at the trilateral level and are probably best left to bilateral initiatives.

17. Pacific Forum CSIS has launched a track 1.5 trilateral extended deterrence dialogue. For the results of the first meeting—a "surprising success" for most participants—see Santoro and Glosserman, "Building Toward Trilateral Cooperation."

18. Martin Sieff, "Japan, South Korea, US Maintain Naval Cooperation," *Asia Pacific Defense Forum*, May 23, 2013. http://apdforum.com/en_GB/article/rmiap/articles/online/features/2013/05/23/japan-korea-talk.

19. Wakamiya Yoshibumi, *The Postwar Conservative View of Asia* (Tokyo: LTCB International Library Foundation, 1999), 169–82.

20. Michael McDevitt, "The Long Littoral Project: Summary Report," CNA, June 2013, 59.

21. Demographic trends also militate against Japanese dreams of reclaiming the islands. Those trends also provide ample incentive for Japan to eliminate obstacles to closer ties with South Korea. For more, see Brad Glosserman and Tomoko Tsunoda, "The Guillotine: Japan's Demographic Transformation and Its Security Implications," Pacific Forum CSIS *Issues & Insights* 9, no. 10 (June 2009).

22. Alexis Dudden, *Troubled Apologies Among Japan, Korea and the United States* (New York: Columbia University Press, 2008), Kindle edition, loc. 84.

23. *Chosun ilbo* interview cited in Yuka Hayashi, "'No Easy Way Out' for South Korea-Japan Feud, Despite Biden's Efforts," *Wall Street Journal*, December 13, 2013. http://blogs.wsj.com/japanrealtime/2013/12/13/no-easy-way-out-for -south-korea-japan-feud-despite-bidens-efforts/.

24. Dudden, *Troubled Apologies*, 25.

25. Gi-wook Shin, "Can the United States Play a Role in Northeast Asian Reconciliation?" presentation at Stanford University, January 21, 2010. http://iis-db .stanford.edu/evnts/5969/Historical_Reconciliation_%282010%29.pdf.

26. On the Abe administration's hope that an Okinawa deal would temper criticism of a shrine visit, see George Nishiyama, "Abe's Style Presents US with a Dilemma," *Wall Street Journal*, December 28, 2013. For the Korean view that Washington is enabling Japanese conservatives, see Robert Koehler, "*Chosun ilbo* Sorta Blames US for Abe Asshattery," *Marmot Hole*, December 30, 2103.

27. Jennifer Lind, *Sorry States: Apologies in International Affairs* (Ithaca: Cornell University Press, 2011).

INDEX

Abenomics, 35–37

Abe Shinzo: alliance modernization, 128–29; constitutional reform, 42–43, 51; defense policies, 125–26; election (2012), 107; foreign policy, 55, 58–59; public opinion, 57–58, 103–4, 110; rollback of Koizumi's reforms, 35; South Korean relationship, 107–9; U.S. force presence, 50; Yasukuni Shrine visit, 108, 177–78

abnormality, 40

Acquisition and Cross-Servicing Agreement (ACSA), 123, 141, 166

ACSA (Acquisition and Cross-Servicing Agreement), 123, 141, 166

ad hoc multilateralism, 138, 197n15

ADMM+ (ASEAN Defense Ministers Meeting Plus), 151

Afghanistan, 170

Agawa Naoyuki, 37

Ahn Jung-guen statue, 161

alliances: ad hoc caucus structure, 138, 197n15; autonomy, 150–53; burden sharing, 33, 50–51, 140, 163; competition, 146–48; external challenges, 2; hub-and-spokes, 2, 120, 137; identity as basis, 20–21; implications of public opinion, 6, 134–35; institutionalization, 96, 139–42, 164, 169, 197n15; internal dynamics, 2–3; minilateral, 137, 162; modernization, 121; multilateral, U.S.-centered, 137–39; NATO-style, 137, 139, 196–97n14; origins, 13–14; personal relationships, 126; politicization, 3; possibilities, 136;

exploitation of, 68; failure to consider, 95–96; generational divide, 75; importance, 6, 97; Japanese occupation of Korea, 7, 62, 93, 103, 113, 114; Japanese rivalry with China, 43–44; Korean gestures, 173; Korean War, 93, 97–98, 130, 177; Nogunri massacre (South Korea), 130; Northeast Project, 160; obstacle to alliances, 93, 154; public responses, 118; reconciliation attempts, 99, 165–66, 200n15; revisionism, 71–72, 100–102, 115, 172, 178; rightwing agenda (Japan), 57–58; sex slave compensation (comfort women), 102, 104, 106, 172, 179; textbook issues, 100–102, 118; U.S. mediation, 177–78; U.S. responsibilities, 179; Yasukuni Shrine, 102. *See also* World War II

Honda, Michael, 104

hub-and-spokes approach, 2, 120, 137

humanitarian assistance, 169

human rights abuses, 81

identity: abnormality, 40; activist manipulation, 14, 54; asymmetrical perceptions, 135; as basis for cooperation, 20–21; changes in, 18–19; Chinese ascendancy, 43–48, 87; civic nationalism, 62–63; competing, 15; confidence, 180; constraints on cooperation, 95; construction, 15; crises, 15; foreign policy, 17–18, 59; intergroup conflict, 16–17; international relations, 14, 16; means of definition, 18; metaphors, 6–7; middle power, 28–29; national interests, 18; public opinion as tool, 5–6; as subject, vs. object, 10; theories, 11–15; understanding of, 19; vulnerability, 55–56, 72–73, 92, 124,

159. *See also* Japanese identity; South Korean identity

Ieo-do/Socotra Rocks, 85

independence, in alliance management, 150–53

institutional cooperation, 96, 139–42, 164, 169, 197n15

intergroup relations, 17

inter-Korean relations: basis in distrust, 71; challenges to U.S. alliance, 129; disillusionment, 70; generational gaps, 160; limits on cultural cooperation, 80–81; public opinion, 79–84; reunification, 61–67, 79; summit (2000), 61–62, 64, 65, 79, 81; views of U.S., 131. *See also* Sunshine Policy

internationalism: ambitions, 67, 117, 168; divergent international dependencies, 87; global emphasis, 70–71, 168; global stability framework, 169–70; international ambitions, 117; *kokusaishugi*, 15; limits, 37–39; nationalism, inverse relationship, 32; position, 73–74

international relations, 11–21

Internet, 8

Iraq, 24–25, 123, 124

Ishihara Shintaro, 45

isolationism, 37

Ito Hirobumi, 161

jackpot *(taebak)*, 84

Japan: atomic bombings, WWII, 172, 178; China, views on, 43–48; Cold War, 29; constitutional reform, 27, 39–43, 51, 53, 171; cultural confidence, 31–32, 35; defense policy, 123–26, 199n48; dignity identity, 25–26; domestic security, 25; economy, 22–24, 35, 57; egalitarianism, 33–34, 52–53, 189n25; generational divide, 36; "great gesture" option,

of Korean schoolgirls (2002), 66, 67, 129, 131; de facto trilateralism, 142–45; force presence in South Korea, 66; foreign university students, 37, 74; Global War on Terror, 24–25, 123, 124, 133, 170; historical legacy, 97, 172, 177–78; impact of Japan-South Korean tensions, 108; mediator role, 8, 21, 108–9, 135, 144, 177–78; Nogunri massacre (South Korea), 130; rape by U.S. Marines, 121, 123; rebalance to Asia, 2–4, 133–37, 153; reconciliation facilitation, 21, 176–77; sex slave issue (comfort women), 104; shared interests, 76, 78. *See also* U.S.-Japan alliance; U.S.-South Korea alliance
United States Forces Korea (USFK), 66, 67, 129, 130, 131
USFK (United States Forces Korea), 66, 67, 129, 130, 131
U.S.-Japan alliance: benefits, 164; burden sharing, 50–51, 124, 128; competition with South Korea, 146–48; domestic politics, 121–29; "high-water mark" hypothesis, 124–25; insecurity, Japanese, 47, 51, 123; Japanese views, 29, 42, 51; Japan's security dependence, 123–24; modernization, 125–29; reaffirmation process, 131–32; reinforcement of pacifist identity, 56; security partnership, 48–52, 98–99, 188n75, 189n84; sensitivity toward Japanese insecurity, 47, 123; tension over U.S. vs. Asian orientation, 52, 55–56. *See also* troop presence
U.S.-South Korea alliance: benefits, 164; competition with Japan, 146–48; Future of the Alliance talks, 131; Korean Joint Vision Statement, 70, 89; obstacle to Korean reunification,

65–66; security issues, 68; Security Policy Initiative, 131–32; South Korean views, 67–68, 131, 178; status of, 56; strengths/weaknesses, 10; tensions, 129–31; terrorist attacks (September 11, 2001), 124; untethering of, 61; value of Japan-South Korea relationship, 108. *See also* troop presence

values: basis for alliances, 4, 140, 154, 197n19; citizen engagement, 176; common, 115–17, 139–40, 168; democratic, 29, 65, 74, 94; interests, 48, 76, 78, 168; Japanese identity, 31–37; perceptions of compatibility, 48, 76
values-based diplomacy, 21, 197n14, 197n19
victim sentiments, 32
vulnerability, 55–56, 72–73, 92, 124, 159

Walt, Stephen, 150
Webb, James, 151
welfare state, 34
working-level bureaucracy, 167–69
World Cup, 62
World Cup (2002), 100
World Trade Organization (WTO), 85
World War II, 7, 102, 104, 106, 172, 177–79. *See also* historical legacy
WTO (World Trade Organization), 85

Yamaguchi Jiro, 34
Yasukuni Shrine: Abe's visit, 39, 108, 177–78; Koizumi's visit, 27, 44, 102, 135, 143; overshadowing by sex slave issue (comfort women), 104; public opinion, 39; symbolism, 102
Yeonpyeong artillery shelling, 84, 86, 96, 139, 143
Yoshida doctrine, 184n7

ABOUT THE AUTHORS

BRAD GLOSSERMAN is executive director at Pacific Forum CSIS and coeditor of *Comparative Connections*, its ejournal. He is the editor, along with Kim Tae-Hyo, of *The Future of U.S.–Korea–Japan Relations: Balancing Values and Interests* (CSIS, 2004). His study of the impact of the March 11, 2011, triple catastrophe, "The Choice: Japan After March 11," is forthcoming. Glosserman has authored dozens of monographs on topics related to U.S. foreign policy and Asian security. His opinion articles and commentary have appeared in media around the world. Prior to joining Pacific Forum, he was a member of the *Japan Times* editorial board, and he continues to serve as a contributing editor for the newspaper. He has a J.D. degree from George Washington University, an M.A. degree from Johns Hopkins University's School of Advanced International Studies (SAIS), and a B.A. degree from Reed College.

SCOTT SNYDER is senior fellow for Korea studies and director of the program on U.S.–Korea policy at the Council on Foreign Relations (CFR). He is also a contributor for the blog "Asia Unbound" and previously served as the project director for the CFR's Independent Task Force on policy toward the Korean Peninsula. Previously, Snyder was a senior associate at the Asia Foundation, where he founded and directed the Center for U.S.–Korea Policy and served as the foundation's representative in Korea. He is also a senior associate at Pacific Forum CSIS. He has authored or edited numerous books, including *North Korea in Transition: Politics, Economics, Society* (2013), *The U.S.–South Korea Alliance: Meeting New Security Challenges* (editor, 2012), and *China's Rise and the Two Koreas: Politics, Economics, Security* (2009). Snyder received an M.A. degree from the regional studies East Asia program at Harvard University and a B.A. degree from Rice University. He was a Thomas G. Watson fellow at Yonsei University in South Korea and a Pantech visiting fellow at Stanford University's Shorenstein Asia-Pacific Research Center during 2005–06, and he received an Abe fellowship, administered by the Social Sciences Research Council, in 1998–99.